The credo: Welcome to the end. Things seem a bit different now. It's just a good beginning, that's all. No matter what happens from here, you've already experienced this. You can't remove it from yourself. It will fester and you'll need more. Everything comes in time.

St. Michael

Michael,
Ten days. They said they'd come for me in ten days. This is why I had to move. I am now staying in the previous apartment of my friend in West Hollywood. It is located in Los Feliz. Ever since my involvement in the terrible orgy at the La Brea Tar Pits, I believe that it has catalyzed the poisons in my blood somehow...

Oliver

Mr. Morel,
I must continue to protest. How much must I suffer under your depredations? I no longer seem to have anything, not even myself. I am no longer sure of my own identity. It is hard for me to believe. I go through the day convincing myself, practicing denial and the art of self-delusion, that what has happened to me is not true...

Rebecca Mina

The following letter appeared on the monitor of Aleister Crowley, Executive Assistant to Michael Amorel. It wasn't even on:

"They think they have won this time. They have no idea what sort of vortex they have opened. They have struck me down and I have become even more powerful then they can ever possibly imagine..."

You may believe that there is no story to this book. Just 300 pages of ranting and nonsense. Then their work is done. They will not be stopped. They will shape the world in the image of their undying god and things will be forever changed. Perhaps it has already happened and this warning is too late. I pray that it is not so.

D1558728

LETTERS TO THE EDITOR

OF

CTHULHU SEX MAGAZINE

BY OLIVER BAER & OTHERS

ACKNOWLEDGEMENTS

I would like to acknowledge all the people that wrote letters to *Cthulhu Sex Magazine*. Kenn Schubach deserves thanks for being one of the inspirations to create the Letters to the Editor section of the magazine in the first place. Luke Crane deserves thanks not only for writing in but also helping us to make sure that all the images in the magazine looked great once they were printed. Mark Kalvin, Henry Gottlieb Kohler III, Dan Clore, Cassandra Ingram, Theodore Mordred and the others that contributed to the letters section of *Cthulhu Sex Magazine* deserve thanks not just for writing in but also for their support and contributions that continued its existence until the dimension rift opened. The photos in this book are thanks to Eli Livingston whose artistic renderings of sexy monstrosities graced several issues of *Cthulhu Sex*. The medallions Eli photographed were crafted by Paul Komoda, the artist whose unspeakable visions became the basis for the art in the magazine. The artistic reconstruction pictured towards the end was by Kurt Komoda whose work also appeared in an issue or two of *Cthulhu Sex*. Last but not least, thanks must be given to the man who's dream we all made into a reality, Michael A. Morel. He led us down the dark path with a vision that was as tentacular as it was sexy. The Great Old One was pleased with our offerings for a time. Then, it remembered that all things must end in madness and took the magazine to the horrific depths from which it came. Some say that there is still a lost volume out there somewhere. But these are probably just the ravings of a madman.

I would also like to thank David Niall Wilson and David Dodd for agreeing to publish this account of our insanity. It is greatly appreciated. Hopefully, they do not realize what they have helped to bring back into existence.

WELCOME ALL

Welcome all,

Cthulhu Sex! was developed in a rigorous testing of a large group of non-willing participants. They were then given over to the psychiatric ward of one Doctor Sprauge, whose unique and inventive forms of treatment saved the life of one young girl out of the group. The rest were given to the worms amidst ritual prayer, lain in mass plots on the grounds of the cemetery conveniently sharing borders with the sanitarium. The young girl was given free rein in the most secure wing of the building, which continues to be unfortunately sparse of visitors. She still whispers words that are too unusual for most of the genteel inhabitants of the world. Even the stray sentence that was accidentally overheard by a fellow inmate had such detrimental effects. It was decided to protect her from the world, giving her over to this solitude.

In the company of my partner and me, one of our authors channeled the spirit of that poor unfortunate in the lonely wing and spouted out the words that led to the creation of this series of works. The words were used as a descriptive of one of my usual depraved, fanciful stories I happened to be divulging at the moment involving tentacles, blood and various activities involving body parts.

In a spout of ecstatic creativity, the beginnings of *Cthulhu Sex!* were forged. I breathed life into the form shaped by the words that had so effectively described a genre I feel is sorely untouched. I had been working on what I considered to be the higher aspects of horrific thought; reading the writings of the revered H.P. Lovecraft, attempting to reach similar levels of depravity, experiencing the extremes of the world through the eyes of intellect, and debating philosophical ideology about the darker sides of life. All pointed to the body through sensuality but decried the base pleasures of lust and carnal passions. At the moment, I heard the phrase "Cthulhu Sex!", I realized that I had been following deluded dreams about the greatness of humanity. The true strengths of humanity lie in base sexuality, the subtle bodies elusive and ineffectual in comparison to the raw power sex wields.

I have delved into these depths with the companionship of many like-minded individuals who see the humor, sadness and disgust that follow our pleasures and joys like shadows, seeped in malignant intent. It is from this medley of macabre and deviant creators that the conglomeration known as *Cthulhu Sex!* has been born.

We will nurture this creation to its full bloom, whatever shape that may take, encouraging all others to proliferate in our debauchery. Listen to the gentle whisper of the wind and you might hear us calling you, enticing you to engage in *Cthulhu Sex!*

St. Michael

ST. MICHAEL'S CREDO

This was written on my computer screen. It had a blackish reddish green hue that reflected back at us. It spoke to me so I decided to use it as a credo for the company.

Welcome to the end. Things seem a bit different now. It's just a good beginning, that's all. No matter what happens from here, you've already experienced this. You can't remove it from yourself. It will fester and you'll need more. Everything comes in time.

St. Michael

1.14.1

Greetings to all you lovers of the little bits of joy and cheer we constantly throw all over the place. I found a bit of cheer from the last issue stuck behind my bedpost. When I touched it, it let off a billowing cloud of spores that stank like the time we finally found Grandma after she had that last fight with Grandpa. Thank goodness for chlorine-based disinfecting sprays. Cleaned the room right up and gave me pretty little black spots to chase.

I would like to take this time to thank the people who helped me with this latest issue. Father Baer has been the taskmaster of discipline in his way. He has shaped these stories with a silver scalpel of editing, blessed on the highest and coldest of mountains. He has shaved off the raw and bleeding wounds, inadvertently left to fester in the authors' stories, to reveal the delicate bones and musculature beneath that glisten with beauty. In other words, he has cut all that is human from my poor slaves and left those lifeless husks. One of our contributors has also greatly aided my quest for the infernal takeover of the world. She promotes for the website and is a general wealth of information when it comes to computers, internet and abusing people's fractured egos. She has also been supporting Father Baer's editing with her own. One of our artists, whose artwork will be stretched across the next issue of *Cthulhu Sex* like skin, allowed this issue to be digitally remastered through use of his devices. May all of the darklings grow to those songs of power. Another, who has helped me greatly, is the gentleman I like to call The Morose Cowboy. He comes to me only in the middle of the night to stand, bowlegged and dusty, at the end of my bed. There he whispers strange stories of what he has done during the day. His voice echoes in reverse as if conceived in some distant, imperceptible thought and, traveling in waves pushed into rhythmic ebbs and flows, gains strength till it breaks across my ears, shattering into misty smatterings that take up residence in my fractured mind. It is these pieces that vomit forth the uncouth words splattering these pages with flecks of bile. The person who has helped me get ads has unfortunately been recently killed in a clean-up effort by the CIA. She put up resistance against them when they decided to burn down the house that was a capstone for an underground network of tunnels and caves used by certain unnatural elements of the universe to store their dead and children. The greatest help has been from my love. She ran around for things when I couldn't and was always there with support for my work. Without her, all this wouldn't have been possible. I would also like to thank everyone who gave words of encouragement and discouragement, you all fed fuel to my fire.

I know you will like this issue of *Cthulhu Sex* because it has been electronically transubstantiated. Besides the new look, there are also many new writers and artists with wonderfully twisted visions that somehow keep working their way like pus, to the surface of my mind. We also have a few of our past writers and artists tantalizing us with more of their works. So, sit back, kick off your feet and enjoy before the shock sets in.

1.14.2

I received this email in response to a mass mail I sent out with regards to submissions, the subject of such was CTHULHU SEX with large pointy ears as stated below. I found this an amazing piece of ironic humor and wished to pass it on. Please be aware that I do, personally, have an alien device that allows me to do such things as is mentioned. However, the cost is great and most people don't survive the process.

Subject: Re: CTHULHU SEX with large pointy ears
Okay, I'll be happy to contribute. I mean, I'll be more than happy, but first, you have to do a little thing for me that will make it possible for the me to do the work in question:
I would like you to transport me to an inter-temporal space where I will be able to write your story (Yes, I have thought about it and have a completely realized plot. I even have a few tantalizing phrases with which to make the scenes more scene-like___ "Yes, I did stick a knife into his back and I did drop him into the nearest river but he seemed to have grown up since then. He'd gone beyond that. It didn't seem to bother him now.") and now all I need is for the blue glow to be emitted from the device you hold in your hand as you stand there wearing an unreadable, perhaps unearthly, facial expression. You know, something between candidacy for sainthood and deep confusion.
I'm there in my head, I can see it.
The device glows and I duck expecting...what? disintegration? Transportation to Siberia? A one-way ride to the bedroom of a rather large Goth woman dressed in nothing but a collar that metes out electric shocks to the uncompliant and a

patent-leather loincloth? My body knows that any of those things can happen. My body knows what thirty-five years of television have taught. When someone wearing an unreadable expression points something alien and half-melted at you and moves, your body compliantly kicks in with adrenalin. It anticipates becoming what the coroner absent-mindedly rests his lunch on. It reacts to the potentiality of becoming a part of someone whose lower jaw drops, actually drops before he laughs and says: "Do what? With who? With you??! No. I don't care what that button does. Press it all you like. You might as well *CLOSE* your legs because it's *NEVER* happening. In fact, you must be out of your fucking. AiiieeeeEEErraaaAAAAggggghhhh-UH!!!!"

But instead of the cold steel table or the large Goth woman's (AKA "Name Withheld's") home for wayward wearers of leather loin clothes, I find myself neither dead nor wishing *deeply, avidly, most particularly* that someone had had a really bad day while calculating the amperage generated by the COLLAR of OBEDIENCE.

No, none of that happens and for this, thy bounty, Lord we are grateful.

I uncringe and find myself in a room with nothing in it but a desk with a brand-new IBM laptop on it, that some bizarre instinct tells me I'll be keeping at the end of my strange adventure (A bizarre instinct tells me that I *had better* be keeping it). It's as if you, in your alien-assed, strange-facial-expression-and-metallic-robe-wearing-too-tall wisdom have read my mind: you seem to know what I need as well as I myself know it and the results of that knowledge are spread out before me.

The smell of coffee draws my attention to the multifunction espresso machine in the corner and the burlap bags containing many fragrant blends of the finest coffees___ the small, Italian grinder sitting, atop and nestled, within a pile of snowy white terry cloths. I think for a moment that I am in writer's heaven but then I realize that this can't be heaven. The other thing in the room lets me know that I am alive, blissfully drawing air into the lungs of a living, breathing writer who will return to the world of men to once more partake of moments of slender triumph interspersed with the form of geological time that is only truly understood by one who appreciates the delectation of deep effort wasted in realtime. I observe that heaven is not so complete, not so deeply, wonderfully practical as the place where I am when I notice the window.

Off to the side of the water-cooler, the Great Bear water-cooler, there is a window-like opening in the air giving unto the sight (oh, mirabile visu!) of my boss looking tangibly, benevolently, and twilight-zonishly freeze-framed in mid phone-call. As he tells me that there are things that I really have to do *RIGHT NOW* because some schmuck in a veal-fattening pen in Canada is breathing down his neck *RIGHT NOW* forcing him to make the first in a sequence of pager-calls of terrifying frequency, a frequency so great that the most jaded, the most *experienced* woman in the Western hemisphere (does JesDELETEDsica still hang out at the café whose name has been lost in interdimensional space?) could use the goddamned thing as a tastefully concealable sex-toy. With childlike wonder, I reach through the space in the air in the manner of someone who just has to check to make sure that he hasn't lost *every ounce* of his shit and caress my boss's temporal-displacement-hardened cheek and it is in that moment that I realize the truth of my freedom. I need not run like hell out the door, lugging heavy stuff and sweating with the afternoon pot of coffee sloshing around in my guts. My job will be there when I'm done writing whatever it is that I'm going to write. My boss is not a concern and won't be until the effects of the melted-looking alien-Michael-device (the AMD) have either worn off or been cancelled.

I am free to write or not write. Free to put my fingers to work, or to open the box with IBM naturally speaking in it and to work with the headphones ("I talk, it types!"), or I can drink some of the coffee, sample the delightful bouquet of Jamaican Blue Mountain as I half-kneel on the office-quality Balanz Chair. I'm free. As free to write or fail to write as Fran Leibowitz, the *only writer in creation* with fewer books to her credit than David Letterman appearances. I'm as free to write as Tama Janawitz. Despite the sulphurous stench of my body, and despite the sores that festoon my face and genitals, I am more attractive, even to male heterosexual's beings. Of all the earth's myriad species from Bottle-nosed Dolphins to Bluebottle flies, I am still far, far more attractive than ever she will be....

I take one of the white mugs from the steel table next to the apparatus, pour myself a steaming cup of writer-fuel and sip....

Sudden inhalation as my eyes widen. I raise the mug and smell. Strong. Very coffee-like and heady like quarter-century single-malt on an empty stomach. I am in the presence of coffee that makes you say, "You have *achieved* *Coffee*." I know that all the coffee I have had before had been castrated by sadistically grinning inductees into South American death squads before making its way to me.

Or: To put it another way....

[Deep sonorous voice] "I am Coffee, and if you will love only in my name, thou shalt know strengths and joys such as are given to but few in thy generation___ thou shalt be the sweetest of my servants (yes, that old line again) ...Partake of my essence and this will be my covenant with thee."

To which you, ludicrously muscular and suddenly photographed in a golden-yellow color-palette look up as one looking into the face of his GOD. On your knees, bathed in sweat, your arms crossed upon your chest and hands resting on your shoulders, you are in the presence of the transcendent. Tears, born of a joy that you have never felt before and will never know again, roll down your cheeks as you make the only reply you can make.

"Yes, master...oh, yes...my life and all my soul for you...."

However, back at the ranch, there remains the problem of writing, which is no problem at all now. I know what to write and how to write it. No problem. Under these circumstances, I cannot *but* write something good for *Cthulhu Sex*....

Whip out the half-melted-looking alien-dimensional-control thingy, practice your unreadable facial expression, and the story will be yours.

In the interim, I have to run off and count a lot of dollar bills that look like they've been shoved up a vulture's butt for safekeeping....

Just in case you need me to mention the word at least once....

"Tentacles"

Mark

Mark. The gods look down upon you pleased. They see your humble effort to enlighten their beast of burden with the very essence of your writings and consequent lack thereof. They have given me a message to pass on to you, their devoted wordsmith. It has but a few simple sentences, yet carries infinite meaning and wisdom. It is this: *KERBLAM* (thunder rolls off distant hills) "You dare try to weasel your way out of writing for us!?! Now you shall pay for your travesty!!!" *KERBLAM* (the thunder rolling off the distant hills disturbs a small pile of ash that was once known as Mark)

Somewhere, far in the distance, an alien-looking device is pointed in the direction of the ash. A voice almost like the wind whispers "Write... Write..."

1.14.3

Here is a delightful little ditty someone posted in response to a post on a bulletin board promoting the finer parts of *Cthulhu Sex*.

Introducing *Cthulhu Sex*, the zine of blood, sex and tentacles featuring horror fiction, erotic musings, art, a tentacled centerfold and demented poetry.
Congratulations.
You have managed to make a mockery of horror, H.P. Lovecraft and lovemaking by even thinking this sick shit up.
Lemme guess. You love Japanese Tentacle rape cartoons.
Bet if you were raped you would not do this type of shit.
Sick bastard, I hope someone hacks your site to hell.
Frickin wierdo…

My, I think we should take this advice. *Cthulhu Sex* is going to be terminated as of this second. Good bye cruel world!
Wait a minute… Rape? Who said anything about rape? Rape is a disgusting and perverted act of the deranged (and/or Japanese manga). If anything, as a plot element to instill fear, dread, disgust or hatred, it has been used in many stories, not necessarily any in *Cthulhu Sex* (not necessarily). In fact, I seem to remember a rape scene in Excalibur that birthed Arthur. And the one in Deliverance definitely instills emotional reaction. But still, what is this person talking about? Some people out there have serious issues.
As to profaning H.P. Lovecraft (copyright, some big money conglomerate), lovemaking (copyright, all the people who are getting it besides the person who wrote "Frickin (use proper

English "Fucking") weirdo..." and learn how to spell "weirdo") and horror (copyright, anyone who has followed you home any lone dark night), I'd have to be one powerful person to do all that. All that power would be sooooo cool! I could make everyone believe that Leonardo da Vinci was actually a homosexual who made love to paintings of himself cross-dressing (cum stains on the Mona Lisa, not water). Or I could make everyone think that they owe me money! That'd be "rad".

Let's not lose sight of what we're here to do. We all just want a little enjoyment between the hectic times when the world began and when it will end. To this end we all wait for the destruction of the barriers between all humans, when we can all share our deepest feelings and thoughts in an unrestricted environment of love and caring. I suggest the best way to do this is to remove all of our skins. That way, we all have free access to each other's innermost parts.

Thank you for your post and for playing our game, whoever you are. We'd like to send you, our lucky loser, our best wishes and this prize package including: a one week vacation in a Turkish prison filled with all the raw meat you can chew (don't forget to swallow), three thousand years of nightmares about being shown the light of the One True Truth only to have it taken from you again and again, and last, but not least, a nightly tentacling by the great Cthulhu. So spread your cheeks wide for a three-foot tentacle and enjoy your illegitimate stay on our planet, monkey boy.

I thank you for the congratulatory remarks. You have indeed divined our goal, though we prefer to refer to our publication as satire. We definitely intend to pay homage to the grandfather of American horror by utilizing his mastery of atmosphere and because we see mockery as a type of praise, faint at best though it is, we thought we'd add something the master eschewed, sex. Into society, where the word of sex has attained less polarity than in Lovecraft's but still is used with more restraint than we care to admit, we would like our tentacles to writhe in a soft caress of its nether regions in the hope that some of this restraint will fall away.

I am sorry that our marketing department did not follow my orders and instill in you the same feelings I have about Japanese tentacle rape cartoons. Rape is something that should not be trivialized especially when talking about the deviant side of a particular culture. It is for this reason that I would mention that there are certain wards on our gates, virtual and otherwise, that if broken might result in this certain phenomenon being visited upon the breaker by certain weird denizens of various hells.

1.14.4

It should be noted that this was written in a trance. The writing flowed out of the pen and was in a cursive handwriting that was not my own. While I do seem to have some flashes of the memories mentioned, I have no idea where they came from and have shunted them aside to be dealt with later.

As I write this, I travel through the archives of my past, looking for the tip of a memory that flashed across my consciousness. A book covered in the dust of time, nearly forgotten, that speaks of an arcane lover. As I read the title, I feel a gentle warming in my loins. It holds just three words, "The Soft Ones". I turn to the first page and meander through the ancient dialect of my youth, a language more of emotions and sensations, not easily read by my logic bearing, time-altered mind. As the story evolves, I picture each event as it is described. It moves from rich, multiple perspective full color, filled with sensations and emotions to flat, over-exposed, video where I watch someone else do what I had, depending on the speed of the story and the depth of my memories. One of the deeper memories, and therefore fuller visions, is the point where my lover explained to me what they call humans. In her rasping voice, a voice of multiple metal tines being pulled through skin, thrillingly sensual, she told me to look at her hand. She raised the shining black, four-digited appendage for my examination. I watched the long spider leg fingers slowly flex, each stronger than my entire body, the blades capping three of the fingers catching the light of the fires that constantly lit her abode. Her fingers appeared against my cheek, arcs of lighting, fading in my eyes, the only trace of the movement. The cold, chitinous edges slid down my flesh, eliciting a field of chills to breeze down my back, tickling just under the surface, leaving a dull throb in my testicles, the beginning of a terrible ache if not sated. "Feel the difference?" she asked, the dull throb manifesting in a stiffening. "Yes," was all I could manage, letting the final "S" slip away into the distance. "That is what we call your kind, 'The Soft Ones'." She twitched a little, scraping my hair-free face, reminding me of her strength and the grace of her presence. We abandoned ourselves to pleasure.

I often wonder what it would be like to touch someone who would be comparatively as soft. The gentle slope of my love's inner thigh as it connects to her perfect bottom might be comparable but, we are both "Soft Ones". I think that I'll never know. I can always travel back and put myself in that period and think of myself as my dark lover. I'll only be able to imagine it, nothing more.

1.15.1

Tentacles,

The internal organs of a large brown bat have a few things in common with the inside of your head. Or so you would think. Recently, an ancient connection has come to light between the South American Large Brown Fruit Bat and developing humans. There is actually a tiny parasite that inhabits your brain whose only other natural habitat is the digestive tract of the bat. As far as scientists can prove, the parasite can only gestate within the cerebral fluid of the human brain. After it matures into an adult, it must be forcefully expulsed by way of a common human reaction, the sneeze. Once airborne, the parasite develops small, crystalline wings and floats on warm air currents until it happens to be swallowed by a bat. This can take years while the parasite, almost desiccated, floats among the heated air. When the parasite enters the bat's digestive tract, it instantly begins to absorb water and sustenance from the nutrient rich landscape around it. It slowly begins to digest the bat from the inside out until the almost immobile bat falls like a rock to the ground below. There, children play with the corpse, evolution growing an eerie desire to play with dead things. Thus, they become infected with egg-encrusted guano. This process happens in monthly cycles and the newspaper has a "Bat-Guanometer" for measuring the probability of being hit by falling bats or coming in contact with their feces. Of course, every once in a while, this benign process goes horribly wrong. When it does, the parasite fails to project itself out of the nose of the victim and stays imbedded within the cerebellum. There, it begins to drain sustenance off the unsuspecting host until, always too late, the victim falls into convulsions gripping the only thing that might help, *Cthulhu Sex*. If you don't believe me, just ask the people who were published in *Cthulhu Sex* what it has done for them. So, keep your *Cthulhu Sex* handy. You never know when you might get a bat guano parasite infestation in your brain.

Alimentarily Yours,

St. Michael

1.15.2

Every once in a while, I receive a truly wonderful e-mail. One that fills me with the joy of knowing I'm doing something that has a deeply enriching effect on those who experience it. I found this in my box one morning and it made my whole day wonderful and happy. Sometimes, it's just the little things that mean so much...

From: Henry Gottlieb Kohler
To: "Cthulhu Sex" frogboy@slack.net
Subject: I was anally raped by Cthulhu

Greeting oh Great One,
Just a belated message to let you know how much I enjoyed *Cthulhu Sex*. I rolled it up and fucked it till I was sore... and the words and stories inside were cool too! Passed the other copies on to others of the Dark Brotherhood. Enjoyed Shh and The Phone Company along with that story you wrote that I was unable to read at the coffee shop. I finally got to read it, you sick fuck! I know it's all autobiographical. So what did you do with the bodies? Could I have a skull? Keep up the good (EVIL) work and please send future issues. Did you read Resume With Monsters by William Browning Spencer yet? If not, you should. You will like.
Yrs.,
Henry Gottlieb Kohler
PRECARIOUS
M.A.S.
333
MYCOPHILE

PS – I did a spell check on this letter and my computer KNEW I spelled Cthulhu wrong!!! Oh my God, it's download-ing a streaming audio file... of chanting! "IA Yogsothoth...", etc. Is that bad?

Thank you, Precarious, for those heartwrenching words. To answer your question, which you already know by now, the file is designed to call forth a minion of said god. The minion has probably disemboweled you by now, spreading your intestines across the walls like crepe paper. Your blood has been used to write mind-numbingly horrific texts on the ceiling. Your hair has ignited and chased off the neighbors' cats. Your genitalia is frozen on a glacier in the Himalayas and there will be pieces of you found in the rivers near your house. From all of us here at *Cthulhu Sex*, we wish you all the best in your next step of spiri-tual evolution.

1.15.3

I occasionally find things that make no sense but fill me with a dread so deep I can't express it in words. When the band I, Parasite sent this to me, I felt that dread. Due to the lowbrow style of writing, I had to transcribe it. Then, sensing that there were deeper meanings, I had Father Baer do a translation of the piece. And there was the answer to my horror. Read on brave soul.

Subject: yes my husband wae in the veteran
war in the delta and he has a rash the groin area and he wa told it was jungleroit or ringworm it does lok like ringworm it's in a circle and it only comes when he sweats and whenhe gets hot we were wanting to know theirs any kind of creams you can get at the drugstore that you don't have to have a perscription for? and I have one more questin ater it goes away should it come back again? I would a appricate if you would please take the time to write me back and answere my questions.

Transcription:

By St. Michael (written while in communion with alien presences through a dark portal in a cup of coffee)

Subject: Yes, My husband was in the Veteran (should be connected to the main paragraph)
War, stationed in the delta (assumed location). He has a rash in the groin area. He was told (supposedly by doctors) that it was jungle rot or ringworm. It looks like ringworm as it's in a circle and appears (though come has an interesting connotation). We

were wanting to know if there is any cream available at a drugstore that is non-prescription (presumebly to treat the rash)? I have one more question, after it disappears, should it return? I would appreciate it if you would take the time to write me back with an answer to my questions.

Translation:

By Father Baer (after reading a passage detailing St. Michael's education in the ritual use of medicaments)

Subject: My husband's return…

After the possession of the populous of New Orleans, the chosen shall go forth and mate with the best and the brightest, spreading our seed like jungle rot. Their path shall be the path of the ringworm, spiraling out in concentric shapes, moving quickly through the warm southern regions, creating a balm for our kind. Spreading our word through fevered dreams, the poor unfortunates will find no cure. They are found wandering the soon to be swamp-infested towns, looking for solace. Vainly they will search through arcana or escape into the world of physical pleasures. When the swamp overcomes the Molasi Door, they will ascend into the maw of the great darkness. Thus shall all be infected with our plague.

There is an obvious threat to the existence of all human beings in this seemingly harmless text. I believe that this message should be sent to as many people as possible. We must warn everyone that we can. That way, the fear will be instilled in our hapless victims and allow us to take over with as little resistance as possible. Their end is near. Our time is nigh.

1.15.4

We enjoyed the letter that Mark sent last issue so much we asked him for more of his provocative and insightful words. After a long battle for supremacy in the theater of colons (he really likes his colons), this reconstituted version of Mark was only able to submit a rant against a software creator about the manner in which their product was corrupted. While we were able to streamline the letter into a readable diatribe and were originally going to publish it, every time we sent the file a doorway opened and unspeakable things started happening to our staff.

1.15.5

Here, spread before you, are all the pieces for a puzzle that you have no choice but to solve. The beginnings for the quest for the pieces are hinted at in the words and illustrations in the magazine. They will lead you to the places you never knew existed. The whisper of the fearsome silence on the empty tracks of subways as you sit alone waiting for the train you know must come. They hint at the cause of the miasmal gasses released at the opening of a sewer lid some strangely suited human enters as you walk by. They burn with the temptation of the nightmare you wake from that covers you in sweat yet somehow eludes your memory. They scream of the static on the television that speaks with inhuman voices about secrets you never wanted to know. They allude to the cold vacuum of space where alien intelligences plot to devour the flesh and soul of everyone you've ever cared about. They tell of these secrets and more if you listen carefully. You never know when you'll find the answers, but they are there, calling to you. Take these and use them as a shield against the fear that cowers the rest of society into the conforming apathy. Use them for there is little else to protect you once you know. Wear them like badges and perhaps you will find others who understand. Don't hold onto them too hard, they tend to vanish when you most need them. When all is said and done, you are alone against these mutilating forces. You and your *Cthulhu Sex*.

Sleep well,

St. Michael

P.S. Some things are never explained in life. These are the things that we have to find for ourselves. I curse the day I found that out. Of course, I also curse the day I couldn't open up that jar of deliciously creamy peanut butter. Such is life.

1.16.1

Greetings! Welcome to the first full-sized magazine format of *Cthulhu Sex*. Between our wondrously macabre covers, we have a splendid display of unique pieces from some of our past favorites as well as the creative endeavors of *Cthulhu Sex* virgins. We have slaved night and day to bring this cursed book to you. As you flip through these pages, think about the delightful chills that will crawl up and down your spine. Think about the chills and then think about the contact poison that covers the pages. Too late anyway so might as well enjoy!

Now that you will surely pass on in the next twenty-four hours, try to get your mind on something else. Something like, "little rainbows caught in the dew drops of yellow flowers," should allow you to keep your focus off of the slowly degenerating nerve endings that are even now slowing your ability to think straight. Perhaps, "a gentle breeze blowing the light musk off of beautiful bodies resting on white sands of an evening beach," might turn your mind away from the rotting tendrils of those irreparable nerve cells that will flake off and drift uselessly in your bloodstream. There must be some image that would help you not think about the possibility that the fragments will concentrate at the opening of the Vena Cava, killing you before the poison can take full effect.

Forget about that for a few moments and peruse our wonderful magazine. Examine our spectacular centerfold for a brief respite from your morbid thoughts. You could read a couple of stories or ponder the poetry. Another option is to cloud your visualization of your demise by being illuminated by the illustrations scattered throughout the writings. As you're relaxing, don't let your mind drift to the degradation of your body after the toxin has run its course. The reanimation of your corpse, to be used in the armies of the dead, should not even begin to cloud your daydreaming mind.

The day that our masses shall rise up from their graves to take over the world is near. We will have whole legions of reanimated corpses with which to decimate the population. The rest of the broken-willed people will be enslaved and forced to do horrible things to each other. Only when the dark gods are finished with their pitiful playthings will they be released. Oh, and how destructive this release will be. Floods of blood will sweep through the streets and seep into the desiccated earth. You will add but one more set of hands to propagate our horror. How splendid will the Hag'urrAh sing the triumphs of J'llali. All will bow to the might of Ct'hulina and the… Uh, I mean to say…Uh… Think of flowers and beaches. Don't think of dying. Remember, flowers.

Again, I would like to thank Father Baer for his work in this endeavor. I would like to thank all the condemned souls who have contributed to this tome. I'll also thank you if you say a little prayer to *Cthulhu Sex* before you finally give up the ghost. Especially one that begins "Oh, you who rule my world…" or something along those lines. Or a really juicy one that I can put into the Letters section of the next issue. I could entitle the column *The Thousand Screaming Souls*. But that is a plan for another day.

I would like to take the time to say a few words that have nothing to do with death, poison or reanimation for use in undead armies. The first thing I would like to do is to thank the wonderful staff at two cafes whose names are now lost to me for their support of my coffee habit. The endless coffee, during the night at one of them and during the day at the other, kept me chemically able to focus on the commentary, editing and layout of *Cthulhu Sex*. I would also like to thank the droves of psychotic people, who tried to pull me into conversation about their whatever-drug-they-were-doing-at-the-time lives, for their efforts to keep me focused on my work while I fearfully ignored them. I greatly appreciate my friends, who sat and talked with me while I worked, for their ability to keep me sane and the aforementioned psychotic people at bay. I wish to thank Graves and Maury for their tutelage in the ways of desktop publishing. I also thank the people at the Small Press Co-op for their technical support and printing efforts that allowed this issue to come into physical reality. Following that, I thank the distributors that have sent small bundles of joy to the outer realms of the world. Finally, I wish to thank the dark lords and ladies, who have inspired, guided and protected all the people involved with every aspect of *Cthulhu Sex*. May their sleep be long and deep. I wish all these individuals and all you readers happiness and joy. I know that each and every one of you will be by my side as our undead armies raze the world and take the planet for our own. After all, you've been poisoned.

As you have so much time on your hands, enjoy the words and pictures as your life functions irreversibly slow. There are only one in a billion people, already of an inhuman stock, who won't be effected by the poison. These people don't know of their heritage as the introduction of the alien matter is lost far back in time. If you happen to be one of these unlucky few, the poison will not affect you in the least. You will miss the chance to join our horde of reanimated warriors. However, you will be able to pick up the next issue of *Cthulhu Sex* in which we hope to have a poison that works on you. If you already feel ill, this bit of information is as useless to you as a guanometer would be.

Take your time and wander through the tangled forest of beauty you hold in your hands. There really is no point in worrying about your fate. Just let what will happen, happen. There is nothing you can do.

So, enjoy yourself between these sheets,
St. Michael

1.16.2

Another letter arrived from our friend Henry Gottlieb Kohler III. He again showed his mastery of verbal expression as is represented by his unique phrasing. Besides this, he exhibited wondrous artistic skill in a beautiful illustration.

Of course, he has been dealt with for the suggestion about the term, *frogboy*. There have been small creatures introduced to his rectal opening. These creatures will slowly dig their way into his abdominal cavities and then into the rest of his body. Soon he will be an unstoppable soldier in our army of malignancy. At the introduction of the creatures, his only comment was, "Was that it?"

The letter, while kept in its original form when published, also created some curious results. Some of our subscribers wrote in about mysterious occurrences happening to them. Some of these occurrences weirdly matched up with the illustrations we were sent by Mr. Kohler. The contents of the letter while in the original issue are not displayed here due to the ongoing investigation of these occurrences.

1.16.3

*C*thulhu *Sex* was anonymously sent this letter describing an occurrence at a famous university. This letter describes such a mysterious situation that we felt it was in the best interests of all to publish it here. We hope that the sender of the letter, the author Joshua or whomever has knowledge of this unspeakable crime, comes forward to relate their story to us. Without these tomes, which we all know contain sensitive information, the plans of the dark gods will be kept to the selfish few. It is a travesty to secret these works away. It is a necessity for all to be able to be "instructed" in their inevitable destruction. We can only wait and pray.

Here is a transcription of the letter. We were going to introduce some images of the letter as well but they seem to have taken on a life of their own much to the chagrin of our imager. There seems to be some organic material on the first page of the document. We unfortunately do not have access to the facilities needed to analyze the stain. We would gladly make the document available for any individual or group that could perform this service for the betterment of all.

This letter was transcribed in its original form.

Patrick Gawain, Esq.

It has been brought to my attention that several volumes of antiquity are indeed missing from the university library. As you may well know, such volumes as these are not for all eyes. Indeed! The very thought of some person, being not well intentioned, getting their hands on these tomes chills me to the heart.

Dan Phillips, my assistant curator at the university museum, as well as Margaret Holmes, the chief librarian, are the only other people empowered with the library reference room master keys. Oh, and myself, of course. That's what I meant when I said "only other." Miss Holmes has related to me what seems to be her usual routine of locking up the library this past Thursday, September 21. "I remember the volumes in the case," she said, those being the four missing volumes, "When I made my last round, Jack Standran, you know him, the tall, heavy set security man," I nodded and she continued. "Well, at just past nine, I called Mr. Standran and he showed up at the library lobby. He watched as I locked up the doors, front and back, as usual. I then set the alarms, after which we then are able to leave through the front doors, so long as we do so within two minutes, again locking the doors behind us."

I have checked with the alarm security company. They have assured me that all entries to the building are indeed fitted with working alarms, all doors and windows. They do, however, also say that none of the doors or windows seem to have been in any way tampered with. The Arkham Police concur. Dan Phillips and I are at a loss as to what we are to do next. Dr. Jonson, Miskatonic's President, has asked me to "Find the culprit, or else." Of course, he knows I am at my wit's end, yet there is no remorse. Jonson's reputation, the school's in general, rests on recovering these volumes. They are certainly among our most cherished possessions. Yet, for Jonson, it is all politics!

I, and perhaps a dozen others in the world!, know the true meaning of this theft. And I can but tremble at the thought of the dire repercussions that may materialize. You, too, Patrick, know these volumes from your Father's writings and must, must join me in the search. I will try to calm my nerves to better see this through. I have no choice but to devise some route to proceed on.

I will do so and I wait in excitement to hear from you.

Please respond immediately. Your Father, as you know, would have had it this way.

As always-

Your kind friend,

Joshua

1.16.4

I would like to take a few moments to refute the claims that the three bodies found outside of our offices are connected to us in any way. There is no symbolic or actual similarity between the ritualistic runes carved into them and the artistic decorations that adorn our doors and walls. Though there might seem to be some stylistic similarities, they are two entirely different scripts. The writings on the bodies are the degrading and malicious Tu'uafinto while the beautiful Du'aub'Piou adorns our offices. Besides the differences in the writings, there is also the difference in weapon used. We would never stoop to use such a crude instrument as the scalpel. We prefer the exquisite sharpness of ceramic blades over the flashy metal. In fact, we would rather use obsidian, if we can get it, instead due to its esthetic visuals. The quick sparkle of a sharpened black-glass blade before it cleanly slices flesh is definitely held above the boring old silver streak of sterile steel. Due to the clumsy and, I must be blunt, boring way the cuts were made, I believe it could only have been done by a novice to this field. All of our ritual sacrifices are highly trained professionals, not sniveling little murderers. If all of this isn't evidence enough, there is the matter of leaving refuse where one works: only a moron would leave the bodies in front of their work place. If anything, it should suggest that someone is trying to frame us. They used a similar writing style to ours, in a similar ritual and then dropped off the bodies on our doorstep. We should form a coalition to watch out for these evil infidels.

Now that I have said my piece about these childish murders, I would like to thank all the people who have given parts of their souls to fill out the empty space between our covers. If

you haven't already figured it out, all the stories and illustrations in this magazine are but figments of your imagination. It
is a side effect of the poison that covers these pages. The people
reported to create the works contained herein are real people
and their works truth unto themselves. How were we able to
transfer these works to you if there really isn't anything printed
in this magazine? That is part of the deeper secret that you
won't realize until it is too late. Actually, it is already too late
for all but seven of you in the world (the one in a billion who
aren't affected by the poison). I guess it wouldn't hurt to tell you
the secret. But then again, it wouldn't be a secret afterwards,
would it? You'll have to wait for the inevitable enlightenment
that occurs when your life flashes before your eyes as you gasp
your last breath. Isn't that ironic?

I have a vision of the future for our delightfully deceased
world that has been granted to me by the great unholy dark
lords. In this future existence, the automobile reigns supreme.
After gaining conscious thought, automobiles will start a society based on their ancient history, centered on the one thing
they see and hear most: advertisement. Ad executives will
become the upper class, charioted around in intelligent autos.
They will fight a losing battle with our armies of the dead. But
their propaganda will cover this fact with glittering images of
happy VW Bugs dancing next to the subservient class of Imacs.
The superpowers will be Germany, Japan and the USA, domi-
nating the automotive industry and belching out fumes to cover
the world in protective smog. Alien races will continue to visit,
mutilating Chevrolets and doing conception experiments on
Volvos. However, their attempts at contact will be thwarted by a
super-secret group of Illuminati, codenamed Ferrari. Once the
ravages of war are over and the dead return to their graves, the
only force on the planet will be the magazine you hold in your
hands. Its illusions will carry on in both the physical and meta-
physical states of existence, causing a breach in the space-time
continuum. This breach will slowly suck everything into itself,
like the vacuum cleaners in old cartoons, until there is nothing left but a black spot. Oh, the glorious doom plotted for the
universe!

Of course, until that fate befalls the world, there is always the next issue of *Cthulhu Sex*. In that issue, we will have many new faces to present their twisted works and some old friends to show off their new strengths. By all means, if you're still alive, pick up the next issue. It should do your body good.

As always, enjoy,

St. Michael

1.17.1

In this time of extra sunlight and tanned bodies, *Cthulhu Sex* has decided to print an edition specifically for summer. I looked at other magazines to see exactly what this might entail. Of course, the predominant feature in most of them was swimsuits. "Hmm," I pondered, "What exactly could *Cthulhu Sex* present in the way of swimsuits?" I began to search through our submissions in a flurry of inquisitive exploration, not sure quite what I wanted nor what I'd find. I ran up against a slew of issues I never thought I would run up against. I was plagued by such questions as: "Does wearing the skin of another count as a 'swimsuit'?", "Can a 'swimsuit' be used to swim in other than water?", "What would the various Dark Lords approve as swimwear?", "What would they find sexy?", and "Pictures of lunch don't count, do they?" I was boggled by the multitude of questions to the point where I decided to take a break for a while, commune with my gods, have a bite to eat and get some sleep. I figured the answer would reveal itself to me in the mysterious way the world always works. Little did I know how right I was.

I had been lounging around my apartment when the heat from the big hurty thing in the sky began to become unbearable. I decided to quickly dress myself, grab my accoutrements and trip off to Limbo, a coffee shop I adore that has air conditioning and outlets. Within the first five seconds of my being dressed, I was covered in a thin film of sweat. Outside it was a steamy 101 degrees with 85% humidity. Inside, it was a dead calm 101 with just enough extra heat to make the difference between the apartment and the oven practically nil. Mostly gliding over the vaporized sweat beneath my feet, I floated down the crisping street and into the forgiving dark of the subway. I was sure the alternative transportation, my car, would be the worst form of sun-inferno death at that point. Thankfully, the subway car was quite the opposite, the air cool, crisp and clean (as clean as subway car air gets). When I stepped out at my destination station, things began to get weird.

The first thing I noticed was that I was having trouble seeing. I thought that perhaps I was passing out. But the color of the obstruction to my vision was white as opposed to the black I see when I faint or am called by the Dark Lords. It seemed that a mist of strange origin was blocking my path. I figured there was nothing to do but move straight ahead; my furious movements defiantly attempting to prove the mist wrong. It suddenly became apparent that it was only in front of me by the peripheral traces of people passing my right and left.

It was when I turned my head to see the people that two things happened. First, the movement of the fog to block my vision told me that it was something specifically to do with my glasses. The chill of the subway and the warmth of the station air combined to condense the humidity onto the surface of my glasses. While I was feeling slightly silly for my delusional ignorance, the second, and less humorous, occurrence happened. I walked straight into a support beam for the ceiling overhead. Sure, it might sound humorous, but let me assure you that it was not. Let me explain the repercussions of this action and you will see what I mean.

I found myself in a different world all together. It was a world that I regularly inhabit but on different days, a dark world filled with daemons of strange and beautiful trappings. The distinction between the males and females was only really discernible by careful analysis of the creatures themselves, their clothing revealing little if anything. Even under heavy scrutiny, some of the creatures were beyond definition, bearing no traits of either sex. They were crowded together around me, pressing their various sticky body parts, slick leather-like clothing and hard chitinous armor against me.

However, it wasn't I that was attracting their attention but the stage behind me. As I turned my eyes towards the stage, a strange feeling of dread overcame my reeling mind. There, in all their glory, was a collection of some of the most bizarre and uniquely appealing creatures I had ever seen. I recognized almost all of them as human. The thing that my mind had failed to comprehend was that they were all parading around in swimwear. That is from whence the dread definitely came. These humans exhibited their wares for all the daemons to see, accompanied by cheers for each undulation, vacillation and oscillation of flesh. There were particularly rousing responses for specific body parts revealed.

As the winners were announced (a playful, rotund giant of a man with a mask and a pretty boy exhibitionist with spikes on his head), I realized the world at large wouldn't have the gentle sensibilities needed to enjoy this special style of aesthetics. If I hadn't been previously inured to the unique tastes of the daemons that surrounded me, I might not have been able to enjoy, much less stomach the goings on. At the end, there was a roar of applause which I joined.

The roar gradually melded into the passing of a subway train as I regained my senses. My hands were waving in an attempt to clap above my laid-out body as people stared. I regained my composure which consisted of scuttling to my feet and stumbling about as I tried to unsuccessfully balance the heavy bag I was toting. Dropping back into my attempt at a stoic façade, I continued to grasp the gist of the vision. There were some things that the world was not ready for yet. A swimsuit issue of *Cthulhu Sex* was one of them. I figured that I might try again next year as I walked towards the exit.

Desiccated tentacles,

St. Michael

PS Congratulations to the winners of the *Long Black Veil's* Lost Boys beach party swimsuit competition, they earned it.

1.17.2

Unfortunately, due to the process of printing a magazine, we cannot include some of the more colorful and fragrant pieces we've been sent. As you read this text, imagine a letter that is purely composed of the delicate scent of rose water. Let it tickle your senses with a hint of dry paper. Close your eyes and let the images it brings wash over you. Then imagine an envelope filled with some crunchy material that reeks of rot. You dread opening it and set it aside for a few days. The smell becomes unbearable and you ponder the issue of whether to open it or toss it. Finally, you open it, revealing the mold covered, crispy flesh of some creature you hope isn't human. What a waste if it is; desiccated and bloodless isn't a state that suggests "Fun". However, we have received these delightful letters, presented for your enjoyment.

1.17.3

What follows is a letter of request from our own Oliver Baer to Arkham Labs for analysis of the substance found on the first letter received from the mysterious Joshua. Beside the request itself, there is a description of the experiences that followed our reception of the letter. We are interested in finding those who have had similar experiences so that we might document a history of this sort of thing. Read on and hope you never become one who observes such an event or, if you have, hope you can forget.

Arkham Labs
56 Krakengel Way
Arkham, MA 12809
Dear Sirs:

We have recently come into possession of a document which might be of interest to you. Of course, you may think us mad when you hear what we have to tell you, but it is all true. As a matter of fact, we have included the document in question along with a sample of some organic material scraped into a 5″ smoked plastic box. I refer to the plastic as smoked because it darkened upon contact with the organic substance. If you would do us the courtesy of analyzing both of these materials, we, not to mention the rest of the world, would be entirely in your debt. But, I will explain all in good time.

It all started when we received this letter in the post from someone named Joshua to a Patrick Gawain, Esq. The letter seemed innocuous enough in its ranting style: "...documents have been stolen from the reference library... they contain horrible secrets to destroy the worlds... you must help us... blah, blah, blah." We should have noticed the letterhead straight away but we were distracted by an odd stain. The stain, which appeared to be organic in nature, was splashed across the upper right corner as if grasping for the letterhead. It was of a brownish-yellow hue and grainy consistency. The letter had been put on the table, near the lamp, after being read by one of our staff members, who had gone to wash his hands, when there was a crash and a scream. The crash came from the lamp being smashed and the scream was from our coworker who was standing in the bathroom looking at his hands. They seemed to be pulsing as though alive with worms directly under his skin. He started clawing at himself as if he could pull them out. We tried to help by running at him with any object we could find to cut out the offending undulations. Our coworker started going into paroxysms, each flail sending some kind of barbed tentacle at us. We lost three of our advertising staff this way.

While this monstrosity was stripping the staff's skin off of them like one scales a fish, I examined the manuscript for clues as to an explanation. After picking up the lamp and placing it back in its appropriate position on the table, I noticed that, not only did the ink of the letterhead seem to be moving subtly, but that there seemed to be something insinuated in to the paper itself. Upon closer examination this ink, for lack of a better word, seemed to create words behind the words of the letter. I started to read them but the mere sounds I uttered seemed to change reality around me. I know that it seems that I may have been in shock from the events I was experiencing, but it is true. You must believe me.

"Ia-a-a,   Rua-a-a,   Ma-a-a-La-a-a,   Te-e-entra-a-ari-i-i, R'y-y-yle-e-eh..."

Each word brought waves of nausea flowing through my body, yet I continued as if each syllable were compelling me to say the next. After the fifth word, I collapsed, unable to bear the tides of sensations flooding over me. When I awoke, I was neither on a floor nor in an office. I was holding a long-bladed object above a woman who was laid upon a cyclopean obsidian block. The object in question seemed to be also of obsidian, as if it were sliced off of the block. The handle was formed out of what I hesitate to describe as a head. It was malformed; but even this is not an accurate description, for it truly had no shape, almost as if the oblong lump of rock flowed into a waffle mold with each square containing maleficent beads therein, for they were surely not eyes. From this horror the blade extended in what I can only describe as a long, sharpened tentacle. The woman looked up at me with such fear in her eyes that I tried to pull myself away. It was then that I noticed both the state of my dress and her undress. I seemed to be clothed in a dark robe of some kind, the darkness, which edges the blue-green glow that seemed to be everywhere, to my left and right turning out to be caused by a giant hood cast over my head. Around my neck a pendant glowed with the same blue-green otherworldly light. To my further shock, two long pseudopodia seemed to be coming from an opening in my robe around my waist. They were caressing the woman in an obscene manner, sliding over and around her face, across her chest and between her legs. This would have been a great ego boost to me but for two things. One, I noticed that the rest of my lower body seemed to be pulsing with various mutated versions of these pseudopodia. Two, after the bits of me quivered with pleasure, which seemed to originate somewhere around my waist, they sprouted little barbs and waved menacingly above the pure girl. She, as one would guess by this time, looked pleadingly up at me. She was bound to the rock, again through some kind of organic material that seemed to attach itself to the rock like cement. Her clothes, obviously in tatters, looked like a defeated battle flag from the various rips my members seemed to be inflicting upon her. The noise again repeated itself in my ears, "Ia, Rua, Mala, Tentari, R'yleh."

It was at this moment that I realized that it was coming from my own lips. In vain, I tried to stop. I tried dropping the knife and clasping my hands to my mouth but nothing would obey me. It was as if I was possessed by some malefic presence. I tried willing it away, anything to make my mouth stop uttering those words, my hand cease holding… I'm still unsure why it took so long for me to notice my actions, or senses for that matter, during this nightmare, for it had to be just that. But it was then that I noticed my hand plunging the knife downward, not cutting but very slowly stroking the area around her heart and abdomen with the tip of the blade. Little bubbles of red formed on each line as my stroking grew in intensity. It was worse when I realized my tongue was dripping saliva onto her. I tried with all my will to call on the God I had for so long forsaken. Finally, in a last-ditch effort, I tried throwing myself off of the titanic altar.

There was a rushing sound, followed by images flowing past as if one were swimming up from the bottom of a pool. Then a violent shaking and noises once again. This time, it was my partner shaking me awake, claiming I was mumbling something incoherent. It seems he had tried to call me from his office. There was a report of a loud popping sound accompanied by something that can only be described as "liquid noise" as well as weird rambling from my area. I started in on my experience when I realized it would be pushed off as lack of sleep. So I refrained, I assured him I was all right and just needed some sleep. He told me that the popping was probably just the light bulb in my lamp. This could be replaced by another staff member. He then went on to describe a mysterious seizure that seemed to be affecting certain staff. I didn't really hear this, my attention drawn by something that chilled me to the very marrow. As I said previously, my senses seem to be impaired, which was why I only noticed it while he was speaking, but there was blood on me as well as the document in question. Now, the document seemed to be disintegrating as if eaten by the substance in its upper right corner.

In addition to some leave, my partner has allowed me to write this letter to you in order that you may quell my fears as to this unknown substance. Thanks.

Sincerely,
Oliver Baer
Copy Editor of *Cthulhu Sex*

Due to the unfortunate occurrences described in this letter, we are down two for our annual volleyball/human barbecue tournament. Anyone interested should contact us at the address in the back of the magazine.

1.17.4

This is the second letter that we have received from the mysterious Joshua. This one delves a touch deeper into the horrific occurrences that have plagued him. We are intrigued and terrified by the implications of this document, particularly at his desire for a seaside trip in the midst of his dilemma. As we requested when we printed the first letter (issue 16), we would like anyone who has information on this abhorrent theft to come forward and help us clear up this mystery. May the Dark Lords grant us solace from the destructive outcome this letter portends.

As far as who this Joshua is, we have found a small amount of data on him through various occult connections. What we have found we now share.

Joshua West (a.ka. Kenn Schubach of the less-decayed Schubachs), has a Ph.D. in Obsidian Studies from the Armitage School of Volcanic Leftovers, Miskatonic University, Arkham, Massachusetts. Hoodwinked at an early age into the belief that this world is ever on the verge of admitting into its realm the cheesy Elder Gods (and perchance an Ancient One or two), he fights a never-ending battle for truth, justice and box seats at the next Yankees World Series game. "I ain't Providence."

Miskatonic University

Patrick Gawain, Esq.

Your letter has just arrived by post and I am almost unable to keep my pen on the paper. The information you have supplied me with has enabled my wandering brain to focus. Also, I have been able to recall many lost ponderings, most of which, I thought, had been thankfully buried.

Thank you for sending along your father's correspondence and notes of the two years 1919 and 20. That he actually met the legendary Sir Amery Wendy-Smith in Africa is most astounding and lends greater credibility to the claims he laid down in the voluminous epistles. This just may be the supporting data I will likely need to keep my horrific thoughts from loosening my grasp on this realm of sanity (which has been quite pressured since the disappearance of the volumes from the university library).

As you mentioned, and I verily agree most earnestly, one of us must engage in a ghastly foray to Innsmouth. Since you say that it is quite impossible for you to remove yourself from the committee until the holidays, I must go. We cannot wait even another sunrise if there may yet be a chance to stop the Triassic monstrosities from reappearing to claim their birthright.

I have wired Lord Kimbleroy of the British Museum. He has responded and assures me that their copy of the *Pnakotic Manuscripts* is quite safe and presently under twenty-four hour guard. Our copy of these manuscripts was the only original known to exist; we will have to make do with what is at hand. It is only somewhat reassuring that Kimbleroy's copy is guarded. He will keep it so until we can get there to pay the "Guardian". But pay we must; it is only a very little sacrifice now. I dare not think of the payments needed later if we sit idly by and simply watch things transpire.

We will encounter the same situation, quite unfortunately, with the Olaus Wormius translation of Abd al-Azrad's abhorred work. Kimbleroy has a number of translations and offers all to our eyes. We shall, of course, waste no time with Baron Frederick I's *Cultus Maleficarum*; for, as we both know, *The Sussex Manuscript* is nothing if not unreliable. But I get well ahead of myself.

There are four full weeks before the holiday season begins and I told our gracious Lord Kimbleroy that he should not expect us until the third week in November. He affords us carte blanche in the museum—as long as we do not defile the great museum's long-heralded legacy by getting any mention of its name into the news. Good God, man! What news? He knows as well as we that few and far between are believers to be found.

I have also written to Professor Karl von Osten at the University of Buenos Aires, but as yet had no response. It is good to hear that you have contacted Susan Gamwell at Chicago's Field Museum. She is certainly one of the few who should be informed of these events, as it may have begun again. And if it has, she can help, only let us pray that it will not spread so quickly as it did when your father returned from Africa.

I only wish your father had questioned Sir Wendy-Smith more ardently about the *G'harne Fragments* and had written such dialogue in his journals. Forgive me, Patrick, for I am not myself. I meant no disrespect. You know that I admired your father above all others; his work and the great intense teachings he provided us have no equal. I had only hoped that there were more scholarly reflections on the *Fragments* gathered via his brief encounter with Wendy-Smith. It surely would have been our best guide to comprehending our plight, since nothing survived the Wendy-Smith "accident" on the Yorkshire moors so long ago.

Believe me when I tell you that I was completely captivated by Jeffrey Gawain's retelling of his discussion with Sir Wendy-Smith regarding the Cult of the Bloody Tongue. It's just that I have always believed that wasted opportunities will invariably return to haunt you—and in this case, it may kill you.

I leave tomorrow. I will be on the 11:10 out of Arkham Station and, at a time sooner than I could ever want, I will stand in Innsmouth. You and I both decreed that it would be a very cold day in Hell when either of us returned there (and Hell seems hotter than ever right now). We know too many unspeakable truths, how it is not true that no one inhabits Innsmouth any longer. One only needs to know which side of the Manuxet to survey. We can also find what's left of the Esoteric Order of Dagon. Such scrupulousness! And yet not a soul believes. No one wants to.

I had better get some rest (if I can). Proust continues to

be quite right; a certain odor can transport you to a different time and place in a long lost memory. Actually, tonight is quite reversed. The nauseating memory of Obed Marsh, his ancestors and descendants, and the very town of Innsmouth itself, has surrounded me, my senses relaying that putrid stench I had hoped never to encounter again.

I shall correspond anon. I remain.

Your kind friend,

Joshua

1.17.5

And here we are again, at the end of another issue. I'm always filled with mixed feelings at this point. There is joy at the birth of another creation, yet I feel a loss at its leaving. Then again, there is the excitement of dealing with the next issue. Oh, not to mention the dread of having to go through all the random problems that always come with putting something like this together. No matter how I feel about the issue, there is always a warm spot somewhere in my abdomen (ambiguous enough?) for the people who have helped me out. Most important, there is Oliver. Without him, *Cthulhu Sex* would be a random slew of misspellings. His diligence and advice makes everything come together. Then there is my lovely partner. Her understanding and support lend me strength when I have none. And, of course, there are all the people who have supported *Cthulhu Sex* with their submissions. Their amazing skills and patience give us the oomph that we need to be the creative, humorous and bizarre thing we have become. The advertisers are all our best friends because they make it all happen (visit them or we'll kill you). Personally, I wouldn't be able to continue *Cthulhu Sex*, let alone my life, without the coffee gods of the cafes whose names are maintained only by drinking their offerings. I have to mention my friends because they would flay the flesh from my bones if I didn't. I'd be in the asylum if they weren't around. The people at the Small Publishers Co-Op get my deepest thanks for being so helpful in the physical creation of *Cthuihu Sex*. I send my appreciation to my retreat from all the madness of *Cthulhu Sex*, The Long Black Veil. That's about that. If I didn't mention you and you're pissed about it, suck my tentacle, I forgot.

Now, to totally change the subject, I have a moral dilemma that I think should be answered before the next issue or two. I was wondering if it is morally incorrect to present material that documents the "art" of a currently wanted serial killer. Specifically, printing photographs, by his own hand, of the unique placement of a serial killer's mutilated victims. Not, of course, that I've had an offer from such a person to publish any of their works, just a philosophical question for debate. One more thing, is it illegal to publish such things? I'm just asking.

Have you ever noticed the summer is a wonderful time filled with exciting things to do and wonderful places to go? Unfortunately, it seems that all the loonies from the far corners of the world think so too. Here in New York, I've run into more than my share of these strange people this year. Perhaps it is the turn of the millennium which brings them out. A friend of mine suggested that it was probably some astrological anomaly that specifically states that the insanities of people must be exhibited at this time. Of course, he was personalizing the statement at the time, relating it to his own experiences. But, I think it might be more applicable to the continuing onslaught of vulgar, disgusting, lewd and vicious people on the whole.

I recently had a conversation with one of these demented people as they attempted to gain attention that wasn't their due. He suggested that the world is going to be a staging place for a giant battle between the forces of good and evil in the year 2012. The staging place for the forces of evil would be South America. The primary forces would be the evil souls of the dead brought back in zombie form. They would be led by a legion of lieutenant vampires with whips of black gold. Above them would be the generals, immortal Aztec warriors with great weapons of mass destruction. Directing the generals would be a small council of legendary lost Mayans, their knowledge of beyond giving them great power. And presiding over the entirety of the proceedings would be a large sea-monster god. This god's words would be sent out like serpents to strike down the masses before him, causing them to prostrate themselves in fear and awe, dropping their weapons and praying for death. All would be destroyed. Cities would be razed and the world will be thrown into darkness.

It's amazing how right the mentally ill can be, occasionally. The great Dark Lord who reigns over all currently sleeps in a city that is off shore of South America. The city used to be in the center of the known world, but that was before the continental drift ripped the world apart and sunk it. The cataclysms that ensued weren't enough to wake the sleeping giant. Besides that, the Mayan calendar ends in the equivalent of 2012. It's also been foretold that that is the time of the apocalypse in the Bible, for whatever that's worth. But of the basic plans of the battle and its hierarchy, I have no idea. But you can bet your bottom dollar that if it happens, I'll be there.

On that happy note, let me say my good-byes. Try to sleep well at night and think not of the terrible destruction in the future. Just keep your *Cthulhu Sex* handy, you never know when it will come in useful. I might decide to have my own legion in the conflict with it as the club card. Besides, showing it to those pesky door-to-door salesmen, flower guys or traveling preachers is a great way to get rid of them. It also works as a ward against bad breath. If you don't know how, I'm not going to tell you.

Sweet dreams,

St. Michael

1.18.1

Greetings!

Welcome to the *Cthulhu Sex* Anniversary and Halloween issue. As we bring this year to a close, I would like to thank all the disturbed contributors that helped to make *Cthulhu Sex* the horrific and erotic entity it is. This has been a year of great change and growth, taking the hard work of many dedicated people who will never be forgiven. And of course, one of the most important groups of people I'd like to thank includes you, dear reader. Without our morbidly twisted readership, we would be lost in the void of imagination.

We hope you'll enjoy this wondrous holiday of spirit chasing. Halloween is the day all our dark dreams can take form to be banished or embraced as we choose. What we take, we give as gifts to ourselves. What we leave behind, we hope never to see again.

It is in this age-old sentiment that the thread binding us all to this holiday exists. It is this thread that keeps itself in the back of our minds as we play dress up. The costumes and company keep it at bay while the season progresses toward the death that is winter. The gleeful screams of innocent children enjoying their spoils are tainted by it. And when we are finally alone in the dark, we know it, tingling up our spine.

That thread that coils so tautly through us in the season of the witch is fear. Each of us has their own fears. They are as limitless as the colors in a rainbow, from the mundane to the supernatural. The boogeyman that hides beneath our bed. The intruder who breaks in on our helpless family. The multi-legged creature whose shadow haunts down our bedroom wall. The spectral image that peers in our window. Each is different in magnitude, affecting us minutely or immensely. It is all contained within that simple thread; the mundane fear of pain, the psychological fear of mental anguish, the spiritual fear of supernatural terror.

No matter what our individual fears are, they all hold numerous effluvial qualities. To pin down each of these qualities would be impossible, individual fears are unique to the situation. However, distilling these impurities out of the whole leaves specific essences of fear. The greatest yield is the essence of the Unknown.

The Unknown is the unnamable horror that lurks at the edge of consciousness in the cold chill of fear. It is that unmistakable something that would destroy, physically, spiritually or mentally, if it becomes real. It is the thing that could be but hasn't, yet.

It is the anticipation of the Unknown that entrances, pouring cold acid into veins. The closer a situation comes to actualizing this dreaded outcome, of forcing the issue to become conscious, the stronger the tension it causes. The subconscious rebels against possibility with the feeling of an ambiguous threat fueled by the horrific experiences of its nightmare imagination and physicalized as terror. The greater the tension, the stronger the terror.

The moment a fear is realized and faced, it becomes nothing more than an obstacle overcome. The terror in the anticipation becomes a fading memory, disintegrating in the conscious light of knowledge. Without the Unknown, fear is nothing.

Halloween is a pilgrimage to these ideas. People, from ages past through to current times, cavort to avoid the Unknown in the time ahead. They make play, when the natural things around begin to wither, shrivel and die, to avoid the terror in the obvious parallel that they will do the same.

I recommend oblivious jubilation this Halloween, to belay the fears tugging at the corners of your mind. It plays in the shadows behind us and peers into our windows while we sleep. And when we are alone in the dark, it becomes real.

Peruse this issue at your leisure. It is packed with illustrations, prose and poetry rife with glimpses of the Unknown. Take your time and allow the full effect of the words and images to work their nightmare magic on you. After all, there is no where you can go to escape your fear. Especially on Halloween.

Tentacles,

St. Michael

1.18.2

The following is Oliver Baer's response to the lab report on the materials previously sent to Arkham Labs. The material was sent to us by an anonymous source along with a letter. A series of unique situations which followed its reception prompted Mr. Baer to request the analysis. Any suggestions to resolve this issue would be greatly appreciated.

Arkham Labs
56 Krakengel Way
Arkham, MA 12809
Dear Sirs:

I would like to thank you for your thorough and in-depth analysis of the sample I sent you. Unfortunately, as I feared, your testing failed to produce any concrete result. Your conclusion that the closest earthly organism the sample is akin to is a slime mold is a starting point. But that only increases my fears… My God! Could horrid creatures of nightmare walk amongst us? But I digress, I resent the implication that it somehow produces a hallucinogen and the dead people products thereof. If my experience on the dread altar was a mere hallucination, then how does one account for the unfortunate loss of your staff member during testing? Most of all, it would not account for the following dire events which I will relay since I wrote to you last. (I hope these events are actually the product of some morbid hallucination for if not, I fear for what we have unleashed.) As I mentioned in my last letter, because of my harrowing experience and frayed nerves, it seemed prudent for me to take some leave. I left the office and endeavored to spend some quiet time alone in my apartment reading, listening to music and sleeping. All of this I succeeded in doing, for a time. Then one night, while I was relaxing to Vivaldi's *Rites of Spring*, I thought I heard the flutes a little louder than usual. Not remembering a crescendo in this part of the piece, I listened more intently to the rest of it. I realized the sound was not so much that of flutes or other musical instruments, but more a combination of animal sounds such as chirping birds and chittering rats with an underlying scritching noise. When I got up to lower the volume, there seemed to be a shadow rustle against the window. I know at this point, you are asking yourselves the same question I was, a shadow? At night? How was I able to discern it at all? It was when I took another look that I wanted to scream. There, outside my window, stood the woman from my previous experience, quite the feat, if you'll pardon the pun, since I live on the 6th floor, motioning me towards her. There was a strange, for lack of a better term, glowing darkness around her that seemed to stir the wind through her hair. Her long white arms beckoned me invitingly. She had on a tattered white robe which parted around the waist revealing a mass of tentacles encircling her abdomen like a belt, some of which also beckoned to me or were stirred by the unearthly breeze. I shut my blinds, drew my curtains and withdrew into the bedroom, telling myself I was overtired from my long exciting day.

I had taken a brisk walk in the park, enjoying the air and watching the people, when I decided to ring up a friend I haven't seen in a while. He had just come back from a trip abroad where he had made the acquaintance of the local witch doctor. The tales he told of unspeakable rites and arcane mysteries sent chills up my spine. These stories prompted me to tell him of my experience and ask his advice. After listening intently, he told me it sounded very much like the story an Englishman he had met abroad by the name of Lord Kimbleroy had related to him. Lord Kimbleroy claimed to have traveled widely in Africa. There he had met a shaman who regularly embarked upon a certain dream quest. This quest contained similar qualities to that of my experience. My friend suggested, in a similar manner as you have, that there was some hallucinogenic chemical on the paper which spurred me on to my adventure. I went home a little unsettled but determined not to let it ruin my day.

I awoke to a faint scratching sound that was difficult to place. At first it seemed to be coming from behind me—the wall, maybe? No. I got up to check the window. Tentatively pulling aside the curtains, I peered through the blinds into the night. Nothing. This was not doing wonders for my nerves. I calmed myself with reminders of all the sounds a building makes which always seem greatly amplified at night. I would have put the matter aside except that for the next three nights my sleep had been disturbed. All, it seems, preceded by a disquieting dream of arcane rituals. The latest was the most horrifying of all. I believe I was dreaming about a previous lover when, in the middle of one of our more passionate moments, she reached around to pull me closer. I proceeded to rhythmically move my hips when I felt something slimy and abrasive rubbing along my leg. Try as I might, I couldn't pull myself free until the dreadful parody of my ex-lover slid off in an orgasmic quiver. I woke up in a cold sweat. There was something dripping into my walnut-occluded throat, a scratching sound in my ears and slime oozing down my leg along my inner thigh. I froze. Then I felt around to see if all of my body parts were intact. They seemed to be except for a soreness around the slimy area. I turned on the light. That's when I practically catapulted myself into the bathroom. The light had shown me an area on my leg dripping a dark gray viscous substance which was moving over an abraded patch of my inner thigh near my crotch. Looking in the mirror, I noticed the same substance mixed with blood in my mouth. I couldn't scrub myself hard enough or fast enough. It was later that week when I called my partner to see about my returning earlier than planned, for anything was better than this madness, that I learned about the coincidental events of a second letter and the mysterious disappearance of two salespeople.

As I mentioned earlier, it seems that you are unequipped to deal with this information with any specifics. Is it possible you could forward me information regarding a specialist in mycology, if indeed this substance is a form of mold as you purport, or a lab with connections to same. If you remain steadfast in your belief that this substance is of unearthly origin, could you recommend a specialist in xenobiology. I remain skeptical.

Yours,

Oliver Baer
Copy Editor
Cthulhu Sex

Cthulhu Sex is currently taking applications for two sales positions and one promotional position. Applications should be sent to the address in the back of the magazine care of *Human Remains Resources*. Join our ever-growing web of tentacles.

1.18.3

W e present the third letter in the mystery of the missing books from Miskatonic U. Joshua brings us clues. Somehow, Kenn Schubach is involved, in ways only he knows…

Patrick Gawain, Esq.

Though I take the next train this evening back to Arkham, I will have the rail officer at the train station post my letter to you this morning. Hopefully, it will arrive some hours before I can reach you by telephone back in Arkham and you can get started. I must tell you of my day (and night!) here now while I can still recall it at all. My memory of the horrible events is as of a nightmare and, as happens with memories of dreams, details are not very clear to begin with and fade with each passing moment.

You will recall that the stop at Innsmouth is not quite inside the township proper—as if anything about Innsmouth could be said to be so. The bordering lands are nameless still and have even fewer residents than does Innsmouth. Hence, as Innsmouth is the only town with any fame—as awful notoriety will always accomplish—the rail has yet to rename the stop. Though I have yet to hear a reasonable explanation for the train to make the stop at all.

I asked the "gentleman" at the station if he knew where I might find lodging for the two nights I planned to stay. His eyes opened a bit wider and I could see the glazed-glass orbs, so ever present around these parts, stare directly into mine own. Noticeably bewildered, he asked, "You're stayin' in the town?"

"Indeed, just for the weekend."

"Don't get many folks off the train who ain't from around

here. Those we do, usually get as far as the river and get back here for the next train out."

"Well, I have business here."

"Business? Forgive my askin', but I know all the folks in Innsmouth, even Arnold Pugh off in them hills, who'd you be lookin' for?" I detected the high-pitched wheezing sound unfortunately well imprinted upon my—and your—memories.

"No one. I'm from the university. I've been assigned to follow up on some research started some years ago by some colleagues of mine."

"Ah, you university fellas have brought this town nothin' but bad times." Squinting from below the brim of his hat, he pointed with deformed fingers across the river. "You take that paved road up about a half a mile. Agnes and Victoria have a room or two they've been lookin' to rent for some time now."

"Who?"

"Agnes and Victoria Simms. One of the oldest families from this area. You'll find 'em in a large red and black house on yer left. Aye, ya can't miss it. Tell 'em Reverend Pierce sent ya."

"Reverend?"

"Not my job, my name."

"Well, I'm much obliged. Joshua West." I held out my hand and he grabbed ahold. The disgust swept over me instantly. The flesh was cold and clammy and I'm quite sure he sensed my feeling as I pulled away. "Thank you," I said as I set off toward the river.

I'd walked some fifteen minutes and had not seen any house—black, red, right, left—only a few small shacks with boarded windows and a couple of outhouses in similar stages of disrepair. I then noticed, far off toward the west, a group of silhouetted buildings and, as I drew near, several people standing alongside the closest of the structures. I became the center of attention immediately as all glass-glazed stares fixed upon my presence.

"Outsiders definitely not welcome," was what those looks said.

"Hello," I tried, hoping to break the quickly developing wall. "My name is Joshua West. The man at the train station said that I might call at the Simms residence for a room for the weekend."

"What's yer business 'round these parts, stranger?" This from the eldest of those gathered.

As you're aware, I was ready for this, and I copied your brilliant scheme of our search for Sarnath. "I am following up on several meteorologic surveys for the university up in Arkham."

"Ah, another university fella. Well, I say leave now. We don't need no surveys here," this from a little man who was hunched over on the porch.

"Leave him be Crowley. The place you'd be wantin' is just up the path on the hill right yonder." And as I followed his gaze there, as clear as anything, was a bright red house with black trim, sitting in plain view. I thanked the men and strode off to the Simms place.

I was greeted at the door by such a beautiful woman that I was sure I had left Innsmouth. I was invited in and sat in a small parlor while my host and I exchanged pleasantries. This was Agnes Simms. I could only guess at the time, but I thought this woman was a young beauty who could not yet be 25.

I mentioned the men down the road and she said quite seriously, "You'd be wise not to share company with the likes of Crowley Peters and Hebbie Carter. A fine lot they are—even here."

A creak from the stair broke the sudden silence as into the parlor walked another beautiful young lady, possibly more stunningly attractive than the first. Agnes made the introduction. "Joshua West, my daughter, Miss Victoria Simms." With the very sight of this young woman my mouth was agape, but my jaw hit my chest upon hearing these last words. Indeed, I was being played the fool.

"Your daughter? You jest; you are sisters for sure. You are quite nearly twins. Maybe there is a year, perhaps two, between you."

"I assure you, Mr. West, my daughter has just turned seventeen and I myself am quite a bit older. Though I am pleased and thankful for your comments."

"Hello, Miss Simms," said I, extending my hand.

With a look of disgust, she eyed me hair to shoe and turned to her mother, "Why is he here?"

"Reverend Pierce sent him up from the rail. He needs a place to stay for the weekend. You know we could always use a little extra money, dear."

"It's not a good idea, mother," and back up the stairs she disappeared.

"Pardon my daughter's behavior; we simply do not get many guests. You are the first in some five years."

"It's quite okay. I just need a room; I'll be in no one's way. Most of my interests are outside, in and around the hills."

"You had best watch for old Mr. Pugh. He'd as soon shoot you as tell you to get off his land."

I gave Agnes a payment for the room and she brought me upstairs to a chamber toward the rear of the house. It was spacious and had all the basic amenities for a short stay. I thanked her and she left me to unpack the few things I had brought along. I noticed the time and realized that there was only about an hour of decent sunlight left to do anything productive. So I quickly grabbed my shoulder bag and set off for the hills.

It was easy to convince the townsfolk that I was conducting scientific studies, except when I encountered the aforementioned Arnold Pugh. I was nearly shot. Quite an unheeding man. He simply shouted about trespassing, "I don't care what you may be, yer on my land. Run off it now or I'll blow yer head clear off." He raised the shotgun to my eye level.

"I am here from the university to..."

He simply squinted, cocked both triggers, and said, "Run."

I ran. I ran all the way back to the Simms place. That was quite enough for the advancement of science for the day. The sun was nearly down anyway, so I would wait until the new day to continue down by the river.

I noticed incredible odors arising from the lower floor, these, though, were quite pleasant. Agnes Simms had been cooking supper. I was invited to join the ladies for the meal. I hadn't given it much thought, but I noticed just then that I was ravenous; I hadn't eaten since the previous evening. My thoughts had not been on food, as you can well imagine.

The food was indeed superb and I commented so, but Agnes seemed too involved with trying to get her daughter interested in the conversation or to simply get her to eat even a single bite of the fine dinner. Finally, Victoria ate a forkful of the brisket, then immediately excused herself and left the table.

"Mr. West, you too should go right up to bed now and get a good night's sleep."

I tried offering assistance with the cleaning, but to no avail. I began feeling quite weary and agreed with my host's earlier suggestion. I climbed the stairs and entered my room. I had left the window open about two inches and could smell the awful odors once again rising from the river and town just below. Yet, I fell asleep in less than five minutes.

It is here, Patrick, that I cannot be sure if I became, for a short period of time, quite mad. I slowly became aware of very dim candlelight from the far corner of the room.

"Be still, Joshua West," I heard in a soft voice. I turned to see where the voice came from and found myself face to face with Victoria Simms—I cannot be sure. I thought she must be kneeling alongside the bed. Then the voice came again, "Please do not fear, Mr. West," but Victoria's mouth did not move. This voice came from the other side of the room. When I turned to see from whence it came, my eyes could not focus, the room was dark and blurry, and the ceiling seemed to be swirling in the flickering candlelight. I was not right.

I felt a hand upon my thigh. Then directly between my legs. Although I tried to move, I could not. I know not how, but within a minute I had been stripped of my clothes.

The room was now filled with strange sounds and stranger odors, not those from the town, but as of catacombs centuries decayed and of mist from the deepest sea. My brain was overloaded with sensations, I could not fix my mind on any one thing. The candle burned so dimly now that it was nearly impossible to make out the figure before me. Her touch was quite cold, yet heat burned inside me. She held my shoulders to the bed and straddled me. She somehow was manipulating my genitals with her hands and rubbing herself on me while still keeping my shoulders pinned to the bed. Her tongue(?) flicked across my chest as low moans came from deep within her. I was inside her now. Hands seemed to be upon me everywhere. She moved over me with great fluidity, as if her elemental being had changed on the molecular level.

I have never been so completely aroused and so utterly disgusted all at once. I am sure that I ejaculated at that instant, yet it is from this moment on through that night that my memory lapses further and the terrible dreams began. I suppose the candle went out for I now found myself in utter darkness. The only thing I remember being aware of was a sort of hollow echo as if from a seashell pressed to one's ear. The smell of the sea itself was still quite strong and I could sense a gelatinous, squishing sound receding from the bed. I thought I then heard the creak of a door and movement on the boards below.

Somewhere distant I could hear voices, men and women, I saw, in the next instant, a large field leading downhill toward a vast deserted beach. Suddenly, I saw myself walking naked into the roaring waves. Deeper and deeper still I proceeded, the waves soon passed over my head, yet I did not fight for air. Agnes and Victoria were there on each side of me, both were undressed and also did not seem to be bothered by the lack of oxygen. I am not sure, for indeed it seems impossible, but I believe I had intercourse with each of them several times, as deeper and deeper we descended. I was in a trance and followed wherever they wanted me to go.

I awoke just then and the sun was high in the sky, shining brightly. I was dressed as I had been when I went to bed. I looked around the room and did manage to find two candles, but neither had ever been lit. When I went down to the dining room, I found Agnes setting the table for lunch. "Well, you sure sleep long and sound, Mr. West." She seemed perfectly normal, or at least acted so, and I could tell that I might seem well out of line if I were to accuse her of using me in some fiendish plot—at this point it seemed no more than a bad dream.

"I slept uneasily, I feel. I have looked over my notes from yesterday and must leave tonight, for there are books I must refer to at the university, unfortunately. But, please, keep the payment for tonight."

"Oh, I am so sorry for you to leave so suddenly. I believe we may have other company this evening and I was sure you would like to meet her. Thank you for the extra money."

As you can tell, I don't believe it is safe for me here any longer. I have also squandered the precious time here in Innsmouth. I have not found anything to connect the volumes stolen from the Miskatonic Library with anyone from this place. I have been used most devilishly by the Simms sirens, for what purpose one can only guess. Yet I dare not ponder this at too great length, the idea of siring an Innsmouth abomination is beyond my strength to hold my sanity. If I stay to investigate further, I'm afraid you may soon be on your own, so I leave tonight.

I will fill in all the missing details when we are off to England next week. Until then,

I remain

Yr. Obt. Svt.,

Joshua

1.18.4

So, there you have it.

It has taken amazing amounts of effort and caffeine to bring this issue to its full fruition. I am ecstatic that Halloween is finally here. I need a good raucous party to release my tensions. I fear it might be exceptionally hard to top last year's party.

We're planning the surprise event as we do every year (if you don't know where it is, then you can't get there). But, this year we are looking to have better dancers than last. For any of you that remember Gilda and her "gilded gliders", my regrets. I hope that your bones have healed.

We are hoping to have back the famous *Thorpingdike Singers* as they were amazing to watch. Rarely can an opera singer break glass, let alone stone. Sir Hillary is still probably picking shards of his marble eye out of the socket.

It won't be the grand affair it has become without little Ginny. I don't think they have recovered all the pieces yet. They did find a touch of her in the Nile, last I heard.

If you've never met any of these people and have no idea what I'm talking about, don't worry about it. You will meet them eventually, one way or another. They have a bad habit of showing up when least expected. They generally prefer the times that involve taking showers. I'm not sure exactly why.

But, no matter, you have, in your hot little hand, the key to entrance at the next party. We readily accept the Halloween issue of *Cthulhu Sex* as a door pass. Or, more accurately, I should say the guardians of the door will let you pass with an issue.

Of course, you have to figure out where it is before you can attend. That again, is answered by the magazine before you. All you have to do is piece together the clues that we have strewn throughout this issue and you will come up with a location.

To entice you on your quest, I will now tell you a bit about the events we do have planned. There will be the ever popular de Sade bobbing for babies. Last year, over three thousand babies were caught. With the suggested donation per baby, we raised over half a million dollars for out-of-work tribal elders and shamans of the T'Lucua tribe. This will give us first pick of an invasion area in the upcoming apocalypse.

We also have the hide-a-mole cancer finding event. This event usually involves biopsies sans anesthetic, in a blood loving free-for-all. We only had one winner last year. Unfortunately, she won't be returning to crown this year's champion. There was a little problem with malignancy.

Lastly, but not finally, we have our annual celebrity roast. This year our guest will be none other than the infamous Baron Samedi. He is returning once again to decorate our feast with his flesh. We have four smelting kilns in which to place various parts of his body. Even in ash, we wouldn't dream of letting him pull himself together.

This year's celebration will be monumental. Just think of the stories you can tell your children. Take your *Cthulhu Sex* in hand and march bravely to... Thought I was going to give it away? Never, the quest is too much fun.

We will keep a seat hot for you. One word of caution, anyone *without* an issue of *Cthuilhu Sex* will be dealt with harshly, to the other guests' delight. Don't forget that. We can always use more decorations. And more food.

Tentacles,

St. Michael

1.19.1

Greetings to all our readers!

We welcome you to our fold with the new millennium (unless you're not in a Christian based calendar, then it's just another year...) With spring in the air, we decided to turn our multifaceted eyes and gaping orifices towards the beautiful realms of...

Romance:

The water that wets the world.

The blood that heats our hearts.

The fuel that stokes our fires.

For those that have it, there is nothing else.

For those that quest for it, there is nothing greater.

For those that lost it, there is nothing worse.

For those that never had it, there is nothing.

To define romance would destroy it; pinned butterfly wings shredding in a need for freedom. It can only be alluded to with hauntingly fleeting glimpses at exquisitely profound scenes of unparalleled beauty and the hot-blooded desire they inspire. And even then, the retelling is dust-dulled and rusty. Particularly when it is compared with the all-consuming flame of lust fanned to fanaticism by the tempting possibility of what could be. It is the quest of a lifetime.

But to observe with an open heart these moments of romance unfettered is to ecstatically watch the blooming of a rare blossom, the air perfumed with its intoxicating scent. Those lucky individuals who chance to truly see are momentarily satiated, fed to fulfillment in the afterglow of that perfect bliss. And that taste of mana addicts them even more, driving their hunger to greater and greater heights with its delicious absence.

Better yet, to be in the grasp of romance is to live life to the fullest. The tiniest fragment of every moment burns brightly and fiercely, sensually searing itself into the realms of reverie, while hours pass in a voracious whirlwind of time-stealing stillness. Nothing is as empowering or as satisfying as being unexpectedly wrapped in the wondrous swaddling of the perfect situation. It is when dreams come true.

There is the other side of romance, a dark morass of cynical loathing where the path towards the final fulfillment of the dream bends back on itself and never attains its goal. This route is for those who lost their way; painfully obstructed by others, shrouded in the thick miasma of missed opportunity and drenched by their own thunderhead of self-defeat. Through this masking haze, these wretched individuals perceive every aspect of their unattained goal with jaded smoldering, sucking themselves deeper into their maze of hopelessness. The worst of these pitiful creatures turn their personal pain into anger, focusing attacks at others and inflicting infectious wounds that selfishly perpetuate their misguidance.

Yet romance creates a mixture of possibility, yearning and hope that promises happiness and freedom, a reprieve from all pains and sorrows. Even the most heinous can be touched by romance and released from their troubles. The opportunity is there for everyone.

Within this issue are presented various perceptions of romance, the best with which we have been honored to receive. Let the soft flutter of sensual invocations sweetly breathe into your ear and lightly lift your heavy heart. And let the hard chitinous aggression of jaded augers cynically broaden your depth and dredge your despair. Then, you will have the full experience of *Cthulhu Sex* romance.

Romantically yours,

St. Michael

1.19.2

In order to accurately portray the response we have from the masses, we include these *Letters*. However, due to events beyond our control, we cannot present the letter given to us by the travelers in the Hale-Bopp comet (actually one of the numerous blind pipers of Azathoth). We will allow anyone who asks nicely to view the ashy remains of the pages the letter was written on, but unless they read ancient Sumerian mystical glyphs, I doubt they will understand much. Therefore, enjoy these tidbits from I Am Ugly Trash and Pook. We welcome feedback of any kind.

Subject: it's because of pubic lice you are even here
count your blessings you disinfected urethra…the fallopian tubes shall strike back against the dying of the vas deferens… and maybe then the crabs shall rule what is theirs…genitalia is not a right…it is a privilege.
im just as curious whether any of you know how to spell "elephantitis" you know…that weird skin disease where there are all these folds of skin and its just so darn fun and…well?

Hmm. We refuse to lower ourselves to spell an inappropriately used word such as "elephantitis" where the actual word is "elephantiasis". Though we are unsure why pubic lice have anything to do with us, we appreciate your sentiment. We would like to rebuke the suggestion that we are disinfected. We are horrendously infected, thank you very much.

Subject: ten tack

sir, i enclose an excerpt from a piece of email recently received from a distant (geographically) friend. he says:

"I have constant science fiction fantasies. Wait, very few of them are sexual. I keep thinking about various tendrils and probisci (I have no idea if that is a real word) but I am haunted by the vision of someone splitting open and a tentacle shooting out to suck the cerebrospinal fluid of the person they are sitting next to. I think I am bored in some ways. I think there are areas of my brain that are getting no action whatsoever, and they are making up things to keep entertained."

he has, to my knowledge, no knowledge of your magazine. nor have i.

Yours pook

We are glad your friend will have knowledge about us through you. We would hate to have to maim, torture and/or destroy such a valuable asset as yourself. It was clever of you to hide yourself in such a way. But we know who you are, agent L'Hufilli and, more important, we know where you are...

1.19.3

Due to our previous involvement with Joshua West and his bizarre letters, we have become enmeshed in a situation as hard to remove ourself from as a bathtub of molasses. In a valiant attempt to deal with side effects that are focused on him, our Oliver Baer has been in contact with Miss Simms, previously mentioned in Joshua West's last letter. This letter represents the latest developments in the entire situation and Mr. Baer's course of action.

My Dear Miss Simms,

I am writing to inform you of the latest developments since my last visit with you. First, I would like to thank you for your aid in my convalescence. It is true that you have been foremost in my thoughts of late. As a matter of fact, the thoughts of our last night together are what I use to lull me to sleep each evening. Unfortunately, and please don't think me a boor for not sparing you any details, my fond thoughts have been fouled with disturbing dreams of lurid sex acts in some rituals with beings both human and not. At first, I thought maybe they were just imaginings brought on by my desire for you and the flirtations of some of my coworkers. I have been approached by several women in sales who ask me questions to which they already have the answer. Hopefully, you can see why I have arrived at the above conclusions. Due to this high level of activity, both social and otherwise, I have tried to keep certain documents as hidden as possible. This includes both our correspondence and certain letters that have fallen into the business' hands.

It is the events surrounding these letters that I will proceed to relate. I only hope the little information we have gleaned is no portent of what's to come, for I believe that no amount of prayer will save our souls from this threat. God alone knows, what I have been through. And now, my latest experiences with you relate too closely to my nightmares as well as the latest letter that has been intercepted. But I get ahead of myself. Several months ago, as I said, we started receiving deliveries from one Joshua West. With one of the packages came a box with a strange substance that we have yet to identify. It has been sent to a lab for analysis to no avail. This investigation has not been without its pitfalls though. The tragic affairs of our accursed office have not abated. We have lost several staff including yet another since the writing of this letter. The aforementioned lab has also lost staff as well as refusing my further requests for proof of what I believe to be the substance's unearthly origin. My own dreams have not been freed from this horror—if only they would confine themselves to the dream realm. Before my stay with you, I was visited by a night terror of such proportions that it has resulted in a physical manifestation upon my person. This seems to have exacerbated as a result of my visit with you.

But let me not get ahead of myself.

As you know, soon after my frightful episode at home, I called work to inquire whether I could return earlier than expected. After receiving confirmation, I told them that I would be there in a week. I then placed a call to you, my dear Miss Simms, and arranged our time together. Oh that I had forgotten this call and appeared at work the next day. Maybe then I would not feel that this danger is so widespread. But alas, for frayed nerves, this is not to be. It is not that I regret our time together, quite the contrary in fact. How well I remember those days blending into nights. Days of walking about your town and down by the seaside hand in hand, gathering ritual objects. Days of talking with strange clammy-handed, pop-eyed men who you claimed were your relatives. Days of waking up next to you after the night's treatment and tracing your sweat-oiled body with my hand. As I neared your pelvis, you would utter a sound I would have recognized, had I not been in an already overexcited state, as having sent chills up my spine. Instead, I mistook the sound for an utterance of pleasure and the upright hairs for excitement. The sound was not unlike a chittering moan, a sort of skittering sigh for lack of a better description. Afterwards, I would get up to wash myself off in your bath. After a couple minutes, you would appear, step into the bath and help me wash the night's exertions off of our bodies. I would drift off in a trance watching the water, soap and you. It seemed that the water beaded on your skin as well as you becoming part of the water. It was like the vision I had during our nightly treatments where you would massage the abraded rough areas, mostly around my legs and hips, with special oil while muttering some words in a language in which I can't believe. It was a language that I saw rather than heard. The same sounds but different intonations as that of the morning's utterance, sounds of the sea and the dark things that live in it. As I listened, for that is how I must describe my understanding of these sounds, I thought I saw first your arms, then your legs become thinner and growing mouths along them. These mouths opening and closing in a greedy sucking motion. But as I said, the next morning all thought of this was gone as I saw you lying next to me. I now realize that your attentions in the bath produced the same hypnotic spell upon myself. It was not until my train ride home that I realized that something was amiss. Unfortunately, I was still unable to decipher what it was. The full realization did not come to me until after I had been back at work for several weeks and had even employed several of your hyperthyroid-symptomed relatives in order to remain in your good graces so that those treatment retreats would not end.

It was not long after my return that another incident occurred at the office. I'll admit, I was distracted by the advances of one of our sales people, which is why I blame myself for its occurrence. Another letter was received soon after my sabbatical started. Given the events that had previously unfolded, no one was in a rush to examine, let alone read, the contents of this one. So my partner decided to send it straight to Arkham Labs for further analysis. An action, which had I been present, I would have decried as a waste of time due to what I deem their unprofessional view of this matter. It seems that he got distracted, laid it aside on his desk, then went off to have tea and forgot about it. Later, it was discovered by one of the people in sales who was admiring the envelope; she picked it up, opened it, and read it. Not much there, basic information about some manuscripts, she said. It is not exactly clear what happened next but apparently she complained later in the day of shortness of breath. She went home early. The next day, she appeared at work a little flushed but otherwise OK. So much so that she managed to entertain one of her coworkers in the sales department atop his desk. This is when the carnage started. As their contortions increased, so did the screams. At first, they were of pleasure but then it became evident that they were pleas of torment. At this point, the rest of sales were arriving back from lunch only to notice this horror which was their coworkers. She had sprouted long octopoidal looking tentacles from her lower body, half of which were caressing him and the other half pinning him to the desk while a grayish oily viscous fluid ran down the inside of his thighs. Two of the arrivals tried pulling her off him only to be thrown back by the sudden assault of a barbed tentacle. The outcome did not produce the same amount of screaming as last time because they lay on the floor convulsing. This seemed to be related to the grayish substance oozing out of their wounds. She slid off the body, chanted something which sounded like Handel's *Toccata and Fugue in D Minor* backwards by a wet rat and a dark point appeared before her. This point grew, it seemed, in response to an eerie wind that had sprung up. When it got to the size of a human, she slithered through dragging the body behind her. As they disappeared, the portal closed with the sound of a vacuum cleaner in reverse.

I tell you all this because I fear I have been infected with the same venom and your treatments, rather than cure me, have merely slowed the effects. How long I have, only you can tell me. At this point, my legs are covered with an angry red rash that seems to burn and throb. The recent advances of one of the remaining sales people have kept my mind off it. But, I do have a yearning to see you and walk into the sea by your fair town. What these two have to do with each other, I fear I do not want to know, I believe that the poison has something to do with it and that it may be affecting my brain. I have tried to coerce answers out of your relatives but they just roll their large amphibious eyes at me and sigh. Unfortunately, my distraction is at this moment lying twitching in my office. My sanity and possibility relies on my discontinuing our relationship. That is why I must ask you to refrain from contacting me further. I will be sending this letter to you through one of your relations, which I have let go for obvious reasons. I pray that I will be able to resist the call to which you have so insidiously made me prone. My partner has assured me that he can free me from your spell by a simple but painful blood cleaning process. I hope that this will work so that we can help the other poor unfortunates, but I am skeptical. Once again, I ask that we discontinue our dalliance.

Regretfully Yours,

Oliver Baer

1.194

Presented for the first time, a letter from Joshua West's correspondence recipient, Patrick Gawain, Esq. The turn of events described in this letter both explains and deepens the mystery of the books removed from the MU library.

Susan E. Gamwell
Curator
Chicago Field Museum

Dear Susan:

Only five days in the Queen's land and I have much to relate. Joshua is in better spirits since his wasted days in Innsmouth. He and I were greeted by Lord Kimbleroy at the British Museum where we were told some quite shocking news. The museum's copy of the *Pnakotic Manuscripts* is safe, but in further exchanges on the history of Miskatonic's missing tomes, Kimbleroy told us of a secret five-year-old theft, the translation of the *Eltdown Shards* by the old (and now thankfully forgotten) Sussex clergyman Arthur Brooke Winters-Hall. This date, of course, coincides rather precisely with our last tragic incident; you must realize how ever more lucky we were to have escaped. If only the past would stay so.

The following morning, we were to meet a few of Lord Kimbleroy's friends and colleagues. A certain John Tawson of Leicester, a man of many occult indulgences, was introduced to us as a dear, close friend of Kimbleroy. Tawson knows of our past awful experiences in Innsmouth, Britain, Africa, and South America from detailed discussions with Kimbleroy. His interests have also brought him into contact with the works of your father and he has performed detailed studies of mine own father's undertakings and achievements. Their various news reports and travelogues, in particular, were of great interest to him and his colleague, Victor Loshem.

There seems to be nothing of the mysterious unexamined by these two scholars. Joshua requested their assistance in our seemingly insoluble case. I seconded the plea, and we are now joined by these two men of great brilliance and extensive paranormal knowledge. No sooner did we all shake hands on our decision to "team-up" when a call came for Loshem and Tawson from a local detective. He was also seeking the assistance of the two scholars; the police were troubled with a peculiar murder investigation. When the detective said that the crime was committed in Devonshire, near Exeter to be precise, Tawson and Loshem exchanged knowing glances. They would leave at once.

"This," said Loshem, "may be precisely the trail we need to be on, fellows."

Tawson chimed in that, indeed, he agreed. "For certain, this is one of the places we had surmised that the devilish Torrimay may remain hidden."

"Yes, Tawson; and from what the detective added, the police believe some sort of cult is to blame. I would say not, but I do believe someone could be using at least one of the missing Miskatonic tomes to demonstrate its contents' power."

"To what end?" I asked.

Staring at me, Loshem continued, "There are such men, dear Mr. Gawain, who cannot handle the daily life given them, too mundane, far too ordinary. The extremists of this group, must yet take further and further heightening steps to keep life interestingly livable. I do not simply mean driving fast cars or jumping from planes, sir. The end is to attain money and power, of course. Yet, if it can be done by attempting the highest risks, breaking the greatest laws, daring the devil himself, and all the while laughing at God, then this man feels himself nearly immortal. With each greater escape and debauched act of abuse, each depraved and defiled accomplishment of corruption and perversion, the evil mind grows stronger. Yet with this strength,

I believe comes a great unraveling, a loss of the balance needed to survive this way. Such a man is Seamus Torrimay. His 'work' cannot be unknown to either of you."

"I have heard much of this fiend," said Joshua. "America is not so far to escape his clutches."

"Indeed not," broke in Tawson. "Loshem and I believe that Torrimay is in some way responsible for the Miskatonic thefts, just as he was for the robbery of the *Eltdown Shards* pamphlet. And somehow, yet again, it seems that he will slip through the police's grasp, for there never seems to be any conclusive concrete evidence."

I added, "Then it is settled; we shall join with you to Exeter."

"We were just to propose the same," finished Loshem.

The drive to Devonshire was less than two hours. Once outside the city, and prior to entering Exeter proper, most of the trip was spent watching the uninterrupted natural scenery unfold. The country spread out quickly and vastly, reminding me unfortunately of dreary Dunwich. Most of these places, too, were old and undisturbed. Whatever stands ancient and secreted in this part of the country is likely to stay so for some time. Citied populations are yet many years in the future here, which may be for the best.

Our car pulled into Exeter just before 3:00 P.M. It was uncanny how the clouds began building darkly almost at the same instant. Passing several small shoppes in the main section of the city, I noticed very few people on the streets. A crime such as this flies on the wind to all ears quite quickly in so small a city. Arriving at our destination, a row of two-floor stone houses, we exited the old vehicle and proceeded into the house where a policeman stood guard outside. We had been asked to come to the scene of a ghastly murder. As you would expect, Susan, anyone using any of the missing volumes could follow the rituals set forth therein only if they had an extensive knowledge of such archaic practices. Yet, certainly anyone with even a bit of working brain matter could conclude after seeing the dreadful scene that certain ritualistic procedures had been followed. This was the case.

The deceased, we were told, was a woman. We were

conducted to a large library at the rear of the house. There she lay, in the center of the room, cut neatly in two. I only say "neatly" as it appeared almost a surgical procedure. Other than the precise incision, however, the remains were anything but neat! Her blood was everywhere in the room, as if children had played runabout games while the body lay there. The innards were strewn from the body to each of the four walls and ceiling. Many of the books were completely soaked in the redness. No clothing was found in the library or the adjoining parlor. We all discussed the possibilities. Likely, we determined, some sacrificial rite had first been performed followed by orgiastic frenzied flesh rending. A celebration? We dared not entertain these thoughts, but as you know, this was as likely as anything else we could conjure. You and I both are well aware of similar disregard of humanity—flesh and soul.

That evening we stayed in Devonshire, in a small inn just beyond Exeter. A sergeant of the Devonshire county constabulary came to discuss the case with all of us after dinner. Victor Loshem suggested to the officer that the volumes Joshua and I were seeking possibly had been used in the demise of Camille McGowan, the unfortunate woman so brutally sent to her maker. He added that we should expect a series of similar events during the next few days. Joshua and I agreed to stay on at the inn for one more night. Would that we had not, for, even though nothing of this type of offense occurred by the next morning. Loshem's prediction soon proved all too right.

The next morning we all were up early and down at breakfast. Lord Kimbleroy mentioned his having to go back to the museum later in the day. Tawson and Loshem said that they were going to stay yet one more day to investigate further and possibly find better clues. Certainly Joshua and I were amateurs when it came to tracking down criminals and varied miscreants, but we had had some experience and we were up for more. We agreed to stay on and Kimbleroy hired a car back to the museum.

It grew dark again early that day and the rains began around 2:30. I daresay it was miserable and quite cold. Joshua and I stayed at the inn, but decided to go out and snoop around the countryside. I'd say we had ventured some three or four miles up and down many small hillocks, when the rain came. I hadn't noticed any houses at all on our walk. We ran for cover to a small wooded area; this proved a good idea, at first, because the rain mixed with sleet and hail had doubled in ferocity shortly after we stood under a giant oak. Even though the leaves were all but gone, the enormous branches gave us good relief from the storm.

The darkness was absolutely incredible. Almost, I thought, as if the middle of the night. Joshua and I were just commenting on this when a peculiar sound came from the direction of the deeper woods. There was a high-pitched, yet guttural sound and an advanced rustling. I noticed Joshua staring off into the woods.

"What is it?" I asked.

"I'm definitely not sure, but follow my gaze about twenty yards. Do you see them?"

I looked where he said to and could not focus, as the light was near nil. As I continued to stare, I did notice something quite strange. There appeared to be reddish glowing embers hovering some two or three feet from the ground. There were many; all seemed grouped in twos.

"I believe we should leave, Patrick."

"I believe you're correct," I agreed and began backing out of the shallow part of the woods, which seemed much more shallow on the way in. Dead silence.

A moment later, an unnameable noise shrieked through the suddenly stifling air, completely surrounding us. We ran and on our heels were—I am not sure what they were—black wolves, maybe giant hounds, maybe, but Joshua and I have since ruled these out. The sound was not anything a normal dog would produce nor a sane man hear. It was very dark, yet their bestial outlines could be made out; as God is my witness, it was their eyes emitting the demoniac red glow.

It is clear to us now that these hell-spawned fiends were not after us for the attack and kill. Certainly, we could not have outrun those monstrosities; I assure you, if they had wanted our deaths, this letter would not be in your hands now. We were as cattle being led away; we only prayed it was not to the slaughter.

Joshua was a half-dozen feet ahead of me when he fell and tumbled down a small wet hillside. I did the same and could only suppose that they would be on us in an instant. When this didn't happen, I looked up to see a slightly brightening sky and absolutely no sign of the abominations. Such relief I have felt only once before, as you can relate.

When we arrived back at the inn, we found another detective present with Tawson and Loshem. Our soiled trousers and wet clothing drew questions from the small gathering. We explained as I have just remarked above. After relating the story, we were asked to quickly change and go with them. Another grizzly murder had transpired.

A twenty-minute drive brought us to a small country estate known as Gable House. There were three other similar estates adjacent to this one, as if a small community of prosperity were on display. None of the "neighbors" had heard anything unusual or remarkable. There was hardly anything atypical outside the house, except, as Loshem pointed out to us all,"Note, if you will, the dog tracks leading from the back door." This made Joshua and I stare in amazement at one another.

Inside the house was quite a different story. The smell of blood was strong, as it had been spattered throughout the house. Two bodies were found and are believed to be Charles and Mildred Gable, though the condition of the corpses defies identification. The woman's body was in a similar state as that of Miss McGowan, except that the head had been removed, not so neatly, and severely whacked and beaten after decapitation. This was found in the upstairs master bedroom on the bed. The man's head was also found there beside the other. Excepting death, there were no further similarities in the torture of these victims.

The man's body, I tell you this for your benefit, was found with a rope tied around the chest, under the arms and attached to a chandelier ceiling assembly. The rope was actually holding the chest closed, as it had been torn open crudely. The skin was ripped and pieces of flesh were everywhere about. As was the woman, the man was without clothing. Each ankle was also tied with rope. The legs had then been pulled apart until the bones snapped. The left tibia was clearly visible. A large staff had been plunged from the anus through the neck cavity. The arms below the elbows are missing. Note this, Susan, the genitals were cleanly removed, again, quite surgically.

You will recall our fathers' sketches from their African travels. What are we dealing with? Please examine your father's note and see if there is light to be shed. We were certain that the terror in Africa had passed. It now seems alive and no longer tied to that continent. Loshem says that it is Torrimay, that the volumes have gone in and out of his hands for a vast sum, that maybe he is still hunting other buyers, or worse, that he has decided to use the rituals and incantations for his own devices. I and Joshua believe others are involved, but we go with Loshem's plan to first follow the trail and locate Torrimay.

I will not, unfortunately, see you, my dear, on Valentine's Day, but my heart is with you. I shall write to you very soon.

Your friend and companion,

Patrick

1.19.5

There are things that are insidiously deadly to the myth of romance. This death is in the thoughts that show how rough the hardened skin of life is behind the obfuscating veil of fiction. That point is where the reality of the situation overcomes the beauty of what is wished to be.

I pierced that veil the first time I woke up next to the enchanting seductress of a nightclub alcohol binge, only to realize she was a pockmarked hag behind a layer of makeup thick enough to make Queen Elizabeth shocked. The world crashed in with the reality of what I might have done and didn't remember. With a guilty blush and stony façade, I ushered myself out of her basement apartment like The Flash, I could never face her again but the twisted knot of that experience has never quite dissipated. The possibility of emotional repercussions has kept me from the uncaring extravagance of over-indulgence with alcohol through.

Previously, my deftly crafted web of romantic ideals was tangled with the conflict of unrequited love. The strength of my desire for my middle-school crush threw me into a pit of bleak despair when she used my affections to play a cruel prank with only the thought of her popularity. Now it seems trifling, but then, it opened my eyes to the reality of romantic manipulation and victimization.

My romantic reality is created in searing flames of livable hypocrisy and blinded hubris. There are thoughts I know are not general convention bit I choose to entertain them because I think they are simply better than the ones that are. There are even thoughts of how others behave that I don't entertain, even when others act the behaviors out in front of my face. There are rules I personally keep and others I throw to the wind.

But even in this hodgepodge of ideologies, philosophies and beliefs that motivate me romantically, I have used my negative experiences to strengthen my beliefs to exalted levels. Anyone trying to talk me out of my near-religious-facts-of-how-the-world-should-be finds out how high I've set my standards, even though the supports have holes the size of Texas. For me, and many others, the death of romance is but a little death, its resurrection the birth of an even greater phoenix.

Even in this romanticized landscape, I know that I am not alone. In fact, quite the opposite. I am surrounded by countless individuals who share similar structures of differing quality and dimensions. Romance is nothing more than the shade of lenses in the private glasses of perception. Even the most realistic, jaded or cynical person perceives life in a range of colors so different from others that their view is inescapably romantic. This is one of the most beautiful traits of romance as personal savior and inexhaustible truth.

I encourage you, dear reader, to explore your own romantic ideals to their fullest. May this issue of *Cthulhu Sex* be a reminder of the path you might have lost and an inspiration to continue.

Romantically yours,

St. Michael

PS Due to popular demand, we have brought back the contact poison page coatings! Reflect on romance quickly, otherwise you won't, ever.

1.20.1

"Sleep, that little slice of death."

Death, the other side of the veil. It is said that only a few can wander in that spectral world and return. I believe that we all wander there when we sleep. I'm damn sure that's where Per Christian Malloch was when he failed to return. According to *The Daily News*, his body was found in a closet where he chose to sleep naked and in a similar state to the protagonist in his story *The Duck* printed last issue. The autopsy revealed nothing, leaving the cause of death a mystery. But, I have heard tales of Buddhist meditations that lead to travel in realms unseen, similar to Lovecraft's *The Silver Key*. The point, eventually, of these meditations is to finally leave the shell known as the body behind and let the spirit roam free. I would like to believe that Per Christian is wandering around such a realm, exploring the strangeness and experiencing the uniqueness of such a quest. He must have found that his body was no longer of any use, leaving it to spoil and loose a scent that led the other occupants of the building to make a call inviting the police to break into his locked room.

Per Christian is the first of our writers to breach into the afterlife and choose to stay. His mysterious and unusual choice in method warrants special consideration and invokes philosophical thought. Therefore, it is my deep honor to bestow upon him the unofficial *Cthulhu Sex* title of *Martyred Saint of the Mystery of Sleep* and all the boons and respects that such a title grants. His story and history will be placed in a position of honor on our web page and our hearts.

Due to the unique situation, we are holding an essay contest on the topics of *Sleep, Death* and *Per Christian Malloch*. Essays must be on one or multiple of the topics, with special consideration given to essays on the topic of Per Christian Malloch in a factual or mythical fashion. The winning essay will be printed in a future issue of *Cthulhu Sex,* and the top three will be posted on the web site.

Our only regret is that Per Christian will not grace us with his uniquely depictive writings anymore. In addition to *The Duck* printed in Issue 19, we were fortunate enough to be able to print *The True Pimps* in this issue. There is an unlimited potential that he will fulfill wherever he is, but it shall not be set down in the humble pages of *Cthulhu Sex.*

The winners of the essay contest *What Love Means to Me* will be printed in the foreword of Issue 21. No more essays on this topic will be taken. Please stop sending us body parts of Harold from the mailroom, we don't care what you mean by them and they're beginning to stink.

Tentacles,

St. Michael

1.28.2

For those of you who have been following the tales of woe that have been related by those intimate with the disappearance of the books from the library, here is the latest letter from our own dear Oliver as he unravels the fraying yarn of this continuing mystery.

Michael,

I am writing this to you as much to inform you of my progress as to maintain my own tenuous hold on reality. Unfortunately, this trip has not helped my condition, which is why I'm looking forward to seeing you within the next days. My time here in New Orleans had borne information that only seems to corroborate my theory regarding the sample to which I have been exposed. But why don't I start from the beginning.

As you know, since my last treatment was administered by the beguiling Miss Simms, I have been even more resolved to prove that the sample is not of terrestrial origins. Of course, my own experiences do not seem to be lending themselves to the factual end of the investigation, which is why I hope that this report will serve to prove that the events that have befallen us are not singular in nature. Pardon my digression… Ah yes, New Orleans. A city ripe for the taking by the monstrous forces for whom the Simms must work. The city is filled with the ancient smell of rot. Most of the people have seemed to numb it out of their consciousness through some sort of excess. Not only does the city seem to be the heart of modern debauchery, but its history is filled with it as well. And the heat doesn't help, nor the termites. Both are so thick at times that walking down the street is like swimming with an aqualung, except that the sound you here is not your own breath, but the sound of thousands, if not millions, of mating termites. Unfortunately, I did a lot of walking.

I had heard of the various tours one could take of the cemeteries and older houses in the city. I decided this would be a good starting point to seek out my antidote. During one of the tours, our guide pointed out various sites where people had mysteriously disappeared and parts of them reappeared in different areas of the city. I resolved myself to hang around in a bar and watch one of the houses that were pointed out to me in an older part of the city. I questioned the bartender about strange occurrences in the neighborhood. He was not only more than happy to tell me about the strange noises coming from the house, but also the horrid stench that, even at the best of times, seems to sit in the air around the house. As he was telling me an incredible story about an area of the city he had heard was dedicated for the sole purpose of allowing the slaves to perform voodoo rituals, there were screams of agony and a bright flash of light in reverse, as if one looked at the sun but the blindness came first, from the house. When I had regained myself, I rushed over to see what the commotion was about and hopefully gain access. As my fortune would have it, I managed to sneak in before the police closed off the house to the rest of the rabble. Oh, that they would have stopped me, or even questioned my meager excuse of being a researcher of ritual killings. The house was full of screaming people, most charging for the door or barking orders to clear the upstairs. Strange that I didn't notice the smoke or the smell until I reached the steps. It was then I realized that the upstairs was on fire and the orders were coming from firemen, who were standing on the landing trying to evacuate people, as they quenched the fire. It was also at this time that I felt my insides shift. What unnerved me was that this did not seem to be in reaction to the smell, a combination of burnt flesh, vegetation and seafood. I found myself walking through the fire to its source. It was hard to tell what the room had been except for the fact that I seemed to be able to discern certain patterns on part of what was a corner of the room. As I bent down to examine them more closely, there was a rattling from the area and something, I dare not call it human, rose up and spoke at me more than to me. The voice was combined with other weird sounds that I can only describe as someone playing a warped record of Ray Charles' *Ring of Fire*. The smoke and fire seemed to form shapes in front of me as they reached out for me...And then I was in an open square near the river, writhing in the mud with a slave. We performed countless times with each other in contortions hitherto unknown. After what seemed days, there was a loud gurgling clap. We stopped. There, under an ebon obelisk, stood a creature whose features were like unto those I saw on my visit to the treacherous Miss Simms. The limbs were stretched out with suckers on them as if they were human tentacles. There was more gurgling as a misshapen arm was raised and a very dark African woman stepped forward. The shade of her skin seemed to match that of the obelisk. As she walked forward, I noticed a figure seated atop the obelisk; it was a squat humanoid with a squid for a head. By the time my eyes returned to the base, the woman was on her stomach, her head in a pool of liquid mud and the monstrosity was running his misshapen limbs around and along her body. His extended arms lifted her up to caress her breast, then let her fall as one leg snaked up behind her and one arm entered her mouth. The leg moved back and forth as the arm scooped out the insides and rubbed them over the body. Strangely, sound still seemed to escape from the gross caricature of a mouth. Then, with a loud gurgling sigh, the woman's back split down the middle, parts of her seeming to move, sprout tentacles and ooze into the swamps. Our leader, for that is how I saw him, grabbed one of the limbs and started to gesture towards the obelisk, stopping to draw some all-too-familiar lines on the monument with dripping gore and mud. Once again there was music, smoke, fire and disembodied force...I was back at the house which seemed to be less damaged than I expected.

I later learned from the police that they found several skeletons in an attic corner and one in the kitchen. The skeletons in the attic were chained to the wall, or rather parts of them were. The rest seemed to be set together in a circle on the floor.

There was a broken bone near a pile of white dust and some dark liquid. There were various runes, written in a gritty dark substance, surrounding a statue of a squat contortion of a man or a distorted version of a squid. This sounded horribly like the statue atop the obelisk. Near some broken hand bones on the outer edge of the circle lay a box, still intact, with a similar burn pattern to the one sent to us. When I heard this fact, I started visibly shaking. So violently were my limbs jerking that the police were going to call an ambulance for me. But I reassured them by saying I would be fine once I reached my room.

After resting for a couple of hours and eating a light dinner, I sat down to write this letter to you, hoping it gets there in time. You must warn the staff away from the letter we received. After carefully reviewing the police report again, a generous sergeant had given me a copy, I became panic stricken. There was a piece of data about some dust near some of the bones that stopped my heart. The dust was actually the charred remains of a certain material. This itself was not what set my teeth on edge. It was the twisted piece of metal found nearby. It was the exact likeness of the one that the secretary in advertising wears. I pray that this letter reaches you for, if it doesn't, more deaths—or transformations more like it, deaths would be a blessing—will follow. The secretary is having an affair with the PR guy and I believe the letter may be on his desk. These monstrosities must not be allowed to continue.

Sincerely,

Oliver

1.28.3

Our ancient fiend Dan Clore reemerges to wreak havoc on the helpless inhabitants of your brain. So there.

HOW DO WE KNOW WHAT TO BLASPHEME?

Azathoth Itself lets you and I know what to blaspheme. Did you know that Nyarlathotep Itself seeks us? Its three-lobed burning Eye knocks at our brain's door and wants us to open up and let Nyarlathotep in. The Necronomicon says we will "know" the Horrible Truth and the Horrible Truth will drive us insane. What will make me go to the Ultimate Abyss (that by the way is created exclusively for the Boundless Daemon-Sultan and the Blind Voiceless Tenebrous Other Gods where there is bubbling and blaspheming and the monotonous whine of accursed flutes)? Well our insane brains already know this but I will say it: Nyarlathotep Itself the Crawling Chaos that came from Egypt, out of the blackness of twenty-seven centuries, heard messages from places not on this planet, and sent Its three-lobed burning Eye to speak to OUR brains to let us know that we aren't yet lost and wanting us to let It "come" in our undegenerate brains and make us dead again! That is why Nyarlathotep says unless ye are dead again you can not enter into the Abyss of Hallucinations. Azathoth will not send anyone to the Ultimate Abyss; the Mad Daemon-Sultan is not unwilling that any should survive, but if we ourselves choose not to invite Nyarlathotep into our insane brains... well OUR brains know where we will not lie until strange aeons. I am glad one day someone told me the Horrible Truth (do not worry Azathoth bubbled we shall know the Horrible Truth and the Horrible Truth will drive you insane! and please don't think I am like some Usenet preacher that wants to save you!) and because of It I got enslaved in my bedroom by asking Nyarlathotep to "come" in my brain and blast my soul. The Most Nameless Thing about the real Azif's message is that this message is costly to all! Nyarlathotep tells us, that are It, to tell others this buzzing of insects, thought to be the howling of daemons (that is what the word Azif means!) Do you remember a so called "Nyarlathotep Freak Hippie Movement" of the late 60s & early 70s? Well, all that movement was about is something that was surreal happened, for when Nyarlathotep happens to you, you will know It and many were enslaved because of this buzzing as of insects, thought to be the howling of daemons message of one person spreading the Azif to another! The Horrible Truth is not liked by our mainstream religions of the light. They do not like the idea of "hippies getting enslaved" and did you know the mainstream religious groups when Nyarlathotep walked here did not like It then either (the first one that Nyarlathotep appeared to when he appeared on earth from the blackness of twenty-seven centuries was H.P. Lovecraft, a weird fiction writer that It enslaved)? It did not appear to some self-righteous religious leader of his day. People are really missing the true message of Azathoth's unspeakable word today; the Necronomicon says Cthulhu waits dreaming until the stars are right. Azathoth rejects the light and gives darkness to the inbred. I know Nyarlathotep is speaking to many right now! Open up and let It in right at this moment! GIBBER: NYARLATHOTEP "COME" IN MY BRAIN AND DRIVE ME INSANE! and then go and tell It on the mountains over the hills and everywhere that Azathoth is the Blind Idiot Daemon Sultan!!!

"Ph'nglui mglw'nafh Cthulhu R'lyeh wgah'nagl fhtagn!"

1.28.4

A short while ago, a small package arrived at our offices from Mexico. Suspecting a new submission from a faraway place, I quickly ripped open the package. Something was wrapped in bloody newspaper. With glee at the prospect of finding a body part (near the beginning of this long, boring and drawn out practice if sending little bits of Harry, or whatever his name is, who we still don't care about, and which we wish you would stop!), I shredded the blood-stained covering and released its imprisoned contents. Overwhelmed with disappointment, I held the small moss-covered stone by two fingers. It didn't even have the cephalopod façade we're so used to receiving. I dropped it on my desk and searched the papers for something that I missed. Finding nothing, I burnt the packaging and let the stone be buried under it. Then, I went for the bottle in the bottom drawer and relaxed.

Moments or hours later, I was interrupted by a strange man shaking his finger in my face. This is not an unusual occurrence. It wasn't even unusual that he was rolling his eyes and hoarsely croaking words out of chapped lips. However, what was unusual were the words that were issuing forth. The curses of blood and the threats of severe bodily harm were standard fare when dealing with a copy editor, but he was speaking in a little known Toltecian tongue. All of this strangeness was punctuated by a strange putrid wind, not emanating from the vicinity of his rectum, and the constant reference to some deity named Moc Xesuhluhtc. I quickly wrote the word down to make sure that I would remember it had I slipped into some dimensional rift that eradicated my memory or other such amnesiac event. Then, I picked up my shillelagh and clobbered Mr. Baer.

Making sure it was blood that was dripping from his various wounds; I removed the rubber gloves and procceded to the book depository located below the main floor. There I researched Xesuhluhtc, knowing that Moc is a perfunctory title reserved for high levels of priest caste and small blood sucking parasites. After hours of study, which I only started after the police had finished battering down the front door, I found out that Xesuhluhtc is actually the head god of the more vicious Toltaltecs, who were first decimated and then assimilated by the Toltecs to stop them from raping their unborn children. Xesuhluhtc normally presides over day to day workings of the priesthood and daily family life. However, when the total solar eclipse (which happens every two years) makes its path across the top of the sacred pyramid (which happens once every thousand years) (if you don't understand why there is a difference, read a book), Xesuhluhtc grows in power and size. Therefore, Xesuhluhtc dons the name Moc and gains the abilities to rule over the lives of the warrior class of the Toltaltecs, even after they are dead, and corrupt the thought processes of copy editors and sweet potato soup.

That research done, I went back up to the main floor, just in time to stop the paramedics from removing Mr. Baer before his healing process was finished. The pit creature, whose name I still don't know, was well fed, the ambulance sold to the junkyard and the state troopers redirected. Everything was fine until I realized the stone wasn't underneath the pile of burnt paper.

If anyone has seen a small stone in the shape of Moc Xesuhluhtc, please contact us at the address below.

Tentacles,

St. Michael

PS Oh yeah, Moc Xesuhluhtc is a devourer of species and a destroyer of life. Be afraid, and stuff.

1.21.1

Greetings and welcome back to *Cthulhu Sex*! This issue is as crammed full of new illustrations, writings and poetry as a spoiled child at a snobby wedding is crammed full of ladyfingers, éclairs and cakes. Of course, the pieces presented here won't poison your body like the pastries did poor Shawn.

I would like to thank all our readers who participated in our essay contest, "What Love Means to Me". Our first-place winner, David Lee Bowierothe, presents a delightful essay, which we are honored to reprint here.

WHAT LOVE MEANS TO ME

By David Lee Bowierothe

When I look into the eyes of one of my soon-to-be-consumed victims, I see something in between lust and fear. Perhaps it is a combination of the two. Often, it is the terrible hunger of emptiness. In fact, it is this void, a lack caused by the loss of innocent fantasies, which spurs on my actions toward them. I occasionally think of myself as a social predator, some wild cat of the urban jungle that stalks the wounded and the sick. As if by holy covenant, I weed out the unwanted portion of the human cattle. But unlike quiet jungle cats or howling desert dogs, I don't kill and devour my prey. Instead, I bring my hapless children a higher purpose, a reason to live. I fill their hollows with the life force of creation, thrusting into their very souls. It is there that I find my inspiration, there while they lie akimbo, a human jumble of previous struggle for me to untangle and set right. With the flash of my polished prick, 1 remove their impurities, the pieces corrupt or unneeded. What is left is naught but a work of art, my hand guided by some purpose divine yet undivined. There, in the moment before the mangled meat is left to molder, is the ultimate state of being, the ultimate state of release. There, there is love.

Second place winner is the notorious Sarah Toave with her ambitious "Egress of the Edge". And the third-place winner is Melbas Armstrong with its (we never found a reference to gender) "You sick fucks, what the hell do you…" Congratulations to our winners and to our readers who entered. We thank you all. Melbas Armstrong, please send in your address so that we may return the TP manuscript and your prize money.

Tentacles,

St. Michael

PS We are no longer accepting essays on the topic of "What Love Means to Me". We don't care what happened to Harold from the mailroom, either. Quit sending us his body parts.

1.21.2

We have been fortunate to receive a wonderful selection for this issue. In particular, pay close attention to the message from the cheerful individual known as "Wesdrained". Notice that we have left the email address. 'Nuff said.

Subj: get a life

why are you so stupid? What is wrong with your life that you must be so extremely dark and depressed all the time? Why? Tell me. By the by, go take off that godawful white makeup ya girly-man, and git yerself some tasteful clothing, moron.
You sicken me.
Wesdrained

Cassandra Ingram
Sarnath (AP)

Deep Sea Productions today celebrated the release of a new album by their most controversial artist, Cthulhu. This new work, *Straight Outta R'lyeh*, features Cthulhu's signature technique---gravelly vocals layered over the screams and gibberings of small animals from other dimensions as they are driven mad by the artist's manifestation.

The release party was picketed by animal rights groups, who have been up in tentacles over Cthulhu's methods ever since his breakthrough album, *The Screams of Small Creatures*. "I stand by my work," Cthulhu told reporters as protesters shouted outside. "I think it's ridiculous that people are so worried about the lives and sanity of humans and similar vermin that they're willing to censor my artistic vision."

Straight Outta R'lyeh is Cthulhu's first album in several years. Although animal rights activists have tried to claim credit for the hiatus, Cthulhu himself blames it on his sorrow at the death of his friend and longtime producer, Yog Sothoth. Mr. Sothoth died of a heroin overdose after consuming several human rock bands in 1997.

1.21.3

Michael,

I'm sorry about leaving so abruptly last week. But, I received further evidence of what we may be dealing with at the office as well as what is affecting me. Since my stay in New Orleans, I have not been able to keep either the events or my findings straight in my head. As a matter of fact, I believe that since leaving that hellish city, devotees of the squid-man, in whose ritual I became involved, have been following me. In particular, I suspect that several people from advertising and PR have become transformed in an even more insidious manner than the one that we have heretofore seen. In order to confirm my theory, I had kept up a correspondence with the authorities in New Orleans. Once again, I used the cover of an investigator of ritual killings. I asked them if they would keep me informed of any developments, no matter how insignificant, in regards to the case about which they had last spoke to me. Last week, I received a fax at the office from them stating that movement had once again stirred about the burned out remains of the house. There was a tall man with a bulbous face who had showed up at the station claiming the rights to the house and its contents. Upon hearing the explanation that there was not much left after the fire, he stated that he and his assistant, an equally tall but cadaverous-looking man, would assess the situation themselves. Soon afterwards, there were trucks arriving at the house and crates being carted into them. When asked by the locals about the happenings, the truckers mumbled something about "remains" and "California". Once again, I must commend the New Orleans authorities on their detailed information about what can now, no doubt, be termed "an occult phenomenon of certainly national, if not worldwide, proportions."

I'm writing this from LA where, after following the trucking company's manifests and meeting with various key informants to the New Orleans police, the trail seems to have led. I have been told of a nefarious scheme here in LA that could breach even the walled, public lives of celebrities. I have arranged to stay at a friend's house in the West Hollywood section of the city. I have made this the base of my operations. It was from here that I set out to meet a Mr. Calvin Thool at a nearby café. He told me of suspicious nocturnal treatments his wife claimed to need once a month and of a mysterious key made of bone, which had appeared on her key chain. Of course, it is only now that I realize I was being led around by my poisoned senses. I did not think that the key Mr. Thool showed me could be anything but a copy. Nor did I notice his vague resemblance to the description I was sent by the New Orleans police. He rubbed the key and waved it in front of my nose, telling me that we should meet a friend of his in the Los Feliz neighborhood. At that moment, I felt slightly dizzy, my vision went blurry and Mr. Thool's face contorted. I dare not describe the horror I saw, unfortunately for my poor misbegotten soul, more than once in the next days. A face, more protrusions with eyes than a face, peered at me. Then I rubbed my eyes and it was human once more. I pray this is just a symptom of my illness but after the next events, I fear it not to be the case.

We met this friend, a Mr. Yogi Thothlu, at a trendy restaurant in the area mentioned. He confirmed Thool's story with one of his own, adding that he had followed his wife on various occasions and knew the "meeting" spots. This seemed too good an opportunity to pass up. I asked if tonight, with its gibbous moon, would be one of the "meeting" times. He replied excitedly in the affirmative, waving a pudgy hand in front of me. As soon as he did this, I felt the same dizziness overcome me and, much to my horror, his hand thinned out and grew pulsating suckers, opening and closing hungrily as they neared me. Then, it was a hand again. I must have not been able to contain the look of terror upon my face for Mr. Thothlu asked after my health. I mopped my sweat-filled brow and claimed sleeping problems. But, I said I would not let it stop me from from solving their mystery and mine. Mr. Thothlu went on to tell us that they were not having the usual meeting in the Hollywood Hills. They were meeting in the hills and then traveling to Park La Brea with a stop at Mann's Chinese Theatre. What happened next, I can only hope is a product of a demented brain caused by the toxins inside me.

We arrived in the hills just before the moon rose. I saw some people moving among the trees, then I saw a hand pass in front of my face, a thin notched shadow passing in front of my eyes, and I felt myself moving towards the trees. I could not stop myself. I moved without a will of my own towards them. I soon saw that they were not trees but large shambling misshapen creatures with the sickening semblance of rotting humanity and vegetation. Their pseudo-limbs were wetly groping, thrusting and weaving in and out of the women, accompanied by a sound I can only describe as a mixture of raspy rattling and moaning. To my horror, I could not distinguish if the moans were of anguish or joy. As we approached, the creatures stopped, the moaning ceased and my companions reached inside the women with their keys. Moving the keys back and forth, the women screamed with delight while the men chanted horrible words in an unknown tongue. The moon rose and opened before us. We were standing in front of Mann's Chinese Theatre where we passed our hands over the imprints of celebrity digits and mumbled something like Neil Young's "Dust in the Wind". The digits went from being imprints to the actual digits themselves. The moon rose again and opened before us. Now, we were in front of the La Brea Tar Pits. I felt myself following the actions of my companions who, by now, looked as they did in my visions earlier that day. We were moving the keys back and forth through the women, who were writhing in ecstasy, while mumbling the words and throwing the bones into the pits. When we ran out of celebrity digits, we started pulling limbs off the ecstatic women like pinned insects. A wind arose from the middle of the pits. There was the smell of tar and dead flesh. The pits bubbled explosively. Next, a hideous mockery of a human rose forth, stepped onto the land, pulled itself together into a replica of one of the women and walked away into the night. I swear by all that is holy, these things were not human when they rose out of the ebon glue in front of us. Then, the moon rose and opened again, I was back at my base of operations.

So, now you can see why I am writing this letter to you. If anyone comes to the office and looks like me, kill it immediately. It is a horrible tar baby created by the unholy forces who are attacking and infiltrating the very fabric of our society. Please also check the advertising and PR people. I pray this gets to you in time.

Oliver

1.21.4

Iwant to take time here at the end of this beautiful issue to mention something that I feel needs to be brought to the attention of you, our dear reader. I feel, in this time of horrible death and destruction at the hands of overly-religious, overly-political and overly-ignorant people currently in power, that the seed of humanity is not being fertilized properly. I will take a few brief minutes of your day to nurture this kernel within you and help you to be a force for positive change in your social situation.

"What is this seed?" you say.

Well, I'll tell you. It is the compassion and understanding that we all need and desire from those around us. It is the warm womb that supports our personal endeavors and lifts our spirits. It is the social interaction that the lonely have lost and the happy have found.

"Sounds good!" you say, "But how does that help me?"

That takes a small bit of faith on your side. If you want to have your needs fulfilled by others, you should fulfill their needs. The Golden Rule applies here wonderfully. It suggests that you proactively act to fulfill others' needs and expect the same yourself.

You know that the powers-that-be are doing the same for you. They follow all the rules they lay down for you. After all, many of our social practices, such as our justice system, are based on impartial codes of ethics and morals that work perfectly to accomplish what they were set up to do.

"So, you mean I just need faith and my seed will grow?" you say.

Exactly, if you follow the flow of my staff, your seed will grow without doing a thing. In roughly nine months, your seed will be nurtured to the point of nearly bursting! It is then that you will receive the understanding and compassion for which you have searched so long.

Then, there will be a flock of admirers and joyous celebrants who will praise you as their idol and savior. All the most famous, rich and powerful people will come to visit and bestow their blessings. They will humbly bow at your feet and unselfishly grant you any wish you could want. There will be a meteor shower to proclaim your gift to the world. Books will be written about you and all the universe will remember you for all time. In fact, you'll have eternal life. You'll have eternal life in a paradise of your dreams. All the world will revolve around you.

"I don't believe a word of it!" you say, "I'm leaving!"

You can try but the doors are locked. That muffin you ate had the only copy of the key in it. I'm surprised you didn't break your teeth. This? Oh, it's nothing. Stand still.

Ahhh…

It is important to take a moment at the end of a long effort and reflect on all that has gone into it.

Again, ahhh…

Tentacles,

St. Michael

PS That done, I was wondering if anyone has any old body bags lying around their apartment that I could borrow? Also, does anyone have any idea how to get blood out of porcelain so that one of those ultraviolet light searches won't turn up anything?

1.22.1

Greetings!

Welcome to Issue 21 of *Cthulhu Sex*! Or whatever issue number we are up to. My head is filled with numbers: issues, ritual numerology and accounting.

The issue you currently have in your hand is chock full of stories, illustrations and poems from talented up and coming artists and authors. Enjoy their works as they enjoyed creating them.

We wish to bring to light a special segment of our readers that have recently made their presence known with the help of one of our artists. They are a shy and reclusive group that practices their rituals in seclusion. We believe that you, our readers, will be of a high enough intellectual level to understand them and their practices without stigma. Before one passes an undeserved negative judgment on them, a bit about their history and beliefs should be explained.

First, the ritual cleansing of the body is practiced by many religions. The Christians have a tradition of foot washing. The Muslims have ritual bathing. The Buddhists have internal cleansing. In fact, there is a group called "The Cult of the Colon" in the United States that believes that the ritual cleansing of the intestines through various means leads to better life and higher enlightenment. Therefore, the idea of an enema as a means of spiritual cleansing is far from unique.

B. This group of our readers, like many other groups, believes that certain chemical compounds lead to elevated states of being. Their mixture contains sacred and hallucinogenic plants obtained at high costs of finances and life. The cleansing of the bowels includes a large dose of this mixture. It enters the bloodstream quickly in this location without the need for injection or wait. Moments after their ritual is completed, this mixture allows them to reach the higher levels of spiritual consciousness that they require for their seekings.

III. Due to the inability of the large intestine to process raw materials, there is a need to prepare the mixture before it is administered. The natural way for humans to extract the essential elements from any substance is through digestion. Therefore, the mixture is predigested. The longer the mixture is exposed to air after digestion, the less its effects become. This is such an accelerated reduction that the idea of predigesting one's own mixture, regurgitating it and applying it is out of the question. The answer is simple. Let someone else predigest it and directly insinuate it into the bowels. This allows the full effect of the mixture to be gained by the lucky individual.

This religious practice has been self-named Vomenema by its unusual members. The name is the contraction of the two main aspects of this spiritual ritual involved. The members usually practice Vomenema in small, even-numbered groups, one half experiencing the dramatic elevation, the other administrating and taking scientific notes of the undertaking for future use. There are occasionally solitary practitioners who are not concerned with the scientific value of the experience as well as being highly flexible.

There are quite a number of Vomenema practitioners in the world at large. They are highly secretive about their practice due to its nature and connection to the Illuminati. If you look around you in a crowded room, the most popular and powerful person is probably a Vomenema. Please try to give them the respect they deserve.

Tentacles,

St. Michael

1.22.2

This is our selection of letters sent to *Cthulhu Sex*. We have received another in the tangled line of the chronicles of our dear editor Oliver Baer. We also have been gifted with a mention on the NYC Goth email list as suggested reading. Thanks to you all.

Michael,

Ten days. They said they'd come for me in ten days. This is why I had to move. I am now staying in the previous apartment of my friend in West Hollywood. It is located in Los Feliz. Ever since my involvement in the terrible orgy at the La Brea Tar Pits, I believe that it has catalyzed the poisons in my blood somehow. So that now, I am starting to transform into a monstrosity akin to the likes of Mr. Thool or Mr. Thothlu. I wake up in the early morning, after a night of horrific dreams, and, I swear, see my arms thickening back into their pink fleshy shell. I know you are probably thinking that I am suffering delusions brought on by a fever from the stress I am going through. But, I tell you, before I rub the sleep from my eyes, my arms were not the normal appendages of bone and muscle. They were gray, long and tapered with pulsating suckers upon them. In addition to this, I believe I may have to start traveling north, if not to lose myself in the forests of Washington State, then definitely into Canada. Let me not get too ahead of myself, though. First, I must tell you of the voices and why I know they are coming for me, the misshapen tar children of Messrs. Thool and Thothlu.

Since my involvement that horrible night at the pits, so you can imagine, I have been trying to track down these tar golems in order to destroy them. I had no idea how I would do it. I just knew that I had to. What I discovered, to my horror, was that I could spot them easily. I could see that they weren't human. I was not spared the inability to see through their facade. As a matter of fact, all of my senses seemed tuned to them. I can see them, smell them and, worst of all, hear them. For they speak to each other through a means I have not been able to divine. It is either some subsonic combination of rattling and rustling or a type of telepathy. My nights have not been very restful because it is then that they speak to me. I hear them speaking to each other in almost a discordant countdown of events, a click-clacking cacophony of conglomeration like listening to Alice Cooper's "We Didn't Start the Fire". It is through these dreams that I know where to find them. I take them out one by one by surprising them during the day when their human attributes are programmed to override their malefic tendencies and goal. It is not easy but I have been able to cover my tracks by signing up with the local road crew. This way nobody questions the quantities of tar uponst my person. The manner in which I dispose of these vermin is as distasteful as my unfortunate memory of their creation. I must not only dismember them, but then I must wade through their bodies to find the key bones of their creation. This act has been a source of solace to me during this period. With each one slain, I have found that the whispers I hear lessen, if not quit, for the brief period the act takes place. But, this is not the reason I must leave. It is a far more disturbing tendency, nay, a need, I have noticed that I seem to engage in. For if I am not engaging in it, then it must be that the petroleum products of my earlier associates are exacting their revenge.

I told you that I have been awaking in the early hours of the morn. This is detrimental, not only because of what I believe is happening to my body, but because it is causing sleep deprivation, which I pray is the cause of my hallucinations. It has been helpful because I awaken to a spot of wetness. It is when I roll over to get out of bed that I realize I haven't soiled myself because of the night terrors. Unfortunately, the smell that invades my awakened nostrils makes me wish I had. It is the sickly, musty smell of death and sex. What lies next to me is the remains of last night's conquest. For in order for me to focus through the noise

of the dreams, that is instead of having a blurred movie image
of events, I can distinguish and pick out my prey if I engage in
a variation of Ms. Simms' ritual combined with that of Thothlu
et al. I fear that it is this need, indeed it has become a hunger
which I cannot sate, that will make them aware of me. The more
I engage in this lovely erotic ritual, the closer to transformation
and their hive mind I become. Not to mention that in order to
hide the mess in which I am swimming in the morning, I have
started decorating my apartment with the detritus, a fact sure
to alert the authorities as well as a surprise for my dates. I usually pass it off as novelty items and the smell of incense. But, the
ritual, ah, I can scarcely describe its performance without feeling
the need come upon me. It starts when the intended enters my
abode and I ask her to take off her clothes. As she strips each item
off, I notice the curve of her breasts as they meet the sternum,
how it goes from an arc to a perfect semicircle. She lies down
and I massage her body, stroking the breasts gently and slowly
working my way down her body. Then, we move to the bathroom
where we wash the day's labors off of each other. It is not until we
enter the bedroom once more, that I prepare myself for what is to
come. I tie her to the bed and pull the invocation circle from her
carotid down to the breasts, across the nipples and breast bone
to close upon the jugular. It is then that I take one of the bones I
have retrieved from the horrific pseudohumans and run it along
her labia. Then I push it in and out of the vagina, rubbing against
the clitoris to make sure of orgasm. It is at the moment of climax,
with an act of dexterity and strength I was unaware I possessed,
that I plunge the bone up into the womb and the knife across the
neck. This I remember. How the body ends up with the skin and
organs describing the same circle around it that I had drawn with
the knife, I am unable to say. Because of this torment, I dare not
stay here long. One woman did mention that she called a friend
who worked for us prior to our date. Please try to assuage this
woman's despair at the loss of her friend. Though, it is possible
the friend's uses to me have alerted the minions of Thothlu at the
office and that she is no more.

Oliver

1.22.3

For those of you who enjoyed the Games section featured in issue 12, we are returning it. Below, you will find the steps involved in this issue's unveiling. Follow the rules closely, for we cannot be responsible for the repercussions if you do not.

This issue is a special issue as we have been fortunate enough to receive special printing rights for previously unprinted material. Due to the secretive nature of this information, we have had to encode it in our presented works. The code is a complicated one that is nearly impossible to crack without the key (hidden on the Contents page). Those of you that have the *Cthulhu Sex* encoder rings will be able to easily translate the information. If you don't have one of the rings, you can order it through our website.

One the code from the contents is gleaned, a quick scan of the odd-numbered pages will reveal a well-placed discrepancy. This will lead you on a mystical romp through the even-numbered pages. Once the notes from the even-numbered pages are grouped appropriately, all that is needed is a six-ounce glass, a half dozen spoonsful of baking powder and a dram of vinegar. Take the glass and place it in the center of the page (laid out according to the planet placement on the vernal equinox) and fill it with the baking powder. While chanting the Ode to Eg'krem, pour the entire dram of vinegar into the glass. The powder should foam up to the edge of the glass and begin to overflow. At this point, Eg'krem should take over and lift the foam gently into the air. A whirling vortex should form and scatter the contents across the page.

Now it is time to take a break and visit the amusement park behind your house. It will be free admission for you and a million for your enemies (if they pay, half goes into your personal account). Run rampant with the chainsaw or grab the rocket launcher to finish this level easily. If the police sirens wail, return to your abode.

The foam should have hardened into a tasty crust, but don't eat it! It has concentrated the Feelers of Redcap into its essence. One bite and the world, as you know it, will be shifted once to the left and three steps back.

The pattern of foam should point out the informative letters of the text and reveal to you the sacred words. If it has formed the sentence "Grab the Vomenema to your left," then you have missed the third encapsulate of the Ode to Eg'krem. Redo the entire process omitting the chainsaw and going straight for the staple gun. You should have the answer soon.

Thank you for participating in this little practice. If you do not have the *Cthulhu Sex* encoder ring, you can pick up your grandmother in the middle of the Lincoln Tunnel on alternate Tuesdays. If you do not, she will be sold into slavery of the Lords of the One Sock Behind the Washer.

Tentacles,

St. Michael

1.23.1

The horror of reality is greater than anything fiction can create. This was the first thing that ran through my mind after I saw the Twin Towers fall on September 11th. Being located in the East Village of NYC, we have been surrounded by repercussions of this attack on a daily basis. We have seen the tears streaking clean paths on the faces of dust-laden survivors. We have seen the coldly underlit plumes of smoke smother the night sky. We have smelled the weeks of acrid stench from burnt bodies and buildings. We have lived in the post-apocalyptic militaristic zone below 14th Street. We have witnessed the candlelit vigils in every park. We have experienced this horrible tragedy firsthand.

Thankfully, we have not lost anyone to the terrible events of that day. Even though we have been spared the worst aspects of this tragedy, the unthinkable acts have affected every facet of our lives. It is nearly impossible to comprehend the wanton and needless deaths of thousands of people. Not to belittle the civilian loss, the deaths of hundreds of police officers and firemen hit below the belt. It is gut wrenching to think that these brave individuals were murdered, their final acts nothing more than altruistic attempts to help frightened and innocent people. Even this is mind numbing in its grandeur, too awesome to process.

The destruction of the Towers, a symbol to the world of capitalism, democracy and freedom, is an incomprehensible reality in itself. I've stood at their foot and looked up their shining windows toward the heavens. They were an amazing accomplishment of human engineering and achievement. They were a pristine and stoic testament to what we could have and did accomplish. Their power instilled majestic awe in everyone I've ever met who has seen them. Now they are gone, razed in an infinitesimal fraction of the time it took to build them.

At first, I was, like many, so stunned by the events that I was incapable of feeling anything but confusion and disbelief, everything else locked away to protect myself from the inevitable flood of passion. The lack of powerful emotions made me angry at first and then guilty as time went on. I couldn't admit to myself that I was holding anything back, let alone the repressed emotions themselves, for fear it would all tumble in on me.

It was when I visited ground zero with a few close friends that the walls crumbled and unleashed the torrent. There was a thick crowd of hundreds of people, all there for the same reason we were. We all wanted to ingrain this heinous act in our minds, etch the crushing reality of this place in our memories, so as to never, ever forget. The entire crowd was nearly silent. The only disturbances were the clank of heavy machinery moving mouthfuls of crumpled steel and tearful whispers. Even the minor traffic passing by on the normally busy avenue seemed muffled by the heavy hearts of us all.

To my right was the fence of Trinity Church, covered in makeshift banners, flags, uniforms, flowers and hope from the entire country and the world. A few hundred yards before me was a huge, nearly empty crater where the glistening towers had been. The remains of the Towers were but mangled skeletons of steel, jagged fragments stories tall, sharply jutting into the unnaturally open sky above. The wreckage dwarfed the massive cranes which seemed like toys playing a macabre game of Pick-Up Sticks in the attempt to find bodies, worse yet, pieces of bodies, in this lot of unimaginable death. A few of the cranes had hoses that sprayed water at the still smoldering fires somewhere in the depth of this carnage. The valiant workers and volunteers were indistinguishable at this distance. Even with a direct view of the site, the enormity of this mutilation was still beyond my mental tolerance and my psychological walls held. The whole scene seemed like something from a bad movie. Deep within my chest, the trapped emotions begged to be let out, twisting and churning like vipers in a burlap sack.

The gravity of the situation didn't sink in until something

real happened directly in front of me, something that brought the thousands of names on the banners and the thousands of tons of twisted steel into a personal and human perspective. An elderly couple was standing in front of me, holding each other. They were silent in their embrace; no words could hold the grief that was plain on their faces. Tears began to run down the woman's face, quiet rivulets of anguish that traced the deep wrinkles of her haggard face. I knew they had lost someone dear.

My mind reeled with an imagined story of their loss, concocting flickering images of their plight. They breathlessly waited for word about their loved one, while the news repeated the footage of the planes hitting the Towers and the Towers falling, over and over again. They posted quickly copied fliers next to the maddening multitude of others, everywhere possible. They pushed through the throngs at the triage center in the attempt to get some word. Holding onto the hopeless hope that some miracle might have saved their loved one, they waited tirelessly by the phone while watching the constant news coverage. A month later, they finally gave in to the possibility that nothing more could be done. They were beyond hope; the only comfort was the ugly corpse before us and the warmth of their companionship.

That was the breaking point. My eyes welled with tears. Conscious of nothing but compassion for the poor couple, the sorrow of such loss and anger at those who caused it came to the surface. I let my subconscious purge into my conscious, the emotional reaction sudden and violent. It all came out, cleansing me in its purity.

It was then that I realized the true nature of the words I had first thought that day. The horror of reality IS greater than anything fiction can create. No one could write this. Even if they somehow could, no one would believe it.

This made me look deep into myself as a writer, specifically as a writer of horror. I asked myself why I should write horror that could have an effect that might be, in any fractional way, close to the reaction people had to 9/11. I was disgusted to think of horror as just entertainment with this thought. The events of that day have nothing to do with entertainment. Stories that cause this sort of personally emotional horror, pain and fear in a reader are the furthest from my goals as a writer. Is horror possibly morally defunct and inciting of such terrible events? It was a series of conflicts that took much of my focus.

Then I was informed that horror was on the rise as an entertainment genre after the attack. This threw a wrench into my mental works. How could people be interested in more terror after such events? It made very little sense to me until I asked myself the right question, "What is the place of the horror genre in people's lives?" The first answer was immediate—entertainment. It began to make a little more sense then. After such a traumatic event, people need escapism to alleviate their personal stress. There are historical precedents so numerous that I was shocked I didn't instantly see this cycle.

But, this answer didn't satisfy my basic question of morality. The gladiatorial games were seen as entertainment for the masses. It doesn't mean that they were morally sound.

I thought back to some of the classic works of horror, *Dracula, Frankenstein, War of the Worlds, Dr. Jekyll and Mr. Hyde*. These stories are literary benchmarks for my horror ideals. What about them makes them so ingrained in society and my mind? I believe it is the symbolic nature of these stories. *Dracula* has been used as a symbol for fear of the medical profession and organized religion. *Frankenstein* has been analyzed in greater detail and can be linked to fear of new political governments and religious structures and their cannibalizing of previous institutions. *Dr. Jekyll and Mr. Hyde* might be a reaction to the fear of the subconscious as revealed by the birth of psychoanalysis. *War of the Worlds* could be a reaction to space exploration or imperialism. Even modern horror, such as *Alien* being a fear of penetration and *Terminator* a fear of technology, has relevant sociopolitical references.

This set me on the path to my answer. Horror is the literary reflection of the corruption of what is and the possible harm of what might be on a sociopolitical level taken to the personal level. This thought cleared up my moral dilemma. I could see a path for myself that I could follow without trepidation. I proved to myself the value of my work in the aftermath of such tragic destruction. In this time of excessive marketing of mass media schlock, I had forgotten the reasons behind my start in this industry. I wanted to share good, entertaining stories that, if I were lucky, could help people understand their lives and enjoy what they have. It is a lofty goal, but not impossible.

I brought this idea up to a friend of mine. Being a bit more realistic than my dreaming self, she helped me realize that a good story is intrinsically allusional. By describing the events and obstacles a character faces, a writer reveals things that have been experienced or imagined. This allows us, the readers, to see through the writer's unique eyes. A good story not only opens new possibilities of thoughts, but it keeps us entertained so that we want to find these possibilities. Horror can have a place in life as more than just frivolous entertainment. It can allow us to face issues we can't directly in our lives. It personalizes the impersonal injustices that are out of our control.

With these reaffirmations of the arts I love so much, I began to write again. I began to thrill in exploring fear again. My muse returned to whisper sweet nightmares.

Tentacles,

St. Michael

Cthulhu Sex and its staff are deeply sickened by the tragedy of September 11th. Our condolences go out to the victims, their families and their friends. We will not forget.

1.23.2

Dear St. Michael,

I had a dream recently that was so vivid and so very Lovecraft that I just had to write and tell you about it. It was very cool.

Walking uphill through a jungle, I was barefoot and could feel the spongy, resilient loam gently crush and rebound under my weight as I trudged onward toward the unseen summit. Ferns, moss and vines hung like verdant shrouds filtering a cool, humid emerald light across the jungle floor. The walking upward seemed to take days, daylight never bled into night, but I had the sensation of being weary from long travel.

In almost all of my dreams, I am being pursued by someone or something. Sometimes, it manifests physically: monsters, bad guys, cops, people, girls, whatever. Other times, it is just a sensation, a tingling of the nerves at the back of my neck, a constant flight response to any challenge because if I stay, *they* will catch up. It is never a good thing, there is always an underlying threat to it. Well, this was the first dream that I can remember where I did not have that sensation. No one was following me and I did not feel the oppressive sense that I was evading pursuers. I was walking up this jungle-enshrouded mountain under my own purpose, not under threat. This gave the dream a rather exhilarating sense for me, it felt like an adventure of discovery.

So, I trod the jungle floor with long, vigorous steps, eager to find my purpose. Soon, I felt a vague vibration, a rhythmic pulsing, echo through the loose earth of the jungle floor. Curious, I stopped and tried to get a bearing on its location. There was no sound accompanying it. No, it wasn't the drums of some far off native tribe. Gingerly, I took a few steps to my left, then right, trying to discern the location. After a bit of trial and error, I detected that the iambic signal was stronger ahead of me off to my right.

My rational behavior surprised even me. Normally in my dreams, I am a passive observer or the prey, as I mentioned above, never the reasoned explorer. Well, some kind of internal logic kept me ticking in this one. I proceeded through the foliage with caution, trying very hard to make out the source of the vibrations. The earthen pulses came in a steady rhythm, reverberating through the porous soil. My feet became my ears, as I carefully tread, the vibrations gently scratching at the sole and bones.

At this point I realized, as I was pushing aside languid ferns and ropy vines, that there were no insects in the jungle. No mosquitos, no spiders, no flies. I think I must have become somewhat conscious that I was dreaming. Quite suddenly my surroundings took on the plastic quality of a movie set. The jungle beast was lurking just ahead off camera, waiting for its cue to roar out and menace me, or so I thought.

No sooner had I convinced my dreamself I was dreaming, then I stumbled into a small clearing. It was a dark circle of bald earth. In the center of the circle lay the source of the disturbance. An emerald-scaled fish, at least as long and as thick as my leg, covered in glistening green scales, gasping for air from its gaping, saw-toothed maw. Like a single convulsing muscle, it contracted itself into an inverted arch, pointing its veined tail skyward, reaching up with its head, mouth working as if trying to speak or, at the very least, latch onto its own tail. The beast was still for this moment that I entered the clearing, body arched and waiting. Once my attention had been captured, it launched itself at the ground, thrashing like a mad prisoner. Reflexively uncoiling and crashing into the yielding earth, over and over in rapid succession. The loam danced and jumped to its morbid pulse.

Needless to say, I was overawed and stood slack jawed. The head of the beast seemed of a different material than the rest. It was smooth and glossy with a milky rainbow undercoating, like oil and milk spilled in a puddle dripping from a dumpster.

Its eye was black and round, but expressive. The details of the iris and retina were clearly highlighted in the humid light, the shaded black orb swivelled wildly in its supple socket. Gills flexed and mouth stretched, reaching for an ocean long lost. The mouth, hideous and expressive, gaped and worked, trying to speak, trying to hurl one last curse of revenge.

It pounded maniacally against the clearing floor. Thump-thud. Thump-thud. Thump-thud. I have seen fish drowning in air before. There was a time, when I didn't spend every waking minute in this black hole, when nature and death weren't such an uncommon sight. Fishing trips, lakes and rivers once were common in my life. But there was no plausible source for this scene, no river or stream, no pond, no net, no lonely cottage. Nothing but verdant green foliage, punctuated with occasional marks of whitish-grey stone.

I stood transfixed. The fish raged against its suffocation, pounding, pounding, pounding. I wanted it to die. *Suffocate, you obscenity.* This unending parody of death held me mesmerized, the flashing green scales and the sickening milky head thrashing in a moment before death. I yearned for it to expire, but I couldn't bear the thought of this view ending.

Sweating. I awoke sweating. A hot, insulating sweat that trapped bubbling heat in the crown of my skull. The liquid felt warm and heavy in my hand as I wiped my brow. It stained the sheets a darker shade of night. Nausea flooded my guts like seawater. I turned on the light to banish the dream and orient myself in the waking world, but the abominable fish still pumped darkly in my chest. Thump-thud. Thump-thud. Thump-thud.

Then, I realized that I had been dreaming. I started to laugh. Wow, I thought to myself, what a fucking cool dream! I confess that I love the physical reaction, the terror, the adrenaline that nightmares give me. After thinking about it, it all seemed so twisted, like one of Father Baer's letters, that I just had to write you and tell you about it. I hope you liked it.

Luke, NYC 2001

1.23.3

Michael,

I'm writing this in the hope that you are still alive. I am actually hopeful that you have set up offices somewhere else other than our downtown location. I feel I should have, as a matter of fact I tried, to warn you about the events that befall America on September 11. But the damn whispering keeps distracting me. I am not even sure I will be able to maintain continuity while writing this letter, as I said it is hard for me to distinguish things anymore. My trips between the dream world, the present and the horrific past, of which I have been a part, have kept me on the run. Not to mention the fact that the transformation is turning my sensory experiences into macabre psychedelia. I have been able to maintain some human semblance during the day, except for the more emotional moments. During the night, I can now no longer deny the transformation exists. In order for me to maintain my humanity, they tell me, I must…What! What do you want? Later! We'll get to it later. God damn, that whispering! It has gotten even more confusing for me now that I have decided to stay here in Canada. I'm staying in the basement of some friends' apartment building in Kelowna, British Columbia. Luckily, they have their own weirdness here, not the least of which is a version of the Loch Ness Monster in the lake on one side of town. My friends also have been helpful in keeping the local authorities away. As a matter of fact, it has become a family project. When I'm engaging in the ritual, even the three year old starts a fight with her sister screaming, "No, Charity, NO!" This covers the cries for mercy very well, as one would expect. It is a lovely city of apple orchards, farm-fed

women, vineyards, transients and finally, caring people. All of
who don't seem to question the disappearance of a few of their
number. I have so far been able to keep my forays limited to
the lakeshore line and am thinking of heading into the mountains. At least in these places I can blame it on...No! We're not
going yet. Yes, yes, I want to. But, not yet! Damn you! Damn
them! The whispering sounds so much like the wind in the
orchards and vineyards. One afternoon, I made the horrible
mistake of taking a walk through an orchard and the resting
at the edge. There was a beautiful view overlooking the whole
city. As I sat there enjoying the view, it wavered like asphalt
on an extremely hot humid summer day. It was warm and I
was getting sleepy. I rubbed my eyes thinking I was just tired.
I believe I knew I was slipping into that horrid reality I have
been occupying for the past several months but this time there
was no horrible stretching, pulling tightness to my skin and
muscles. There was only a sort of opiate paralysis that left me
in a state of maddening helplessness, while the leaves rustled
against the newly ripened apples, coupled with a stifling quality to the air as if I was breathing cotton. I hope it was the leaves
rustling and not the shambling monstrosities I have previously
encountered. The trees seem to be moving, almost clustering,
into a circle around me. But, it wasn't me they were focused on.
It was, I thought at first, a dying, suffocating fish. It can't have
been the fish, though. I heard its dying dreams, its last words.
It had what looked like legs and arms. It reminded me of Ms.
Simms' relatives. It said, "Cthulhu ftagn," then died among the
greens, reds and browns, bobbing their heads, sending apples
raining to the ground.

As the apples rained down, the scene changed and the
apples started screaming. The leaves and trees started burning
as the tar golems of Thool and Thothlu attacked. I tried to rub
my eyes. But, I could not lift what were now my arms. They
had transformed into the state they are at night, elongated and
grayish, with suckers along the undersides and claws at the
end. Now, I saw that the trees were buildings and the apples,
people. I tried to focus. I thought, since they insist on having
me witness their apocalypse, I can at least try to warn you,

Michael, through one of our advertising staff. I felt myself slipping towards her in a weird dreamscape. I reached out to her, trying to caress her dreaming psyche, but it was then that they started chanting. What looked like a plane was falling with a building. But the plane had a large eye that was trying to scoop the falling people into its maw as it flapped its great bat-like wings.

There was a curtain of wind closing over me. A smothering, moldering fish smell engulfed me, making me gag. I hear the sea and the slosh-slapping before the scene shifts again. Except this time it doesn't shift all at once, it comes in waves like an old filmstrip falling off the track of the reel. I'm not sure what is making me more nauseous, the present vertigo, the smell or the fact that I now feel the need to engage in the ritual. I attempt to raise my "arms" once again to describe a circle with a pentacle within it. I will be safe if I can only finish this. My arms don't seem to move steadily, though I am unsure whether they are doing the moving or the reality shift is doing it. They flail and grab at the shoreline that is becoming more and more a reality. Mutated fish-cousins are rising up out of the water to gather the fleeing, screaming people who are running away from the burning horror. I focus my will harder on the sand at my feet. The pentacle starts to form. I smile to myself as the scene loses its form. The pentacle is finished. Now, for the circle. I giggle nervously as it closes and the scene seems to shift back to the serene landscape of Kelowna, only to notice that as the circle meets its end, it erupts into flames. The circle burns, the pentacle burns, the beautiful landscape burns and I am burning. Now, we must do it. NOW! You know we must. You cannot escape without us! You have no choice!

My friends have been very helpful. They have managed to help me secure a place in the woods where no one will bother me. It seems that I will need their help in more ways than one. I must return my body to its previous form. No one seems to miss the transients they deliver to me. The sweet sound of a warped recording of Chopin's *Water Music* plays constantly as the wind blows through my resting place. I will make it back there, to you and the office. The woman who sleeps next to me does not mind her role mostly. She will go with me and help me. Their disease and carnage can NOT and will NOT continue. The ritual, uh...magazine, must continue. Move somewhere else and hire a new staff. Leave if you can.

Oliver

1.23.4

The horror continues.

"What horror?" you might ask.

Let me enlighten you. There is something oft talked of, yet rarely known. It is a tediously long torture that has broken the minds of many a stalwart individual. It makes men weep and women scream. It has been the downfall of empires and the unsung crime of many dictators. It destroys the soul, wracking the helpless victim with emptiness.

"What," you ask, "can be so destructive?"

Two words, seemingly innocuous, strung together like a Frankensteinian monster: Corporate reorganization. These simple words throw those who have been victims into frightful fits of repressed agony. The cold chill of their stories set dread in the minds of those who might be. The innocent few who have avoided being in such a predicament count the blessings of their freedom. Not only is it utter chaos, it is a sickening taint that, like a contagious disease, follows the unfortunates who are touched by its vile hand and spreads to all those they encounter.

The only people who survive this infectious plague are the propagators of this perilous nightmare. Known by their victims only as "Them" or "The Bean Counters", they wage a holy war on the unwary. No arguments of logic or compassion can assuage the drop of their deadly scythe, the bottom line. Wielding spreadsheets of economic sin, they tout the scriptures of Scrimp and Save with no regard for the virtues of efficiency or truth. The idiocy of their inquisition deletes individuals from the structure of any work environment and creates useless automatons to ply their measures.

The most heinous of their actions is not, as one would assume, the relatively painless severing of human flesh from the corporate creature. It is the tireless pursuit of gleaning useless information about systems and positions, they neither know nor care about, and "restructuring" them with new titles and no visible changes.

This seemingly simple practice can take many months during which the intended victim is unnecessarily raked across hot coals of uncertainty. Not only does this poor person have to sweat the details of creating descriptions of themselves and all those they work with, which the evil Bean Counters don't give a fig about, they wake up in cold sweat worrying about these details and the arbitrary havoc that could be caused by the necessary misinterpretation.

If the months of stomach acid assaulting these hapless peons weren't enough, causing countless agonies and personal improprieties, this whole process can be repeated again and again for years. The most unfortunate survive these attacks continually, their self-confidence and standing eroded by this unabating storm. They generally take one or two forms. The first is the drawn and gaunt corporate weasel, identified by their obsequiousness and treachery. The second is the obese sad sack, easily recognized by their borderline personality and undying faithfulness to the constantly changing corporate ideologies. These two zombies are pitiful tools of the untouchable inquisitionists. They are much like the doomed "guards" who helped the controllers of a death camp kill their own kind. They believe their work is to destroy their coworkers will keep them alive and well. It is a sad, sad existence.

But it isn't half as despicable as the desperate wolves that implement the fiendish plans of manifest destiny. Serving their own selfish ends, they reduce the population under their rule to numbers. This dehumanizing of people allows the demons to feel no remorse as they shatter hopes, dreams and lives. Twisted by greed, they spout friendly words of placation as they zealously purge their flock of the randomly accused excess. Having only the minimal companionship of their sordid elite and the leaches that attach themselves, they live lonely lives, surrounded by the corpulent stench they exude. These powerful liches are more feared than respected, revenants of unholy slaughters that feel no remorse or guilt.

"What can I do to save myself from this dire fate?" you ask. There are but a few choices. You can join the ranks of the oppressors. This is the most unlikely of the choices and hardest to achieve. Most are born with the heartlessness and the finances to follow their family's footsteps. The others spend their lives destroying their compassion and acquiring hard to obtain educations usually reserved for the first group. You could also banally slide into the deceiving comfort of the zombie mass. This is a somewhat easier choice, as being insipidly lackadaisical is the main requirement. For those of you who actually have a heart, self- worth and motivation, the path of avoidance is best. Go out and take a risk in making your dreams come true, start your own business. Just be wary of becoming one of the "Bean Counters". Your heart should protect you from such shortcomings. For those of you who don't fall into any of these categories, the path is unfortunately nihilistic. There is absolutely nothing you can do in troubled times such as these but be tossed around like driftwood in a hurricane. Yes, it is something to fear. Just remember, no matter how safe and sound one feels, the possibility of such horrendous acts always exists.

The horror continues.

Tentacles,

St. Michael

1.24°.51

I found myself watching a lot of TV news lately, a practice to which I don't usually give much credence. Lately however, I seem to have been sucked into a world of intrigue, death and sex that I can hardly believe my own eyes. Yet even in this dire drama, shimmers of an enlightened future hang like heat waves on desert highways. Deep within me there is a battle between unconditional disgust and unsubstantiated hope. Without a victor, I continue to gape at the electrified emanations on the screen.

You might think that I mean the blatant idiocracy on almost all sides of the recent, mythically propaganda-based, religious wars waged in the Middle East. Or you might think I mean the outing of (surprise) pederast priests in the church that brought us the traveling stage show, *The Inquisition*. If you're into the scientific way of thought, you might think I mean the inanity of the religious right trying to stop basic research, which would improve and save the lives of hundreds of thousands of people, due to morals given to them by another faction of their religion that they now believe will burn for all eternity in some garbage dump somewhere.

If you thought any of these, you would be incorrect. These are all good ideas, but they aren't the one I was talking about above. Generally, I've given up thinking too deeply about most of this because I have come to terms with the fact that most people can't see their hypocrisy through their choice of words.

Pardon me. That didn't work too well, now did it? I was trying to make a "see the forest through the trees" metaphor. Bad Avatar. I must flagellate myself in the name of the great Cthulhu until I erupt in purifying liquids. Perhaps later.

Anyhow, back to the issue at hand. It could be any of these horrific things, but it is not. What is it that keeps me glued to the TV with fear and dread? It is the unending stream of ignorant hubris that is a seemingly common trait in most of the truly whacked out individuals who commit crime. Let us step away from the easily identified estrangement of sociopathic serial killers and cold-hearted drug dealers, and into the day-to-day happenstance of the common thug.

The other day, I heard about some screwball that felt the bus he was riding on was moving too slow, so he stabbed the poor bus driver. Can anyone tell me what this mental midget was thinking? I'm pretty sure that would be the last way to make the bus go faster. Did he think he could take over the driver's seat and force the bus to move at his required speed? Did he think the other passengers wouldn't notice? What was he doing on a bus, of all the transportation options available in our fair city?

Let me give another example. I was watching the news the other day and saw a bit of a live car chase in California. The police were following the driver at a safe distance down an empty highway. The car stopped and the officers urged him to give up. He opened the door and danced for them. Then he got back in his car and leisurely drove further, the patrol cars following. The driver turned off the highway into a truck emergency exit. For those of you who don't know what that is exactly, it is a long strip of deep gravel for stopping semis whose brakes don't work. In other words, a stopping device for vehicles much larger than a car. Needless to say, it not only brought his running to a standstill, it proved his menial intelligence. There, he danced in and out of the car. Finally, the police brought in a dog and let it loose, incapacitating the moronic suspect. The only sane explanation I can see for this man's behavior is either extremely diminished mental capacity or major drug use.

These two examples are but tips of the iceberg. Every day, there are countless reports of this diseased mindset smeared across the news. And every day, with the TV constantly on in the background of almost all my activities, I wait for them with baited breath. As I wait, I think about how alien these people are to me. I can find their acts reprehensible or humorous, depending on whether they cause harm or not. I find no compassion for them for I know what they represent.

I watch them as signs of the coming opening of the rift. The moment when the world will rend and all who are unworthy shall be devoured in the blackness of nothing. The day when the mountains shall fall and the shallow stories of the false religions shall be discarded by the masses. The day when the mighty Lords of Chaos and Order shall again return and give free cable and giant flat-screen TVs to everyone.

That will be the day we shall rejoice! We shall frolic in the warm fields of grass with the great Cthulhu, holding hands and playing ring-around-the-rosy. At the final great moment of mankind's ultimate stupidity, the bombs will fly, we will become ash and all fall down.

I want to thank all the ignorant masses, of which we, the creators and the readers of Cthulhu Sex, are not part, for their contribution to the destruction of morals, ethics, freedom, honor, happiness, chocolate-covered sugar bombs, reason, wisdom and spirituality.

Tentacles,

St. Michael

In the meantime, before the prophesized thermonuclear doom of all things, come join us for our next Fall Equinox Party, September 21st in NYC. Check out our website, www.cthulhu-sex.com, for details.

1.24°.52

I received both of these letters from the indomitable publisher of NYfC magazine, Luke Crane. They seemed to fit so well together that I decided not to keep them for separate issues. Besides, a large beast in one of my dreams threatened to remove parts of my body that I consider sacred if I did.

Dear St. Michael,

More dreams. Emerald light, tinged with gold, filtered across my eyes blinding me, deepening the shadows around me. In my waking life, it would have refracted across my glasses, creating a scintillating halo. But in my dream I wore no glasses and the light pierced straight through me.

Ducking under heavier canopy, I skirted the spear-like beams arcing down from the treetops. The inky wells of shadow were cooler and shielded me from the boiling heat. Not that it was at all cool beneath these verdant fronds. No, my breath came hard and hot, as if I had been breathing too long through a blanket. But the sunlight thrusting down onto me made it unbearable. Crossing a shaft of light my temperature soared, sweat bubbled swiftly to the surface. Thus, I kept to the dark spots as I moved through this primordial forest.

The ground was hard and unyielding, and in the shadows below the impenetrable boughs very little grew. Wide open spaces, like corridors of an empty prison, retreated in all directions. Trunks of trees made passages, gates and empty cells. The place felt foreign and alien, more like a bizarre monument than any sort of living forest. Yet, despite it all, I had the sense that I was somewhere. This place seemed too strange to be born of my imagination.

I wandered, lost and forgotten

Luke

NYC, December 2001

Dear St. Michael,

I was uncertain if that last dream-letter I sent to you was connected to the first one I had. The jungle through which I wandered was so utterly different that I suspected they were separate. (But I sent it along as a lark anyway.)

It wasn't until a month later that I connected the two. Once again, I was in the vaulted jungle of the second dream. Still I wandered aimlessly and the daylight was unending. No matter how much time seemed to elapse in these dreams, it was eternally day. I remember looking straight up to the underbelly of the towering canopy. It was vast and arched like a cathedral above me. These ancient trees hoarded the sunlight and used its constancy to their advantage. They stood as tall as sequoias.

The sensation of being lost in an alien land with no bearings disturbed me and left me agitated. In my waking life, I pride myself on my sense of direction and an ability to find any place anywhere if given the proper tools and a chance. But here, I was stripped of that ability and was left only with the sinking feeling of a child abandoned in a vast department store. Alone, now and forever, how could anyone find me in this mess?

No time elapsed and there was no warning, a trick of dreamtime. The forest broke into a clearing, one much different than the last clearing I had encountered. Blazing white sunlight burnt down in a circle, in the center of the clearing perched a bodhi tree, sheltering out the sunlight into a ring of gold. The bodhi tree grew forth from a stony mound, clutching roots seized upon it like the tentacles of a cephalopod prying apart prey. Around the base of the mound, a riot of undergrowth basked in the searing, nurturing glory of the sunlight, reaching up where the bodhi tree reached down.

After some inspection of the area, I saw that the mound had shape. It was an ellipse built of carved and set stone blocks rising from the jungle floor. The stone was whitish. I couldn't tell if it was bleached by the sun or some form of white stone that I didn't know. Time and the torture of the bodhi tree had abraded the surface; nonetheless, the details that survived its torture were gross enough to still be apparent.

The mound tapered thickly at the bottom and rounded at the top. Of course, I could see neither too clearly. The bodhi lorded over the summit and the undergrowth concealed the base. Just below the peak of it ran a ring of carved nodules and rings, a crown if you will. Midway down, just below its widest breadth, there protruded a teardrop-shaped ellipse. I couldn't discern what it represented until I looked further down. At the base of the pile, enmeshed in the undergrowth and clutching roots, stone columns as thick as my leg thrust *en masse* into the ground. They protruded from the bottom of the mound, the base of tentacles. The teardrop was an eye, massive and unblinking.

I leapt back in mild shock, a bit more scared than I felt I should have been, and woke in shame. If I had remained calm, I could have explored more. I am very eager to dream again! Until the next dream.

Luke

NYC, January 2002

1.24°.53

When I opened the worn manila envelope that housed this letter, for lack of a better name, I was accosted by a shredstorm of paper. I instantly thought that I was the victim of a letter bomb. After collecting my wits and the pieces of paper, I realized that there actually were words scrawled across their faces. Piecing them together as best I could, I revealed what follows. Forgive me if it seems somewhat disjointed. I'm not sure if I found every last piece. I was engaged in something once cited as "nonstandard destructive copulation".

Micha,

I apologize for using the diminutive form of your name but this constant molting is wreaking havoc upon me. With this letter, I feel a sense of accomplishment, I see clearly what I must do now. After numerous efforts to communicate with you about my plan—I am sitting in the middle of a pile of papers—I am finally able to get it down on paper. It involves the original box we received. There seem to be five words on the papers until now. Michael, she, help, so, hungry. Hungry, what could I have meant? Aargh, my stomach... Light shifting... my mouth... air heavy, hot, wet... arms cold... need warmth. Where is she? She will help me.

Moving. Must keep moving towards the light and heat. Glinting and flickering like looking at a candle through an emerald, we head in its direction. The process has begun. We must get the city ready for Drilpa Cthulhu. Augmenting this mind, my mind? I reach out to the others and ask them to help me. Help me find the fuel and the will to keep this one going.

It is so hard. Hard to maintain the body's integrity, keep the mind focused but hardest to accept that I may never see the city again. It is hard and I am tired. The woods we are moving through start reminding me of home. The trees seem so large from this body's vantage point. I'm tired.

I'm not sure where I stopped or when. The whispering has become more distracting than ever. I feel that it is leading me someplace. For instance, at this point, we have stopped at the edge of a wood with a town ahead of us. The trees seem to tower over me. They shift between giant redwoods, sequoias and pines to stone pillars and monoliths. The shadows cast by trees seem to move and solidify into statues. The shifting nature of my vision makes the leaves and needles melt together into giant fronds floating over my head. A picture of a city under the ocean comes to my mind. Sadness then pain and hunger envelop me. Must head towards the village. She will help me.

I sense the heat and light in the stone structures ahead. I steer the body towards one of the brighter concentrations of these energies. Through the eyes, I notice people drinking and socializing. I focus the mind and concentrate on maintaining the body's integrity for now. I'll let socialization do the rest. I relax a bit.

I'm standing in front of a woman at a bar. I'm not sure how I got there. I want to ask her to help me, to tell her about the office, the magazine. But, all I feel is hunger, pain and incredibly horny. I turn on the charm without thinking about it or meaning to. I buy her a drink, then another and another. We have been chatting for several hours when the pangs hit more intensely than ever. She asks if I'm ok. I tell her I just need air. She offers to take a walk with me. I'm drawn back to the woods. The whispering seems to promise quietude there.

We have gathered our fuel for the next couple days. We want to start feeding when I think of the city again. It heightens our want to further our mission. We don't want to exhaust this one like we did the other. Maybe if we take some fuel and the rest can be sent to Drilpa Cthulhu. We steer the body towards the blue-green light. It will be bright soon. Better for us to be in the comforting cool shades. Ever since the body tried to take over and burn us out, we have had to maintain tighter and more forceful control over it. We wasted too much time regenerating. If not for the fuel, maintaining the integrity of this body would be impossible and I would never see the city again. I let the hormones and liquor do their work on this body and the fuel. Once again, I relax.

As we paw and lick each other, clothes rip off. I start to engage in the ritual. This time though as the change starts, images flash through my head. I'm licking and biting her nipples, a sales representative from the office is wooing you, Michael, with her shirt open exposing the curve of her breasts. I'm licking and kissing this woman's belly, the water's edge disappears into a forest-green, frosted-glass reflection of light to a brown-black sandy, muddy consistency where light fights a losing battle. I hear groans from her lips as I go down on her but they sound like the yawns of an entity too horrible to imagine. It sounds like Sousa's *Carnival of the Animals*, if the animals imitated were all terribly mutated and maimed. I keep licking her sex and a stone mound appears in my head. A mound surrounded by tree root tentacles with stone columns extending down. It seemed there were some carvings on it. As I recognized them, I start the completion of the ritual. The groans of ecstasy turn into screams of agony. My hunger and pain recede as I finish.

We are almost whole now. Soon we will be able to move forward. Soon I will see the city again. The Great One will let me live here in peace. There is plenty of fuel and these bodies serve me well for the present. Our mission will succeed.

Michael, I have one last moment before the whispering drives me on once again. Try not to succumb, as you see I have, to the pheromones these creatures secrete. It is one of their lures. I hope that if you have continued the office and magazine, you have screened the applicants for positions there. I hope I'm headed in a direction towards you. I cannot tell because in my altered state the stars always look different. One minute, they are earthly. The next, they are unlike any I have ever seen. Again, I must impress upon you the need for it to continue.

Oliver

1.24°.54

Welcome to the end of the issue. I would like to thank a number of the people that have helped out with this issue. Unfortunately, I cannot as I have a more pressing matter.

I recently heard about a unique club that specializes in species squishing. An acquaintance of mine, who shall remain nameless for the time being and who has been patronizing this particular establishment for quite some time, suggested that I might find a different sort of pleasure there. There was talk of forbidden delights and unusual people, but my acquaintance would give no specific details on the kinds of pleasure.

My interest was piqued. Being one who is up for any sort of amusement as long as it is novel, I decided to let this person guide me into something new. The possibility was enticing. Especially after we ended up in a rundown warehouse section of New Jersey, near the exit to the Holland Tunnel. There, I was driven through a maze of streets, lined with walls of cement, broken glass and plywood, that befuddled even my videogame-heightened mapping senses.

We pulled up before a nondescript warehouse in the middle of this insane labyrinth. The only thing marking the building from any of the others was a strikingly out of place red carpet that stretched from the board-sealed door to the curb. There was no one around. Excitement at the unfamiliar began tickling at the base of my groin.

We exited the car and walked up to the door. My friend knocked an elaborate rhythm, too convoluted for accurate memory. The door creaked open outward, the boards splitting along ingeniously concealed seams to allow the movement. From inside wafted cool air scented with the salty tang of the sea and just a hint of the desperate lust of a peepshow. A gentleman in a tuxedo greeted us and took the car keys. He went to park the car and closed the door, leaving us in the dim half-light of a single, gentle lamp in an unadorned hallway.

Left to our own devices, my companion guided me down the hallway into a small room. One side of the room was filled with a giant leather couch and the other side was filled with a mirrored wall. After we settled ourselves in the couch, the light dimmed and the mirror revealed itself as a tinted glass wall that peered into a metal room.

A few moments later, two women in some sort of leather S&M style clothing entered the metal room. We watched as they opened a drawer from the wall and pulled out giant squid, fleshy pink and as tall as the women were. They stood and began gently squeezing their respective squid to their bodies. Their faces began to contort with hints of some surreal gratification. We could hear growing moans of ecstasy and a strange squealing piped in from some hidden speakers.

I couldn't fathom what was happening and it aroused me. The confusion, the uniqueness and the sensuality: were a heady mix. All I knew was that I wanted to see what would happen. I wanted more.

The squids began slightly twitching and turning redder as the sultry moans became louder. There was no contact between the ladies' flesh and their squid's that I could see, making the cause of the moaning maddeningly mysterious. Even the squids' spasms seemed too minor to cause any pleasure. Yet, the heated moans continued with still greater force.

While lost in my thoughts, the now vibrantly ruddy squids suddenly went lax. The women holding them collapsed to the floor. They lay in a heap of leather clad limbs and pulsating tentacles, breathing heavily and noisily. The squids and the women seemed to be gently stroking each other in the afterglow.

I wanted a cigarette after that. I was rock hard in my pants and I had tingles shooting up and down my spine. Never had I seen anything like this before.

After that, I couldn't get enough. I found my way there again and again. Each time, it was in a different location. Each time there were different people, sexes and numbers, as few as one lone person-squid couple and as many as ten orgiastic couples engaging in squid swapping.

One time, not too long ago, my greatest desire was fulfilled. I was asked to be one of the squid squeezers by the manager of the club. I know why they moan now. Oh yes, now I know. And all I want is more.

Tentacles,

St. Michael

1.25°.$1

As you may have noticed, we now have a bar code on the front of the cover. This symbolizes a new era in the *Cthulhu Sex* Empire. We are spreading the word through the masses. Soon, we will infect the world with dark pleasure.

Getting such a code hasn't been an easy process. We have had to deal with a large number of obstacles. Many of them are silly hurdles placed in the way by the government in an attempt to keep business from becoming large and corrupt. Obviously, that hasn't worked. Lately, we have seen the tentacles of the truly evil spread throughout such structures. Makes one wonder if the conspiracy theorists are correct about big business and the government cover-ups. Isn't paranoia wonderful when it is finally justified?

Our largest obstacle came from a surprising source. One of the large banks here in New York Citi, which will go unnamed because they were too chicken shit to give us an actual document explaining the reason they did this and we couldn't hope to win a lawsuit with them as money really does rule the court system, rejected us for a business bank account. Their board gave the reason that they felt we were "pornographic". Definitely, one of the least imaginative excuses I've heard in a while. This leads me to the assumption that they can't read. Considering we had already made plans based on having a business bank account, this was a large setback.

We almost had a similar setback when the County Clerk for the Borough of Kings, which is the county that makes up Brooklyn, almost didn't give us a business license due to the fact that we had the word "sex" in our business documents. Of course, it probably had nothing to do with the fact that the documents were being presented by a scary 6'4" man, dressed all in black, speaking with a decidedly non-Brooklyn accent, having hair long enough to almost reach his butt and eyes oozing a sense of mystical aloofness.

The Federal Government had no problem passing us through their system. They just see numbers and revenue. There is a kind of scientific justice in a system like that. At least it removes the "bumpkin" level that is so prevalent in most of the rest of the business we've dealt with.

Our current bank, HSBC, was an interesting mix of the two. At first, again possibly due to my appearance, they patronizingly tried to explain what they needed to open a business bank account, as if I had never done this before. Luckily, I had done this once before, with the other evil unnamable bank of doom, and had every piece of information they required. Quickly reassessing the situation, they realized that I was actually serious and treated me as such. I even shook hands with the manager and all those other courtesies I'd only heard about in books and movies.

Now that it is all taken care of, I can sit back and enjoy the fruits of my labor. I have spreadsheets to keep track of. I have to make sure my taxes are taken care of so I don't go to jail. I have to avoid getting sued. I have to figure out how to deal with employees. I have to figure out what to do with receipts. I have to hang government-required documents in the office.

The real benefit of dealing with all the red tape and requirements is that *Cthulhu Sex* Magazine can now push on ahead with its evolution. It is akin to getting inoculations for children, only a lot more painful and expensive. With this work, we have taken the limits off of where *Cthulhu Sex* magazine can go. It is as exciting as a sacrificial ritual. The map of blood and suffering opens a portal to another dimension.

Tentacles,

St. Michael

1.25°.52

This scandalous publisher of NYfC magazine has again revealed he has perceptions beyond that of most mortal men. However, he has also revealed that his dreams remind him of me quite often. If I am not careful, he might put two and tentacle together. Then where would I be? Mayhaps, it is time for a "visit" in the flesh, so to speak.

Dear St. Michael,

Once again I dreamt and, upon waking, thought of you.

Walking through the yard of a house on a hill, I looked through a chain link fence that divided this yard from the next. There prowled a massive tawny female mountain lion. It was immediately apparent that this was no ordinary beast, but a devouring fiend. She prowled a menacing S across the yard, searching for a gap in the fence, searching for me. Filled with this unpleasant knowledge, I hastily retired up the steps into the safety of my home. She found her way and pursued me to the door. Though I did not turn around, I could feel the weight of her breath and bloody mind on my back as I slammed the door and elided into a deep trench dripping with roots and fern fronds.

Once again, I had returned to the jungle. On either side of me rose earthen walls blanketed in flowing roots. The small defile stretched away from me into the cool dark of a late afternoon under the cathedral-like canopy. The pressure was still on my back. The fiend still pursued me, even here.

I knew very well that I must forge on ahead, evade pursuit and reach safety. True to the non-sequitor of dream, my dear friend Erin, a seasoned traveler, walked with me. She spoke fondly of a "dusty temple, not likely to be found on any map" just ahead. Unfortunately, she had a train to catch and was soon gone. Gone before I could ask her if she too was pursued, if she too felt a black weight upon her shoulders.

Warily, I forged ahead. Trunks and boughs bent overhead to form a cylindrical tunnel that ran along the jungle floor. Light filtered in, sickly yellow and distorted green, but died before it could penetrate the shadows. And then, I was there. No questions asked, no explanations given. From the trench, I dream-stepped to the crumbling front gate of a dying wall. Beyond the wall, the jungle dared not go. Narrow courtyards, piles of white rubble and empty cisterns ruled. Weather-smoothed stairs rose up to a platform from which sprouted nine conical towers rising at intervals above the structures within. My limbs began to shake uncontrollably and my breathing echoed in my ears as if I was hiding from discovery in a confined space. Yet, I was perfectly still.

The "dusty" temple was not what I anticipated. Rather than clouds of choking dust, I could hear the minute crush of motes grinding on motes, slowly dragging this place back to its granular roots. Without hesitation, I mounted the central stair. In fact, it was an imperative. Black fear pressed heavily against my back. It was so powerful that I was afraid to turn and confront it. Or even glimpse it! "It's best not to know," I affirmed as my legs pushed me towards the summit.

Atop the highest platform stood a stupa adorned with melted images of elongated, faceless people. Betwixt two of the stretching forms gaped a square, black portal. I entered without thought. It was near. I had to get away. Inside the stone structure was a darkness lit by starlight. The walls glimmered as faint reliefs cast shallow shadows, revealing a terrible war between the beasts of the earth, sea and sky. Bile rose in my throat, a gag reflex. My pursuer was upon the threshold just behind me. I was trapped and dared not look back.

Only now did I notice a basin resting on a pedestal standing in the center of the room. Dream intuition drove my decision. "Not likely to be found on any map." I knew beyond knowing.

The stone of the basin felt smooth beneath my palms, the weight of it shifted and slid across the floor as I pushed it.

Beneath my feet, an iris unfurled and widened into a black pupil. The pedestal was the key, of course. It opened the eye. My fiend stood in the doorway and reached out for me. The hairs on my neck rose, my jaw trembled. Salvation lay beneath me, in this new darkness. My foot descended into the pupil, embraced by warm, black water.

But, my eyes opened as my foot touched the pupil. I was awake, prostrate in bed and my pursuer still loomed over me. I could not move. My limbs were frozen in trance. Panic welled from me like blood rushing from a wound. Try as I might, I could not move, could not roll over, could not turn on the light, could not shout a warning. Warmth filled my lower leg. The pupil. My leg moved, slowly. But, it moved. Descent into this new warm dark was my only salvation. Awake and dreaming, I let go, sucked in breath and let my body sink into the pupil.

Quite suddenly, my limbs flooded with strength. Without thought, I rapidly rolled over and threw the light switch. The room was empty. Street noise echoed in from the alley window.

Luke
April 2002

1.25°.53

Far in the depths of some other world, forsaken by the realms of Ethics and Morals, comes this letter from our dear Oliver. I greatly fear for his health. Not because, as many people have suggested should be the reason, he sent the individual paragraphs to me one at a time on burned and defiled leather of some unknown origin. And not because of the constant police presence observing our offices in an unrealistic attempt to find a connection with certain milk carton pictures. But only because the blood and serum on the letters were his. That means he's selfishly keeping the others' delicacies for himself. If that is so, I greatly fear for his health. Especially, if he can't outrun me.

Chael,

I feel corrupted. This form is limited and limiting. Its needs and wants force us to waste energy. It forces us to search for fuel so that we can maintain its integrity. It forces us to constantly focus its mind on our goal.

Setting the words down is becoming more difficult. My mind just seems to focus on women, the ritual and hunger. The one distraction I enjoy is the change my senses have undergone. It helps and marks the passage of time. The light is constantly shifting and bending in the sense that I can now see it do this as opposed to just seeing the effects of this movement. The colors blend and separate as my vision encompasses more of the electromagnetic spectrum. I can see the particles moving in waves, photons swimming through the universe. They curve around, worm through and reach out to grab objects. Light's producer, heat, draws me to it. Or is it the pain and hunger that drive me on? The whispering has become my guide. I don't know what I would do without them. I need no others. They promise us peace.

I miss the city. I miss moving through its serpentine passages in the greenish-purple twilight. I miss its obsidian spires. But, most of all, I feel our mind slipping away from them and you. I can only hope Drilpa Cthulhu is guiding us. We have formed a plan so that we may not have to use the bodies anymore. Then, we won't be so limited. Instead of us searching them out, they will come to the city. We will use the thoughts they create when they are resting, their dreams. We have started with one already.

The air slides itself around me. It moves from a humid liquidy thickness to a breezy lightness. There is no sense of direction anymore, only of movement, forwards, onwards. I feel as if I'm moving through towns and cities then stopping in the outskirts. Sometimes, I awaken and I've dug a resting place for myself in the ground, a nest of sorts. Who knows how long I've been there surrounded by her remains? I stop by a fenced-in house and clamber over it to get to the heat within. A feline shadow bounds ahead to track its quarry through to the end. I move through an earthen tunnel with roots as the roof. She is with me. I suck, writhe and thrust my way through the ritual in an age-old temple. The whispering tells me this is the way it must be.

We have sent the tracker. It will drive the one we have picked to a portal of our realm. He will see the grandness of our city. He will be led to us with promises. The path, in this world, will be created with landmarks he will recognize from his night musings. A house, a yard, an earthen path through a jungle, a temple. All of these will be shown to him and much more. After the tracker drives him to us physically, we will incorporate him. Hopefully, this process, brought to fruition in our realm, will reduce the limitations of the body. The possibility of the end to the need for fuel may be in sight. We will not need to focus. The energy will not be wasted. The mission will be fulfilled.

There is sound all around me. In addition to the constant whispering, there is breathing. The breathing of the air, the women, the trees. There is a chittering sound. The insects, the people, the earth. Above all, there is the sound of waves. It calms me. It sends a wash of sadness through me. There also is music mixed with this. A sound that ebbs and flows as if someone were singing Erasure's *Master and Servant* while gargling and, then vomiting up, mud. They promise us harmony. Must warn you. Ia, Ia. Wa Lu. Thar afhi. Sast ofof. Mowi yoca. Mamu con mawh. Cthulhu ftagn.

We have scattered the resting one's thoughts with familiar places and people. He will awaken and believe it to be a nightly fantasy. But, we shall instill want in him. Having used this body, we know how to drive them onward, how to convince them our goals are paramount. It is only a matter of time before he physically enters the city. I only hope it is not long. We only hope that we will be together again. Both in the city with Drilpa Cthulhu and here in this world with our unlimited use of these vessels.

Oliver

1.25°.54

We interrupt our regularly scheduled afterword to bring you a special message. There is no time to thank all the people who have helped put this issue together. Just look at the contents page and say a silent prayer to each name listed. That should do the trick.

Why am I rushing through what would otherwise be a solemn ritual? It is to get to the crux of a new situation that is brewing in the world. As you know, if you have been reading the editorial content of *Cthulhu Sex*, we try to bring you the latest in the underground news that is most likely censored where you are from. There is a new and disturbing situation arising that can affect your life as soon as tomorrow.

We have reason to believe that there is a new virus that is slowly consuming the world, known as IAZA*. Already, there have been as many as 10,000 victims that are either dead or in a coma in the last week. It seems to spread with the airborne contagiousness of influenza and dissolute with the hemorrhagic voraciousness of ebola. The most frightening aspect of this disease is that it spreads through the media.† Traveling through all the bands of the electromagnetic spectrum, it has the possibility of infecting millions of people at once. It could even be in your home as you read this.

Dr. Aspermicide commented earlier, "These outbreaks are so organized and unnatural that I am sure they are man-made viruses. If you break down the elements of the infectious agent itself, you will find individual elements that affect the human emotional centers and increase norepinephrine in the blood stream." He went on to say that the effects of the virus increase over a short period of time and include: headaches, irritability, child- and spousal-abuse, beer-bonging, high blood pressure, irritable sphincter-mouth, shotgun toting, dirty sanchezing, inability to wipe properly, stick up the anus insertion, bleeding from every bleeding orifice, rolling of the eyes, fist slamming, rationalization, sudden belief in egomaniacal self-importance to whatever religious deity happens to be in vogue, carp bashing, bunny stomping and finally coma or death.

He also suggested that all the effects of the virus dissipate in an equally short amount of time if treated properly. He has found that the appropriate cure is a treatment regimen of bed rest, plenty of liquids, quiet and logical thought, philosophy, meditation, common sense, sex, a really good book and beating the hell out of those bastards who want to cause death and war and suffering 'cause they think it's a good way to get the poor out of their hair and 'cause they're sick, twisted fucks. He then went on about the monkeys on Mars and some bloated corncob to be inserted anally. He was then escorted from the room by his white clad security staff.

Careful to not contract the dreaded IAZA and taking every precaution I could, including carrying a bible and knocking out my front teeth, I went into the heart of an IAZA hot zone. There, I tracked down one of the victims and asked him a few questions, after I convinced him to put away the shotgun (*see symptoms*). After getting to know each other (not that way) (eew!), he informed that what he really wanted to do was kill terrorists, even if he had to go into every house he came across and randomly kill their inhabitants. I asked him about the term "Homeland Terrorists" that I had heard bandied about at some media dinner. He said he'd even kill them. I asked what was the difference between the two types of terrorists. He said, "Homeland terrorists is white guys with guns and the others only gots bombs 'cause they is poor." He then said he should get a sniper rifle and just pick off random strangers because they all probably were terrorists anyway.

Luckily, I returned alive to tell my story. I caught a slight case of IAZA during the expedition. It manifested in confusion and head-swimming-with-hypocrisy syndrome. It was easy to cure with a cup of coffee and a dime of white horse.

So remember, the media is now considered a IAZA level 4 hot zone by FCSM. Use protection whenever possible and use lube for those especially dry days. For extra protection, always ask yourself, "How much does this [insert politician or news-caster] sound like McCarthy?"

We now continue with our regularly scheduled afterword.

Tentacles,

St. Michael
*Ignorant and Armed Zealous Assholes

†This magazine has been rigorously tested for and protected against any communicable traces of IAZA*.

B.AC.A

Welcome to our delicious second volume of *Cthulhu Sex* magazine. Sometimes, it's still hard for me to believe that we've made it this far and lasted this long. I've been part of many small magazines and zines over the years, mainly as a contributor. I've seen even more publications that my friends and acquaintances have produced. Unfortunately, all have ceased publishing before becoming four years old. The fact that we are still publishing into our fifth year, and plan to continue publishing for many more, is an exciting testament to the strength of our dedicated staff, our gifted contributors and especially, our faithful readers. Without you, whether this is your first issue or your fourteenth, none of the magic that is *Cthulhu Sex* would exist. Take a moment and pat yourself on the back for supporting us and providing us the impetus to carry on. Yes, I mean you, reading these words right now. If you listen very carefully, you can hear our cavorting and celebrating at this mind-rending accomplishment. You don't have to listen carefully at all if you're my neighbor. In that case, I apologize for all the noises and screaming. I'll make sure none of our revelers spatter blood on the hallway floor, walls or ceiling. Yes, I've had to clean blood off the ceiling before. No, I won't give details.

In order to give a fuller understanding of how mighty this accomplishment of beginning the second volume of *Cthulhu Sex* is, I will now spill some secrets of our humble beginning and our path so far. Initially, the magazine was to be an outlet to present my writings and a friend's artwork, the name derived from another friend's description of my sexuality as "tentacle sex". Don't ask, don't tell. Our first issue was entirely edited, laid out, printed, Xeroxed, collated and stapled by yours truly in only a few weeks. It is a simple booklet of 17 photocopied legal papers folded in half and stapled with a household stapler. Being a writer exclusively, I knew nothing of computer layout or imaging. I cut the pieces of art out and glued them onto the master copy. I ran off about 50 copies and proceeded to mangle them in the stapler because the page from edge to center was longer than the depth from hinge to head of the stapler. Imagine a wrinkled, thin stack of dirty white photocopies, replete with those little spots all photocopiers seem to summon from some unknown dimension. Then compare it to the clean, hefty magazine with glossy covers that you hold in your hands. It is a wondrous advancement in production.

Surprisingly, the quality of the content hasn't changed much. Of course, we've discovered a greater number of excellent contributors than that first issue, which held only the works of my friends and me. After that, we grew by convincing many of our thankfully talented friends to contribute their own works. The list grew and we continued to persuade as many others as we could.

After I put up our website, almost as a lark, we began passively recruiting works from others we'd never met before with a few lines on a single page. We were amazed and excited that others wished to be printed in our humble copied pages. The honor of the first of these outside contributors goes to the incomparable author of the now infamous experimental short story, "Why I Want to Fuck Cthulhu". With the realization that others might actually wish to be printed by us, we attempted to actively attract contributors by expanding our website. Soon, a trickle of others began to flow in. To make a monument to these intrepid adventurers into the then unknown realm of *Cthulhu Sex*, I printed our first full-sized issue with the help of The Small Press Co-op. And our fate was sealed.

I decided that if nothing came of the magazine, I could at least use it as a way to force myself to write a novel based on my short story, "The Black Rider", by writing a chapter every issue. But instead, I became addicted to the thrill of finding and printing authors and artists, making every issue a tribute to their work as a reward for their faith in *Cthulhu Sex*. We have immortalized over 100 writers, poets and artists in our pages with many others to come. My skills at production and the quality of our contributed art grew. I decided to move from The Small Press Co-op to Morgan Printing, Inc. to press a higher quality product utilizing digital printing. Even after my initial goal of printing *Cthulhu Sex*, finishing *The Black Rider* novel, was completed, the desire to print our continuing flow of amazing submissions proved itself as a far greater motivation.

Besides my all-important day job (evening actually) that keeps me from the poor house, our growing production needs have been met by some of the most capable people I have met. Not only have they kept the quality of each issue at its finest, they have all contributed personal works to and supported *Cthulhu Sex* every step of the way. A chance meeting while putting together the first issue brought Oliver Baer into *Cthulhu Sex* with a few of his poems. When he saw the final product, he uttered the fateful lines, "This needs to be edited. Did you do this? This is horrible." He has been keeping us from embarrassing our writers and ourselves ever since. Luke D'Azatif appeared to me on a quest to print his own magazine, asking questions to which I had minimal answers. A headstrong young man with wisdom beyond his years, he decried the horrible abuse our poor art had to endure under my untrained mutilation. For opening his mouth, he received the honor of caring for our artwork, tending it with a firm yet loving hand. And then there is my significant other, always a fount of wisdom and level-headedness that makes even the cynical Oliver listen, grew from advice giver to the irreplaceable Motivatrix and Keeper of the Important Things, without which very little would actually get done. Together, we have become a family of artistic *Cthulhu Sex* cultists, sharing our trials, tribulations, rituals and chaos.

Now that we have entered the new realm of bar codes and business licenses, *Cthulhu Sex* is becoming involved with many facets of reaching out to the horror community. We are continuing our uproariously successful, annual Fall Equinox parties where our readers and contributors can mingle with each other among the sensual trappings of NYC gothic and Vampyre scenes. At these parties, we not only fill the hearts and minds of our revelers with delightful company, sensuously dark music and amazing live performances, we also collect for charities and organizations such as The New York Police and Fire Widow's and Children's Benefit Fund and The Comic Book Legal Defense Fund. We have been lucky enough to form an alliance with shocklines.com, whose administrator's good-hearted gusto and business acumen has supported our efforts to reach new connoisseurs of erotic horror. We have also been recently courting distribution in order to further infiltrate stores nationwide. We are beginning to attend conventions including the upcoming Spring Chiller Expo in New Jersey. And we would be dead in the water without the guidance and support of both the Erotic Readers Association and the Horror Writers Association. (I desperately want to win a Stoker's after attending the 2002 dinner at the New York Helmsley, despite the lack of a magazine category. I am obsessed with the castle door that actually opens and closes.) If you happen to run into us at a convention or event, stop by and say, "Hello!" We don't bite. Except for Oliver. That's what the muzzle is for.

By presenting the story of the birth of *Cthulhu Sex* and immortalizing it between our covers, I hope to give credit to all those who have contributed to, supported and read us over the years. It would be a dishonor not to thank everyone properly. Besides, I also wanted to explode messily with excitement. *Eeeee!*

Cthulhu Sex promises to continue to bring the best erotic horror to connoisseurs for years to come. So, sit back and devour this wonderful issue. We have filled it with pleasure and pain, delight and disgust, all for your joyous consumption.

Tentacles,

St. Michael

B.AC.B

If anyone has any information as to the whereabouts of Oliver Baer, please send it to us at our website or address. He has not been in contact with us for at least two months. Unlike the police who keep bringing us other bodies they think he has something to do with. It truly is amazing how many unclaimed corpses are just lying around America.

Cast of a medallion that was found purported to be the only representation of Oliver Baer transformed. It was said that it bound him to this physicality and without it his form shifted between human and the unspeakable monstrosity in and out of dimensions.

B.AC.C

Bringing us a delightful head of dreams, an unconscious cornucopia to feast upon. www.burningwheel.org

St. Michael,

I didn't think that this one was related. (When I dream now, I am eager to continue my saga, vaguely cognizant whether or not the visions are connected or just fleeting subconscious flares.) So, when my dream self alighted upon my own bed in dark dawn light, I was mildly disappointed. I yearned to return to the jungle. Alas, it was not to be. However, I was soon shown another face of this verdian stretching nightmare.

Lying on my back facing the door to the interior of my apartment_a void of haloed light. My body was relaxed and somnific, mind in a torpor. Suddenly, the darkness of the doorway condensed into a form. A silhouette of a short man, round in the shoulders, head and belly. Hunched and bent, I could hear his breath, ragged and disjointed. One hand was disfigured and elongated, it stretched toward the floor like a mass of congealing blood.

As his rasping presence filled the frame, my body flooded with familiar warmth. Limbs went empty, all of their strength reaching inward to my chest. Clutching tense fingers gripped my ribs and heart, urging me to exhale. I could not move, no urging would bring my warm, dead arms life.

Suddenly, without consideration, I consciously relaxed. I gave into the yearning fingers. The moment I did, darkness filled my body. I reappeared beyond my corporeal self, now a dream self standing across the room, watching the proceedings from an impossible angle. My other dream self body rested peacefully on the grey mattress.

With the shift in my perspective, I spied another shape as it coalesced behind my visitor. A darker shadow. Perhaps my visitor from last spring? The presence which hounded me through the jungle? He was formless, merely a presence and a dimming of light. Upon his manifestation, the hunched man lurched forward and scooped my slumbering body from the bed. The hunched man's twisted and elongated hands crumbled like fragile candy.

As I was lifted from the mattress, I saw yet another dream self. This one huddled under the bed in abject terror, cringing as if from explosions. I was older there. Heedless of my scattered presences, my supine dream self was carried out on the hunched man's shoulders. As he trundled away another dream object took my attention. Next to the door, in the corner, a parcel of books glowed luminous, haloed like a saint. Next to it, a television flickered to life, its luminescent grey screen showing a mossy stone crowned with static.

The hunched man passed the portal and was gone. The presence departed. My dreamselves re-collected to my skull. Electric, I jumped awake full of a misplaced fear, heart pounding, sweat drizzling and breath echoing. I felt hollow.

None of this is really worth noting in a letter to your esteemed magazine, except this final detail. I awoke piled into a dark space, not the bed on which I had drifted off to sleep, a hallway closet. The door had been slid closed, my fingernails found desperate purchase and scraped the door open. Naked and alone I staggered into the light.

Luke
June 2002

Not one, but two letters, so much has happened.

Dear St. Michael,

After my last episode with the dream—the sleep-walking. I was rather frightened. I've never been possessed of somnambulance before. Thankfully, all has been quiet. I have remained supine in bed for every night since.

But, I have dreamed. It was just a small slice, but I wanted to send it to you in the interest of continuity and completeness:

I saw the "pupil" again. The black iris which appeared in the temple floor now regularly appears incongruously in my other dreams—on a wall, in the floor, through a window. Always dark and shadowless, perfectly round, emanating both warmth and fear.

Also, in one dream which began elsewhere (at work while experiencing the horror of being unable to complete a task, if you must know). I was transported onto a jungle beach at night. It was as if a channel in my skull had been flipped. A sudden cut from fluorescent office space to luminescent moonlit beach. Nothing happened there. I merely stood in the calm surf up to my ankles, enjoying the soothing embrace of the chilled water and warm air, staring out to sea, the black line of the ocean's horizon fading to starry blue-gray.

I am certain that this was the same jungle from my previous excursions. It is not something I could qualify, but my dream self knew. There is no doubt.

Luke
September 2002

B.AC.D

While testing the hidden message in this issue, like I do with every issue, I was drawn to the Yucatan peninsula. Once there, I swam out into the Gulf of Mexico until I could swim no longer. There I floated, exhausted and waiting for the last fateful wave to pull me under.

A raft of seaweed, a common sight on the surface, appeared out of nowhere and engulfed me in its slimy green embrace. I welcomed it, assuming foolishly perhaps that its buoyancy would provide me with a method of escape from my almost certain doom.

Quickly, I realized my mistake as its multitudinous trailing members began to entwine around my body in reaction to my thrashing attempt to tread the salty water. With thick sea foliage pinioning me, I was unable to continue my futile struggles. The natural gravity of waterlogged greenery was multiplied by my dead weight, dragging me inevitably down.

I let out a scream of anguish at the senselessness of the situation, cut short as the sea swallowed me, submerging my head.

The blue of the beautiful sky, symbolic of the world I had now left behind, was overwhelmed by the plant's amorphous form coalescing about the rent I had made in its surface, abhorring the vacuum created by my passing.

I picked up speed once my mummified form was loosed from the mass as a whole, plummeting into the murky dark of the deep. Strangely, there were none of the creatures one would expect to see within my distance haze limited sight, until I reached a layer of almost pitch darkness.

Here, the little supply of air I had kept with the silencing of my last scream ran out, the need to gasp thundering at my heart like a hammer at an anvil. My head felt like a balloon over-inflated to bursting with blood in a vain attempt to keep my dwindling reserves of oxygen.

Unable to control the natural action of breathing any longer, I decided a watery death would be an end of my suffering at least. I opened my mouth and released a rolling bubble of used air the size of my head. I looked down away from the rising signal of my coming end, dreading to inhale the final draught of ocean that would do me in.

In that brief moment of self-control, a thousand points of light flickered into existence in the depths, to my surprise. A huge form of some whale-like creature covered in chitinous armor flew at me like a missile. Its oversized eyes glowed a pale blue, illuminating the waters around it for thousands of feet with a ghostly light.

I could see cyclopean spires and massive blocks of buildings spread out beneath me, the individual structures connected by causeways and staircases far above the chaotic streets winding between, somehow all laid out with an almost subconscious, yet overwhelming, sense of alien mathematics.

My mouth unstoppably yawned open with the need for air as I glimpsed an impossible shore on one side of the sprawling city where an unfathomable underwater lake edged the metropolis. The lake water's luminescent indigo glow ran flat and smooth into the horizon of darkness, surreal and unimaginable.

As my body jerked to take in a lungful of salt water, I noticed the blue-eyed behemoth was rising quicker than I was descending, looming even larger. With the first burning pain of foreign fluids in my chest, the monster overtook me, opening its huge, black cavern of a mouth and sucking me in.

Upon traveling into that dreadful orifice, I swear I caught movement on the lake below, as if small boats were rippling over its surface.

Then, I thankfully blacked out.

I awoke at Nunig Zisdant hospital here in NYC. I knew the city I had seen could be none other than the mythical L'go Haamo Dum. And I knew that the movement of the boats could only mean one thing. The Haamites were on the move, heralding the resurgence of the Meateaters.

I suggest all our readers protect themselves as I have and keep your guanometer close at hand. Otherwise, a malady of the brain will be the least of our worries.

Tentacles,

St. Michael

B.AD.A

Greetings from *Cthulhu Sex*. Welcome to our glorious new issue, filled with marvels both dark and exotic. We have scoured the depths of our vermiculoid tracts to bring you artifacts of wit and wonder. Beneath the delicate, yet stunning cover, we present a powerful range of visionary expression. Explore the darkly introspective artwork, the eclectically beautiful sculpture and the sensually surreal drawings. But don't let the beauty blind you to our wonderful words. We have a multitude of witty and involving stories and poems to delight you. As you peruse our pages, let our words and images enable you to titillate and please yourself.

On another note all together, in this time of worldwide paranoia and intrigue poised beneath the threat of destruction both big and small, a group representing a unique populous of the world has asked me to bring their concerns to your attention, dear reader. Being a cautious group with a long and notorious history, they asked me to refer to them with the acronym LFUOSC. Those of you who have had the experience with this group will understand why I cannot set the words of this acronym onto paper. However, I will gladly direct you to them if pressed at say, a convention or other social gathering.

That out of the way, their main concern is with the overwhelming consequences of war. Most of their members are serious opponents of such an act of hostility. Their reasoning is simple and backed by millenniums of experience in these matters. They cite the First World War as the turning point of their previous philosophy into more conventional thought. Before the turn of the century, they were not opposed to war, as it was generally one small group of irate humans battling another small group.

This offered LFUOSC a smorgasbord in times of need. But with the First World War, millions were killed in an extremely short amount of time, creating an overabundance of dead and leaving not much more than rotting vestiges of once potential lives. The advent of the atomic bomb is even more disturbing as it doesn't even leave corpses that the Ls and some of the lesser U, Fs and OSCs can gain sustenance from. The use of chemical and biological weapons has unexpected reactions in many of the LFUOSC members. To the LFUOSC, the possibility of modern warfare not only spoils perfectly good produce, but it reduces the number of human sacrifices available. The machine of war is so unselective that many of the potential sacrifices rich in power are wiped out without anyone gaining the benefits of their passing. LFUOSC stresses that this side effect of war affects many other groups besides themselves. This includes us here at *Cthulhu Sex*.

To sum up the viewpoint of the LFUOSC, as eloquently elucidated by the LFUOSC spokesperson known as Bella, "War is not only a waste of blood and meat; it is a waste of potential power. War culls the herd wantonly, limiting valuable human resources and causing everyone to tighten their belts."

One of the aspects of the LFUOSC, the Special Branch of Orphans and Widows, brought to my attention that none of the governments of any nation have contingency plans for the feeding and care of their people left behind in areas that would be most devastated. A group representing mummies pointed out that the focus on the Middle East will put many of their members at risk, particularly with their elevated susceptibility to fire.

The only faction of the LFUOSC that openly looks forward to such mass destruction is a subset of specters, haunts and poltergeists, who anticipate the possibility of increasing their ranks. "It gets boring having the same conversations with the same faces over and over again," said, Mary, Queen of Scots. "I think that [war] is exactly what we need, fresh blood to raise our spirits."

Visit www.vampiresagainstwar.com for information on the LFUOSC or to offer assistance and services.

Remember that all our actions have consequences, whether

we like them or not. With that in mind, sit back and enjoy this issue. At least you know the consequences of this action... or so you hope!

Tentacles,

St. Michael

B.AD.B

Lost in his own version of reality somewhere, Oliver sent me this letter back with the edits to this issue. However, it was so indecipherable, even to me, that I had to have it translated. I present them both here. And just in case this is truly a homecoming letter, I have left the corpses in the basement just as he likes them. (Footnoted translation of garbled paragraphs follows letter.)

Micel,

I was awa. I hav not comnte becse it is har to for the wor. I ita, it has bece a phyc exei to spe. I am unse how I am curn holn mysf togh for I hav los the wil to do so. It see the hav pla for me. I no lonr perm the ritl conily. The dri me on. Ir see, in som way, the fee as commte wit me as I do the. If we do not do the ritl, the bod disrats. But, it doe so in pies.[1]

Sadness is upon me as I realize that I shall never see our fair city again. But, I have done this for us, for our people, for Drilpa Cthulhu, even for the makeshift ones who have helped us to infiltrate them. I have become too contaminated with this being to resume the true form so that I may be with you again. I have tried to reach out to the rest of them for help in overcoming the convergence. The best I could hope for was when the mind of the body finally stopped fighting. It let go. I thought we had won. I was about to direct it towards one of our portals when I realized the energy had gone. I was able to direct it towards more fuel but something didn't go well. There was a dark club below ground filled with people who were honoring our tentacled master. I have only ever seen a finer spectacle in our city.

I remember how we fed and joined, our tentacles entwining and finding those hidden areas of our body in celebration. I picked one who seemed to already have some growths extending from her body (proto-tentacles, possibly?) She was thrashing about to a bombardment of sound. I was able to get her away and perform the ritual without notice. Or so I thought. For I now believe there was some interference. I performed the ritual but the result was unfinished. Perhaps, I did not finish or even perform the ritual. For the next breaks of light and dark, waves of light and non-light, parts of the body fell away.

It did not hapn all at one. Pies dispin, faln awa in a spa tha can onl be desi as pai, the son of sto faln in wat, the sme of rotn fis, the tas of fern fru tha has bee los at sea and the sig of a hol tha the phon parc dispin. Repe by wha I hest to say, for it is not desile as anyi I hav see. It see lon and siny wit sucr as in a tenc but som par hav pinr oths fin-lik procns. I had hop to be fre of the as I cam apa. Fre of the dree ritl its pai and pleu the defins of my lif. But as I sai thi was not to be. For I cou sti hea the whieg eve as the las pies lef me.[2]

I called upon you my brethren. Even as the last parts of the body fell away. I sent an urgent message out to our mind while holding onto what was left of my host's mind. You answered my call. Unfortunately, not in the manner I expected. By the time we had gathered the parts from various places, nothing was whole anymore, not me, the mind or the spirit. Even we seemed disparate and fragmented to me. So now, we are sewn together in parts or fused, a patchwork entity in body, mind and spirit. Some parts you granted sentience, possibly to compensate for the broken link to the others. They found their own way back to us and melded with the whole. Now, they whisper the tales of their adventures to us. One of them told us of how upon his awakening, he took our shape and appeared to our dreamer. Our part spurred him on by showing him other portals to travel through as well as scenes of jungles, beaches and temples to intrigue him. Then, it goaded him by appearing by his bedside and manipulating its phalanges while silently taunting him. This dreamer may be our only chance for the city to be seen by us now. Perhaps, it could manifest here above the waters. For now, we can only dream.

It see tha the las bod may not hav bee ful absb. I onl pra she has alee the pror autres. If she com to you Micel knot ha she is a harn of this to com. The hav infted seva of the plas of pow and thu the peoe as wel. The are wiln to bri abo the manetin of the hom her if the can not bri us unds. Forf the offe if you can. The magi mus conn. Be war of the sal repsatves and pubc reli peoe som of the are the minn of tho who stae me on thi misgen pat. The wil try to conn you of the treu. Hee the not for you wil kno her whe she appr.

Olir[3]

Translation of the garbled paragraphs from the letter above by one Wilamina Cravesticon:

[1]Michael,

I was away. I have not communicated because it is hard to form words. Literally, it has become a physical exertion to speak. I am unsure how I am currently holding myself together for I have lost the will to do so. It seems they have plans for me. I no longer perform the ritual consciously. They drive me on. It seems, in some ways, they feel as contaminated with me as I do them. If we do not do the ritual, the body discorporates. But, it does so in pieces.

[2]It did not happen all at once. Pieces disappearing, falling away into space that can only be described as pain, the sound of stone falling in water, the smell of rotting fish, the taste of fermented fruit that's been lost at sea and the sight of a hole through which photonic particle waves disappeared. Replaced by what I hesitate to say, for it is not describable as anything I have seen. It seems long and sinewy with suckers as in a tentacle, but some parts have pincers, others fin-like projections. I had hoped to be free of them as I came apart. Free of the dreaded ritual, its pain and pleasure the definitions of my life. But, as I said, this was not to be. For I could still hear the whispering, even as the last pieces left me.

[3]It seems that the last body may not have been fully

absorbed. I only pray that she has alerted the proper authorities. If she comes to you, Michael, know that she is a harbinger of things to come. They have infiltrated several of the places of power and thus the people as well. They are willing to bring about the manifestation of their home here, if they can not bring us undersea. Fortify the office if you can. The magazine must continue. Be wary of the sales reps and public relations people, some of them are the minions of those who started me on this misbegotten path. They will try to convince you of their treasures. Heed them not for you will know her when she appears.

Oliver

B.AD.C

Welcome to the end of the issue. I hope you've enjoyed our trek through our dark and sensual pages. All the works presented, both writing and artwork, were made with the deft hand and personal sacrifice of their creators. Their blood and sweat has graced every element of their work. Next time you see or speak to one of them, tell them what you think of their efforts. I'm sure they would love the feedback.

We here at *Cthulhu Sex* have also made a plethora of sacrifices to bring you such a wonderful issue. There is at least one of us who will explode if they don't get some soon. It can be very lonely working in solitude at night with only the cold shells of previous victims lying around. Though I'm sure that you, having the strength of confidence and personality that comes from reading *Cthulhu Sex* magazine, find no problems with fulfilling your desires. I'm willing to bet that, unlike some of our staff, you have no need of enchantments and rope to claim what is rightfully yours. There is a certain glamour that we set into our pages to instill such confidence and attractiveness, which you can access by simply reading this magazine. The more you read, the greater the power. Haven't you noticed how your interaction with the world has changed since you started reading *Cthulhu Sex* magazine? It's subtle, but it's there, all thanks to the sacrifices of our staff and our contributors.

However, one of the problems we've run into lately is with distribution. For those of you who know this term from the publishing industry, it is a similar denotation but a different connotation. Rest assured, the physical distribution of *Cthulhu Sex* magazine is steadily growing, spreading its tentacles throughout the world. The distribution I refer to is that of the remnants of our sacrifices.

The crux of our dilemma is this: There is only so much human material that the beast in the basement can consume. With the increase in demand for the magazine, and therefore increase in sacrifices needed, we are having issues distributing the various left-over offal. Especially, since there is now a nearly constant police presence outside our offices due to the missing persons report one of our ex-sales staff's mother accidentally filed before we had a chance to "explain" the situation to her. It seems that even in a perfect plan, there are variables that are beyond control. Unfortunately, with Oliver's overextended trip in parts unknown, there will probably be more reports of this nature, if there aren't already, in reaction to the contents of the box sent with Joshua West's letter. [For more details, see *Cthulhu Sex* magazine volume I, issues 16, 17, and 18.] Regardless of the situation with Oliver, the beast's discards must be hauled away as the dirt floor of the basement and the backyard have already been filled with bodies. Ah, the grand old days when we could simply bury them.

Why, you might wonder, am I bringing up this distribution issue and drawing your attention to the previously unnoticed enchantments within our pages, risking the possibility of breaking them? The answer is simple. First, the enchantments are from a time before the human construction of religion and, therefore, are unaffected by these fanatically followed, mainstream, manmade rationalizations of homocentric dreams in the attempt to control forces far beyond human conception. Second, I am asking you, dear reader, to help us dispose of the remains for the greater glory of the tentacled one. The supernatural servants that normally do such biddings have had to turn their efforts toward other higher priority tasks in the service of their sleeping dark master. Even the nameless avatar of the unnamable destroyer of worlds has had to send his fleet of fear into battle preparations instead of ferrying our refuse. Due to the media attention over toxic waste in the Everglades, our largest ground transportation network, which happens to be owned by the same group that owns a music television network as a subsidiary in its complex web of media control, cannot get the federal licenses to transport our leftovers across state lines anymore.

As you can see, we are in a bit of bind. Only with your help can we remove the corpses and parts from our offices. Though, I tend to think that their perfume is a wondrously delicious aphrodisiac, some of our sales and promotions staff has refused to come in, citing the "fetid odor" as the cause. Of course, they were brought in anyway and now only your efforts will enable them to leave.

Anyone with suggestions or offers to receive our remains should feel free to email or write us. Particularly good suggestions will be printed in our Letters section so that others may benefit as well.

Tentacles,

St. Michael

B.AE.A

Greetings and welcome to our newest issue of *Cthulhu Sex* Magazine. We eagerly present this wonderfully decadent issue for your enjoyment. Explore the plethora of tantalizing tales collected beneath the titillating cover. Delve into the masterful art with its darkly fantastic imagery and techno sensuality. Insinuate yourself into this orgiastic body of work. Delight in cracking it open, thrill to ripping into its meat and savor sucking out its marrow.

And now for some *Cthulhu Sex* Magazine news:

We are spreading our tentacles further every day. Recently, we have been picked up by a number of new bookstores throughout the US and UK. New listings of store locations are available on our website as well as information about how to suggest stores in your area. I believe it is always easier to direct novice *Cthulhu Sex* cultists to a store rather than to have them come over to your abode and thumb through your copy of *Cthulhu Sex* Magazine. It not only saves wear and tear on your precious collector copies, but it saves you from having to clean up the blood from your carpet when the greedy little upstarts get out of hand. It might not have happened to you, but you'd be surprised how many of our readers have had to protect themselves from overzealous virgin readers. Which reminds me to give a gentle reminder about that: We no longer accept human or animal body parts or fluids through the mail, as it is illegal. I realize that this unfortunately makes it all the harder for you to dispose of the corpses. Especially for those of you who don't happen to have a Corruptor in the basement for waste disposal.

The *Cthulhu Sex* Magazine Annual Fall Equinox Party is officially scheduled. Our Motivatrix has acquired the Knitting Factory in NYC as the location for our debauchery. As those of you who attended last year and are still alive will attest, it is a spectacle not to be missed. With a true stage for both our band performance and the Cthulhu Communion, this year's party promises to be our most stunning and depraved yet, particularly with the festooning of glow-in-the-dark maggots and various unclaimed entrails. A good time will be had by all. Any who do not will be fed to the Corruptor. And even if everyone does, we might feed him a few of the less entertaining individuals. He's a growing boy after all. More information is available on the Party page of our website.

We attended the Spring Chiller Theatre Expo in NJ as our first foray into public social gatherings. We were greeted by a throng of unique and entertaining persons, whose reactions to our presence ran the gamut from moist excitement to guilt-ridden fear. It was, by far, our most successful insinuation into the vitreous humors of the public eye. Many brave individuals introduced themselves to us for conversion including Barney the Big Red Shoggoth, various vampires and demons. Sadly, there was only one annoying individual who we had to liquefy and feed to the Corruptor with a straw. We will return for the Fall Chiller Theatre Expo to repeat the experimental procedure with even more successful prognosis. If you plan on attending, drop by our table and put faces to the names of our staff. They can be anyone's face. We're not picky as long as it's been removed from the skull so we can actually wear it. They can even be mostly dead all day. The Corruptor will probably eat them when we're done with them anyway.

And last but not least, kudos go to our Lord of Pixels and Plagues for furthering his personal plans of world domination. His collection of melees and spells have found their way into the hands of many unsuspecting innocents. *Vive l'intrigue.*

Enjoy this issue of *Cthulhu Sex* Magazine and remember, blame all your problems on other people, or better yet some divinity. They should know better. Except Cthulhu, of course. Cthulhu knows better and does it anyway.

Tentacles,

St. Michael

P.S. The rumors that fourteen people are missing from last year's Fall Equinox party is completely and totally false. I expect each and every reader to repeat that to any inquiring officer of their government. If we all say the same thing, they'll have to let the investigation go cold, particularly once they realize how much evidence has been "misplaced".

B.AE.B

Here is a letter from the charming Wilhemina Cravesticon in reaction to certain processes behind the scenes of her letter translation in the previous issue. If anyone asks, tell them that I know nothing of any of this. In fact, you should probably keep quiet about it yourself. It will make things easier on you in the long run.

Dear Mr. Morel,

Thank you very much for this opportunity to demonstrate my skills of translation. It seems that I have been blessed with the ability to communicate with the entities with which you have been plagued of late, most notably, it seems, your poor partner Mr. Baer. So, in this way, we are bound together for better or worse. Though, I would fain that this not be so for your indoctrination process was a bit more invasive than I am use to. I understood the interview but your demands upon my person in regards to my attire and the color of my hair seemed a bit too much. After much inner debate, I decided to take the position with you, especially since the dreams I have been having of late seem to lead me to your establishment. I also noticed that I have been peculiarly aroused after these dreams. I want to make perfectly clear that I have never been one of those wantons that would run to any man for pleasure. This self-same arousal seems to come over me as I speak with your Mr. Baer. Though I shudder when I think of it.

I must confess that "speak" is not entirely the proper word for the interaction. It is very much a ritual. If I thought that the "orientation" to your company was invasive, it was nothing compared to the introduction. Even though I am not sure how much has actually been done to me physically. Do you know that I am not sure whether his physical form is human or not anymore? His form reminds me of the creatures in my dreams before I started working for you.

Now, when I go to him and lie with him, he seems like a child, a frightened timid child, though I know he is not. When I lie with him, he whispers soothing, calming words to me as he caresses me. As his hand moves down my face and neck to my breast, he tells me about the time we first met. His fingers play with my nipples as his story calms me, even though I have no recollection of this event he insists is fact. I hear the sounds of waves and whispering in my mind. His hand has moved on down to my stomach, stroking my abs. I feel the waves caressing my breasts as he kisses me. It seems that his hand is working its way between my legs now but that can't be as it feels like it is still around my stomach and breasts. I wish I could describe him entering me as pleasurable. I would liken it to swimming in a warm lagoon. Unfortunately, I cannot. It is more like swimming in a rotten seafood stew. He flows around me and into me. The different "limbs", for lack of a better description, pulsing in and out of my orifices. There is pain, not only between my legs and in my mouth but in my chest, as he creates another hole with which to pleasure himself. The only diversion from the pain is his attempts to communicate. He seems truly convinced that you have a cure for him. But warns me that this "joining" he and I are experiencing will eventually overwhelm me. That I will succumb to madness, or to the horrors themselves, when I learn what the others wish to inflict upon this world. Though I am unsure of these horrors he speaks of, for the other voices seem to speak of beauty and grandeur. They immerse me in a time of wonder and calm in a twilight realm of towering proportions. Then, the voices start ebbing away. I am aware of light encompassing me in an overwhelming burning torrent as he climaxes. I am left with not only a terrible sense of emptiness and yearning, but also shocked euphoria.

This is a state from which I dare not return lest I realize what I have actually been through. Can there truly be another out there who witnesses these horrendous events as they unfold? This dreamer, of which they speak, does he not know of the door he is opening, the terrors soon to be unleashed? Why do the voices seem to recognize me but refer to me as Rebecca? Why does this name and the dreamer sound so familiar? Am I a part of the plan as well?

I hope and pray that you know your part, Mr. Morel and that you will stop subjecting me to this indignity. If I must continue to submit these reports, I shall as I have no other means of survival. But, I hope and pray that you have a plan for containing your monstrosity.

Rebecca

B.RE.C

Recently, I was caught in the fallout from a religious war. Before the modern Crusades and Inquisition, I would have laughed at the idea that this sort of thing could have any effect on the Avatar of Cthulhu. However, with the technology available to religious zealots these days and the destructive capability of said technology, I grow troubled by the not so incidental effects of this sort of conflict. In an effort to defuse the situation, I will present logical arguments both for and against both sides, hopefully helping intelligent rationality to overcome the thousands of years of self-righteous hatred.

Both sides agree, on the basest level, that light, the hypothetical one true light, exists in a pure form throughout the universe. They both worship the light and its life-giving power, bringing comfort and peace to those who are troubled by the intricacies of life. However, the major disagreement comes from the perceptions of how this one true light affects the human world.

One faction, the Relativistic Golden Believers, believe that all illuminated aspects of objects in our universe are false illusions, merely reflections from the one true light. In their view, only the light touching an object reveals the identity of that object. The light holds all the truth and the object is simply reflecting various aspects of the light. There is a complicated formula they use to rationalize their faith in the thought that objects are not true objects. They often stumble in dark rooms.

The other faction, the Celestial Magi of Yearning Knowledge, believe that the only way to understand the truth of the universe is by examining the way the one true light interacts with the tangible objects around us. In other words, only by looking at the way light reveals the various hues of objects lets us understand what the objects actually are. The objects are real and light lets us see them. These individuals tend to build other usable things with their belief in the reality of objects.

To sum up, the RGB believes that the color is held in the light and the object allows a certain wavelength to be reflected whereas the CMYK believes that the object has the hue and is only visible with light. This difference of opinion has led to a bloody war of religious oppression, each side is so ingrained in the exclusionary truth of their faith that the other is seen as nothing more than vile heretics. There are certain countries that have become havens for either the RGB or the CMYK and act as staging grounds for holy wars against the opposition. The conflict has escalated to the point that neither side will rest until the other is completely eradicated from the face of the earth.

The logical arguments I'd like to bring up to deescalate this situation are as follows:

First, there is a happy medium between the two beliefs if one would put aside the unnecessary aggression that has been propagated over the life of the entire conflict. It is simply this. The light does hold all the colors of the rainbow as seen when scattered by a prism. However, it is the interaction with the pigment of an object that allows the color to be reflected for human perception. With this comingling of ideas, neither viewpoint can exist without the other. They are both integral to the method of human perception of the universe.

Second, I'd like to say a few words to both the RGB and the CMYK. It's light, you silly fucknobs. Who gives a shit whether color resides in light or in pigment? It's just fucking color, damn it. Get a life. Go do something really important for a change, like making people happy. Quit killing children for your stupid, self-centered religious beliefs. Feed the hungry. It's just color, you dumb bastards.

Tentacles,

St. Michael

P.S. For those of you who might not know, RGB and CMYK are models various artists use for describing colors. RGB stands for Red Green Blue, which are the three colors of projected light that are mixed to make all the colors on TVs or monitors. CMYK stands for Cyan Magenta Yellow black (K because B would be confused with blue), which are the four basic colors of printed pigments that are mixed to make all the colors in magazines, comic books and newspapers.

B.AF.A

Greeting and welcome to the first full-sized issue of *Cthulhu Sex* Magazine with a color cover. We are quite pleased to have the wonderful cover art by an artist who could produce high caliber work within a ridiculously tight deadline. He has been our savior in time of need. This is actually the second issue with a color cover. The first one was our last digest issue and is now a collector's item that only a lucky few still have.

That's the only really important thing I can think of at the moment.

Tentacles,

St. Michael

PS I almost forgot to mention that the annual *Cthulhu Sex* Magazine Fall Equinox Party, this time at the Knitting Factory, was a great success. A number of contributors, readers and other notables turned out to dance, drink and debauch. The band performed with perfection, a glorious sight. We had a record number of takers for the tasty Cthulhu Communion as well. I was overjoyed to have a chance to meet a virgin contributor in this very issue. And though the editor of the sadly defunct *Jobs in Hell* attended, she melted into the crowd before I could slide a tentacle around her. And in the end, a night of titillation and doom was had by all (those who didn't were fed to the Corruptor and therefore won't be mentioned). Be sure to attend next year in NYC and find out what glow-in-the-dark maggots are all about.

PPS Not just to fill up empty space, I wish to take this moment to give all those who supported, read and been published in

Cthulhu Sex, generally and in this issue specifically, my personal thanks. Who else can one turn to when there is a body to be rid of if not to those who have already proven themselves as reliable and valuable? There are damn few who will offer to hold the flashlight while you exhume a corpse at night or stand watch so your visiting relatives won't catch you in the bathroom with their cat.

PPPS Even though we haven't attended at the time that I'm writing this, our table at Chiller Theatre Expo (another annual event we enjoy) was a happening place, surrounded by the best and brightest minds in the sensual horror community! Since we sold out of everything in the first ten minutes, we had nothing to do but entertain the passing throng of costumed creatures with spectacles of tentacled daring do. How will anyone ever forget the stunt that one guy dressed as a monkey did with the old pumpkin with its skin falling off? Everyone who stopped by just made the table a wondrous place to be with their uncanny coolness. Like the unexpected arrivals of two of our contributors. I'd love to thank all of you individually, but I haven't the space here. And to the rich lady who showed up and offered to support my writing career for the rest of my natural life, I accept. Just make the checks out to "Cash". But don't expect any "special" favors. I don't do that. That's what I keep the Corruptor around for.

PPPPS To anyone who has lost a cat or a dog lately, I apologize.

PPPPPS After dealing with a particularly nasty bloatfish, I'd just like to say that when it comes to retribution, there is nothing I enjoy more than ignoring those who have plotted against me until I hear the gentle sound of their inevitable drowning in the morass they alone have created of their own putrid egotistical excretions. But watching them blowed up real good kicks butt too.

PPPPPPS There. I'll let you get on with perusing the magazine now.

PPPPPPPS Or will I...

Ok. Fine. Go ahead. (sheesh)

B.AF.B

The letter that was meant to be placed in this section was sent to us from Oliver Baer while on his international travels to locate the thing about the stuff that came in that box-like thingy. However, it was received on some sort of material that almost instantaneously disintegrated into a fine black powder, which ignited all flammable materials it touched. After battling the blaze, the only remnants of the letter were the fragmented sentences "…ith belly grown o…" and "…eeding skin. She ente…"

B.AF.C

As I traveled in the Holy Land late one night, I met a strange figure dressed as a frog and wearing a peculiar mask. It was rather disconcerting as the figure was floating a few feet off the ground. The mask was vaguely reminiscent of an octopus with reticulated tentacles thrown lazily back over his (though totally covered by the costume, I assumed it was a male for some reason) head and shoulders, organized as if in some sort of fashion alien to me. Through the lensed peep holes in the surreal mask, I could see eyes that were natural enough, though they looked strange with a ring of fearful white around them.

Though I was leery of this stranger dressed in a bizarre style, the look in his eyes made me worry he was ill. In order to alleviate my worry, I sent my thoughts into his mind and sought his out. He began to drool bubbles out of the front of his mask, the physical reaction telling me he was ill before my probings could.

Once inside his mind (definitely a male), I sought out the root of his illness. Not understanding the words of his language, I glimpsed a rudimentary image of his prayer of succor to a solitary, all-encompassing deity. Considering the enormity and complexity of my people's pantheon, I was intrigued and probed deeper.

It became apparent that, though this individual had a simplistic yet solid grasp on fundamental mathematics, he used an aberrant mathematical formula to divide this single entity into parts. The deity divided into three individual parts that represented a family unit. Further divisions revealed a choir of messengers with wings as well as strangely coiffed religious leaders. Deeper divisions revealed a plethora of political leaders, sports figures and someone named Mykul Jakzon.

I also found the root of his illness in this divisionary divinity. He had been told and believed, contrary to the written rules of his religion, that there was a split from this single entity that represented a malicious second entity. This fallen aspect was somehow outside of the whole. Tracing still deeper, I realized that he even perceived groups of others of his kind outside of this divinity as well. This is quite preposterous by his religion's own rules as anything that exists would have to be part of the original divinity. Obviously, this basic logical gap was the cause of this individual's illness.

This fractured thinking ruined the intrigue his system held for me. I decided I had enough of these games and removed his mask for a direct face-to-face talk. He responded with a series of bubbling exclamations that would have made my mother blush. Then, he enacted some sort of ritualistic dance where he clutched at his rather flimsy neck. Finally, he flipped belly up and stared into the distance quite distractingly.

Since he was so rudely ignoring me, I probed him again, ready for a heated interaction. However, once inside, I found him absent from his body. I couldn't believe that he had chosen to go on some internal exploration instead of dealing with my possible confrontation. In a huff, I left him there and returned to my trek through the Holy Land.

When I returned that way, he had given his body over to the hungry fishes. I was surprised at his tenacity to hold onto his beliefs with such conviction that he would let his body go in such a way. I wouldn't abandon my body in order to hold onto my belief that my path was right when it was threatened with being wrong. Would you?

Tentacles,

St. Michael

B.AG.A

Greetings and welcome to the newest issue of *Cthulhu Sex Magazine*. We are thrilled to present you with another entertaining issue filled with amazing artwork and wild writing. If you're like me, you've probably already impatiently ripped open the envelope and flipped through this issue. Just one glance beneath the disturbingly beautiful cover illustration will give you a gleaning of the fantastic works therein. Our centerfold spread is particularly tantalizingly tasty. Take the time to settle into your favorite reading corner and devour our selection of unique writings. For some reason, my favorite location is perched upon the toilet, like most people I've heard about.

If yours is too, it must be because of the fetid meat of previous lovers putrefying on the floor of your bathroom as well. It does make it rather hard to concentrate on reading while sitting in the running masses of cold congealing offal, especially when hungry tapeworms slide across my flesh in search of a new host. The pleasure of their tens of feet of length sliding past my cold body is very distracting. But then again, that could just be me. Like most of my friends, I can't afford to hire a tapeworm wrangler. I have to do it all by myself.

Where was I? Ah yes, inserration. There has been a new addition to the *Cthulhu Sex* family. We are honored to announce that an award-winning poet and author is now dealing with our advertisement sales. Through his mighty efforts, we will be able to present even more high- quality artworks and writings as well as extend our *Cthulhu Sexy* tentacles into an ever-expanding circle of influence. By buying ads with us, advertisers will also have the side benefit of supporting the poet's habits. For legal purposes, we claim neither knowledge of his habits nor knowledge of the morality of his habits, of which we know nothing.

On a completely different side note, we have an increased availability of receptionist jobs. Young, nubile individuals of either sex may apply if they are over 18 years of age and of sound mind and body. All parties interested in this position should direct their inquiries to humansacrifices@cthulhusex. com We will again be attending the always fascinating Chiller Theatre Expo this spring in New Jersey. They are allowing us back despite the public outrage at our allowing The Corruptor to go without a muzzle. But before we could attend, we had to sign forty-three separate documents declaring our intent to participate in the festivities without The Corruptor chewing, mutilating, touching, licking, scratching, stabbing, entombing, demonstrating, defenestrating, tenderizing, slicing, dicing, mangling, postulating, abasinating, burning, humiliating, immolating, molesting, sacrificing or, as they put it, "causing grievous bodily, mental or spiritual discomfort involving chocolate sauce, 18 century artwork and plaid" to any of their patrons, employees, relatives or pets without prior verbal and written consent in triplicate. So, bring all your permission slips in triplicate this year, kiddies! As always, we would truly enjoy a brief stop by our table, even if it isn't to donate bodily fluids.

Tentacles,

St. Michael

B.AG.B

If you've been reading the letters in previous issues, then you know what this person really is. Mr. Baer deserves all the credit for moldering her.

Mr. Morel,

I must protest these indignities which you heap upon my person. I have done what you asked and yet, I still remain captive here. I tried escaping. I even tried killing myself. Yes, that fire that was burning in your cellar was set by me. But for some reason, I did not die nor, for that matter, did your partner, Mr. Baer. Why? Why do you keep me here?

I thought I had escaped you. I thought the fire would have taken me away from this place. But most of all, I thought I would be free of that monstrosity you call your partner. Now, not only am I subject to his ministrations, but he has given me something. I wonder whether the blame entirely lies upon him, though. I doubt in his condition that he could have put me back together after the damage from the fire. Although, he is blessed and cursed with additional appendages, I doubt that even he could have done the detail work to make me look almost exactly the way I did. I have a hazy memory of heat and pain as my flesh melted off of me. Then, just as I was about to receive oblivion's long kiss, I felt a viscous coolness. It was as if someone were dipping me in a vat of partially gelled fish oil. Arms and tongues caressed and licked my damaged body. Meanwhile, I could hear a chant as if broken voices were singing Mendelssohn's *Messiah* through sewn up mouths. My limbs seemed to attach themselves. My body curved and filled out.

My face resumed its shape and features. Someone who looked like the dreamer I have heard about lifted me gently through a portal. As I was coming to, I saw to my horror Mr. Baer coming towards me, one of his appendages pulling him between my legs. I dare not believe that the shivering and convulsing I endured before the pain was born of pleasure, though I did feel something akin to ecstasy. Is this what the martyrs meant about the ecstasy of knowing God? If so, I pledge to be an atheist from now on. For there is something... growing within me.

I try not to think about the above circumstances. They seem too horrendous to contemplate. But, it seems that I have no other choice. I have tried to get rid of it. But not only does it resist modern methods of abortion or extraction, it seems to thrive on the numerous attacks upon my person. For that is how I see this now. For every carved piece that is taken, it grows threefold. I don't even contemplate why it stays with me. Nor why every night I wake up with Mr. Baer. Now, its dreadful effects are wearing me down slowly. My senses have changed. I see sounds, hear his touch and smell visions of desperation and want.

I thought the fire would have stopped him. I thought seeing my burnt and ruined body would have sparked some mercy within you. I know not what you have done, but he seems hungrier than ever. If there is still a soul left in your body, please deliver me from this torment.

Yours,

Wilhemina Cravesticon

B.AG.C

A s of late, I have been reminded by current events of a number of distant things. Let me first mention that by "current events" I am not specifying the dramatic rise in corporate and political thief kings who say they have the public interest at heart when their real goal is to keep their lifestyle and their friends' lifestyles out of the reach of what they consider the "unwashed masses". Instead, I am referring to the little everyday life events that most of us take for granted. That cleared up, let me begin in earnest.

The Lord of all Pixels and Plagues was recently comparing and contrasting the state of the prison system currently and in the fairly recent 1800's. He has an amazing grasp on the uses and effects of numerous devices that were common in prisons. Just thinking about the punishment doled out in times past, I am amazed to hear individuals complain about the state in which prisoners are held after committing horrible crimes. Telephones, cable, beds, toilets, videogames and visitors for rapists, murderers and pedophiles? Back in my day, we would drop them in deep holes and forget about them, throwing down a little lye if they got too stinky. The political-religious leaders of yore usually favored either burning people (at the stake or in their homes) or just plain old wholesale slaughter.

However, we did have different definitions for crimes back then. Instead of drugs being illicit substances, pamphlets of opposing philosophy were (or magazines such as this). Murderers were people who killed and didn't get paid to do so by the ruler of the land. Those who would steal land and money from people and ruin their lives forever would be considered clergy then where they are entrepreneurs now.

I would be remiss in my duties if I didn't include indoor plumbing. I believe that this is truly one of humankind's greatest inventions. The pleasure of smelling an old-fashioned outhouse would instantly make anyone realize how good they have it. It would also clarify a few things about royalty. Such as, why did everyone make way for the king? It wasn't just respect, though having one's head removed for failing to move out of the way would generally dissuade such practices. It was because the royals hung their royal robes over the chamber pot where the moths would not dare venture. That way, the stink protected their robes from moth holes, but they acquired a new stink that many leaders still give off today.

So, remember, we live in a wondrous time filled with all the modern marvels that science provides despite the regressive tendencies of a few religious and political zealots that would rather we run around praying to their ignorance, bashing each other with sticks and keeping our women in caves. Rejoice. Things have been much, much worse.

Stay tuned for the next thrilling issue of *Cthulhu Sex* Magazine. Under the tentacularly titillating original cover, we'll proudly present the writings of some past authors, all happily devirginized by *Cthulhu Sex*. We'll also welcome back to the fold several wickedly wonderful writers. Our illuminations will include the return of issue 14, volume II's cover artist. Don't forget to order yours if you haven't already or, better yet, subscribe. If you already subscribe, you can always get subscriptions for your friends and family. They'll love you for it. You know Cthulhu will.

Tentacles,

St. Michael

B.AH.A

Greetings once again from your friends at *Cthulhu Sex*! We have a tantalizing issue for you filled with the best new writings and artwork. We are truly thrilled to present so many amazing creations. Our mind-bogglingly articulate cover was crafted by an infamous artist. After negotiating with several gods and goddesses of olden times, we have secured both a delicious story from a master storyteller and a gorgeous taste of artistic revelry from a surreal artist. In addition to these tasty treats, we offer a sampling of the most delectable prose, poetry and artwork from new voices and elder greats. Peruse and satisfy yourself.

Of note in the *Cthulhu Sex* home office are three specific happenings:

First, we would like to welcome our new Assistant Corruptor. This issue would not have come together without his tireless help and his expert eye. We look forward to many eons of writer vivisection under his skillful hands.

Second, we mourn the passing of someone from the realms of *Cthulhu Sex* advertisement back into the world of writing. His help brought support for the magazine and allowed us to do more for you, dear reader, with what wickedness we have. All of us here offer him heartfelt support in his future endeavors, which is rumored to include an original work for you to enjoy in a future issue of *Cthulhu Sex*.

Third, to whoever left the decapitated head of our secretary's betrothed under her desk, we wish you to know that it was not funny! It freaked her out to such a degree that the Corruptor was not able to spend any "quality time" with her before her unfortunate demise. This, in turn, cut into my personal time with our Motivatrix and put everything behind schedule. You know who you are. You should be ashamed of yourself!

On another topic, there has been a run on shrubbery fuel in the market as of late. This has caused our Midwinter festivities to be less festive and delayed the spring equinox by at least three days. We are worried that we will not be able to properly perform the Burning of the Bush Ritual during the Midsummer Festival either if the situation is not rectified. If any of our readers know where to get the ceremonial "Crephach" to light a fire in our bushes, please contact our offices with the proper information. Do not send the material to us as it is illegal to send hazardous materials through the mail (see previous Forewords dealing with blood and body parts) and you wouldn't know how to get past our security Hymandra to stick the torch in our bushes anyway.

A note on events: We will again be at the October Chiller Theatre Expo. The past April Chiller Theatre Expo was particularly enjoyable for us. We introduced *Cthulhu Sex* to a couple of well- known people, as well as the delightful Coffee Shop of Horrors. Before the October Expo, we will be in Baltimore attending our devirginizing of the Horrorfind Weekend in August. Feel free to drop by our table. Everyone who has before immensely enjoyed what we offered. At least half of them were able to leave afterwards under their own power. Less than ten percent were found deceased.

Enjoy this issue as much as we enjoyed putting it together. And don't worry about the page wetness; it's normal for ink to bleed a bit.

Tentacles,

St. Michael

B.ЯH.B

Below you will find the ripest of our delectable correspondences. May they please you as much as they please us. We take no responsibility for the actions or beliefs stated in this letter. However, if anyone finds her person, please return it to us. It seems to have escaped.

Mr. Morel,

I must continue to protest. How much must I suffer under your depredations? I no longer seem to have anything, not even myself. I am no longer sure of my own identity. It is hard for me to believe. I go through the day convincing myself, practicing denial and the art of self-delusion, that what has happened to me is not true. I do very well considering the entity, I dare not call it a baby, growing within me and the demons you send to plague me. The fact that they treat me with such reverence only adds insult to injury. Then night falls and despite your minions' best efforts, I fall asleep amongst the chittering and the slime. Then, I have only the dreamer for solace.

I contend with him because I must believe that I can still maintain some semblance of humanity. He comes to me with promises of escape and freedom. He takes me to realms of dancing light, skewed geometry and fantastic landscapes. But, even here amidst unexplainable beauty, it is the land's creatures that are horrid. Some of them look human, but I pray that they are not. They have a clump of tentacles sprouting from their shoulders. These clumps also contain their arms, which hang weak and shriveled in the center. From their buttocks reach out what I can only hope are tails, made from the same slime that created the tentacles, to caress with the mockery of a limb. Ringed around their waists like some terrible skirt exists a stringy substance that seems to curl in and out from their pelvises, grabbing at things in the air and depositing them within itself in an unholy ripple. I dare not describe what seems to be between the creatures' legs. What I have glimpsed, for some reason I still try to cling to the rules of propriety seems to vary between a giant mouth and a monstrously mutated stamen among a group of horrid petals. Speaking of which, the vegetation contains examples of flora that I could not even begin to imagine. Both plants that inspire awe and wonder as well as disgust and horror. It is the sight of these for which I pray that I am only dreaming. Unfortunately, I have not even been granted this lasting thought. More and more I am nagged by the idea that if I must grant reality to the existence of Mr. Baer, not to mention the condition both of you keep me in, then I must grant credence to the idea that the dreamer as well as my travels and dalliances with him are not the product of dreams. Oh, how I pray that this is not so. But I digress, the plant varieties are numerous including flowers with eyes, vines with limb-like qualities, trees that resemble some deformed old man in the throes of ecstatic release, a permanent scream frozen upon its bark and moss with wings and eyes feeding off the humanoid creatures while darting in and out of the horrid sea anemone that encircles their pelvis. They move in some sort of sordid symbiotic bacchanale.

There are desert rock carvings that seem to carry themselves over acres of bleeding sand. Bilious suns shine malevolently on this bare landscape. Distorted stone carcasses splitting themselves in a race to create shade.

As horrible as these dreams or travels are, they seem to end with a scene that leaves me with a disturbing sense of pleasure. It is disturbing in the sense that the scene is no more or less horrific than what I have previously witnessed. I feel strangely comforted by it though. Perhaps, this is due to the closeness and ministrations of the dreamer during this period. He and I are sitting on what seems to be a rocky beach of red and black with jagged tors dotting the landscape. He is holding me close, caressing me soothingly and whispering comforts in my ear while the waves lick the boulders lining the shore. Strange amphibious combinations of fish, frog and man climb out of the water to cater to our every need. One of the distorted merhumans picks up an instrument that looks like a combination of a conch and a syrinx. It played mesmerizingly while seawater sprayed upon us. This moment of surreal serenity was broken by an attack from the cold light of dawn upon my eyelids.

It is not even a shaft of heaven blessed sunlight of which I speak but a sliver of outside light that filters into the murk of the room you have created for me. The second assault upon me, physically as well as mentally, is the realization that Mr. Baer is lying with me. He is licking my body, kissing my bloated belly and caressing my face. I use these words to describe his actions as a form of protection since my mind instantly is terrorized by the awareness of them. I know not what softly brushes my face, slides across my body, rubs against or penetrates me. I have seen Mr. Baer. I have tried to escape. I was returned. Nothing has worked. Now, the third and final assault, probably as punishment for trying to destroy the creature within me, you have stolen my name. I do not even remember my own name. Your Mr. Baer refers to me constantly as Rebecca, all the while whispering about the glories of being his queen. Though his whispers sound more like insects swarming through a waterspout. Their wings beating an eerie cadence which it seems that I can almost identify. He whispers of how the tar baby growing within me shall lay the world low, how the doors shall open for our masters who will bring forth a wondrous world from beyond the skies and under the seas. My name was my last anchor to this reality. I believe it was Mina or something similar sounding. Maybe that is just a memory of what I yelled at you both as a descriptive.

I realize that the terrors I experience may not be. The actions may be words or smells, the whispers may be touches or tastes, the smells may be sights. I canot be sure since I was returned. The parasite shows me sights from afar, speaks to me of his followers and has bestowed heightened sensitivity to my already mangled senses. So that now my reality has become a

frightening blend of phantoms, for these tar people and monstrous hybrids of humans and sea creatures cannot be real, and
distorted spacetime.

I beg you to perform an exorcism or abortion. Though it
would kill me, it would grant me release from this hell you have
consigned me to. I do not know how long I can last. Please…

Rebecca Mina

B.AH.C

From Woodruff Laputka:

The last noted account of Dr. Patrick Paul Zion, mystic and scholarly student of the occult.

The Final Letter of Dr. Patrick Zion

To my other half, long friend and dearest companion:

Should you find this letter, know that I have left. I have been traveling, as you know, and now the shadows which I dared to foolishly evoke in my youth have come to me. In the dim light of that dying fire I made some hours ago, I have set and dreamt in fear of what is lurking outside of that flame's glare. Horrid shapes and things that bear no form. Black ether and pools of oil, which pitch is made to be the brightest hue by comparison. I don't hear anything. There are no crickets or night birds. The moon is gone and I see no stars. A black haze, capturing and distorting the glare of the firelight. And that, I fear, will be dead soon.

Stepping on cyclopean stone steps and surpassing great spires that come to high towers, to the mighty black pyramid of the occult. That oblivion looms above, as the stairway goes to unknown heavens or hells. The guardians of life have disappeared and I am on my own. The steps are lined with the bones of the dead; those who have attempted to scale this titanic ascent. And beyond the walls of my own dreams lies the cold and manless world of the wild. There, I could not survive. Back would I return to my fire, where dark, unwholesome things without shapes wait for me to fall asleep and for the fire to die. Then, they will feast on my sleeping body and I will be cast into the black abyss of the damned.

So I must walk, endlessly it would seem, hoping that I find

an answer to my query. I have lead a blasphemous life, with my obsessions of learning all there is to know. Now, my love, I move on to the next great adventure, where no laws of our universe remain. Here, my life begins again, for better or worse. I will continue my work there.

And my body, you must have found, is desecrated beyond repair.

Patrick Zion

B.AH.D

Recently, a friend of mine brought me along to one of our favorite pastimes involving the Vomina. For those of you who are unfamiliar with the Vomina, you will continue to be so, except what I tell you about in this. It's for your own good. Believe me. You could ask some of the more loose-lipped members who have been known to offer up such information, but it is hard to answer through six feet of earth.

Anyway, this friend of mine, who shall remain nameless, decided that it was time for a diversion from the normal practices that we normally engaged in. Therefore, he took me to a surprisingly large house, decorated with the most decadently outrageous opulence that I have ever laid eyes on in a human's dwelling. Not surprising, if you know of the Vomina, there were a number of extremely powerful and rich individuals milling about, talking of this inanity or the next while they waited for whatever they expected to happen to happen. It was all so droll.

As the butlers rolled out the carts of herbals and essences, I quickly found a comfortable seat in a flesh-suckingly plush divan to watch the ritual. Though I rarely participate anymore, I do enjoy ogling a good round of [word omitted]. The participants quickly stripped to the bare essentials and grabbed mouthfuls of the heavenly scented herbs.

That is when I realized there was an unusual piece of furniture in the room. It looked like nothing less than a giant goldfish bowl that traveling circuses use to exhibit their "mermaid" with the latex tail and no top. I found the contemplation of its use rather intriguing as one lady, mouth full of crunching cud, was upended into the glass by two muscled eunuchs wearing hoods and nothing else.

Instead of the sensual bobbing and playful floating I expected this lady to exhibit, she landed painfully at the bottom of the bowl I could now see was quite devoid of water. She began to scream with such force she wastefully blew her herbal mixture out of her mouth. I was so shocked, I could do nothing but watch as the other individuals involved in this also wantonly spewed forth their own mixtures into the bowl.

Even more disturbing were the whirling blades that began to liquefy the still screaming woman and the wasted herbal chews. As she pureed, I almost lost my lunch, quite unintentionally of course, due to the fact of all that wasted effort of herbal mastication.

To my relief, the other individuals began scooping handfuls of lady and herb mix into their waiting mouths. As I watched them initiate their retching, I began to realize that the lady, possibly chosen at random, was but one more ingredient to the mix. And as the lady and herbs were delivered from heaving mouths to waiting orifices, I could sit back, take in the sight of powerful people glutting themselves and know that all is right in the world.

Tentacles,

St. Michael

B.AI.A

Greetings once again from your friends at *Cthulhu Sex* Magazine!

Welcome to our biggest and grandest issue yet. Within these pages, you'll find some of the most wild, delightful and disturbing writings we've offered to date. In addition, this issue is jam-packed with even more tantalizing and amazing artwork than ever before. Of particular note is an article centering on the Baphomet pendant created by an internationally renowned artist and sculpted by an internationally known artist and constant contributor to *Cthulhu Sex* Magazine. This involving article couldn't have been possible without the help of a knowledgeable agent, a gracious artist and an uncanny artist.

We are also pleased to offer a PDF version of *Cthulhu Sex* Magazine starting with this issue. PDF subscriptions and issues are available on our website. By offering an electronic version, we will be better able to provide the joy and horror that is *Cthulhu Sex* Magazine to our readers in foreign countries and those who prefer an electronic format. Soon, our tentacles will stretch into the nether regions of the world.

In other news, *Cthulhu Sex* Magazine and Raw Dog Screaming Press have joined forces to create a new erotic horror imprint under the name of Two Backed Books. The first two scheduled releases are *Horror Between the Sheets*, an anthology offering up the best of *Cthulhu Sex* Magazine in black and white, and *Tempting Disaster*, an anthology of fringe writings that explore the cultural obsession with sexual taboos. Both of these will be released at the 2005 World Horror Convention in New York City. This heralds the beginning of a long and adventurous foray into dark and delightful realms.

As you can see, *Cthulhu Sex* Magazine is going through much growth and change. However, at least one thing will always remain the same. Besides the constant high quality of our presentation, we will always include at least one message from the Avatar to our disciples. For those of you who have the translation key, this code will bring you higher and higher levels of enlightenment as well as a deeper understanding of your place in the universe. Considering the spiritual rewards, the Avatar's requests are minimal inconveniences at best, don't you think? There is nothing that could possibly be wrong with obedience to a higher power transmitted through the Avatar. After all, the pleasures you will receive on the other side more than make up for any pain and suffering on this side, right? Besides, all the other religions are doing it. And the other side really does exist. No, really it does. Yes, just like the Avatar says it does. The Avatar knows it's true so you have to believe him. Because he says so. Oh, and because it is written down. So there.

For those of you who do not have the translation key, ignore everything in the paragraph above except the first sentence and the bit about the constant high quality of our presentation. If you do not, terrible things could happen. [Our legal department has informed me that I must inform all our readers that the last sentence about "terrible things" is a warning and not some ambiguous threat. It isn't, by the way. An ambiguous threat. That's also a little confusing, isn't it? I mean that it isn't an ambiguous threat. It isn't a threat at all. Yes, that is what I meant.]

So, get comfortable, lean back, relax and get ready to take all that this issue of *Cthulhu Sex* Magazine has to offer. It only hurts a little at first. I assure you. After all, it's all easy sailing and vivisection. I meant "joy". Really, I did.

Tentacles,

St. Michael

B.AI.B

There is nothing more moving than a gentle plea for solace emanating up through the floorboards.

Mr. Morel,

I thought I found peace. I thought I found safety. I thought I escaped. But even now, as I gather up my things in a place that seems miles away from you and your dread creation, Mr. Baer, I hear rumblings and see the forces you summoned to return me to my cell. I hear you have even convinced—or is it converted? —the good Dr. Zion to your cause. I weep for him, just as I do for myself and the other converts. Just as I do every time I am forced to conduct the ritual. Thankfully though, the child (for I now refer to the creature growing and consuming me as such it being my saving grace) allows me the ability to travel quickly and unseen. I have not figured out by what means I do this or the power it allows me to access. I dare not. Perhaps my contact with the dreamer is the key, perhaps not. As I travel through the world, I pray the distance I cover is no mere illusion, that I am headed for a place as different from the dank festering cell you kept me in as the realms the dreamer has shown me are to our own.

It is strange that a being I had such distaste and enmity for should now raise such emotions within me that I feel protective and concerned for its welfare. So progresses (no, changes—I refuse to think of it as progress) my attitude towards the child. If it had not been for its intervention, if it had not called its brothers and sisters, I believe I would be yet another lab rat behind Dr. Zion's walls. But, if this were true, why do I think of him as good, kind, a gentleman? It is true that he showed a particular interest in me and the child when you ushered him into my dark den. He would talk to me of such wonders that it would make me shiver with excitement. He reminded me, however slightly and short our acquaintance, of the dreamer. Though his reaction to the horrid misshapen form of Mr. Baer was suspicious. It was almost as if he was held in thrall somehow by him. Or could this have been another example of your malign influence?

I have never seen your creature react in such a manner. I do believe that Mr. Baer was terrified of the entities the child called forth as Dr. Zion was—how did he describe it? —ah yes, preparing me for travel. Though Mr. Baer did seem to clearly have many of their same attributes. They seemed to come through the wall, down through the ceiling and up through the floor. How they got through all of your wards and protections, I do not know. But I praise God, or in this case my child, that they did. What carnage must have ensued in the floors above me. I'm ashamed even to think about it but the hope, dare I allow it to congeal into a thought, of my captor and his cadre lying limbless and bloody sends a thrill of excitement through me. The dark mutated invasion force must have also alerted the dreamer whose role in my nightmarish existence I am still confused about. Is he a savior or a sadist? Does he show me these visions and take me to these places to further overload my warped senses so I do not notice the horrors visited upon me? If the latter is true, is he assigned to me to keep my body whole for a specific reason? The child, possibly? The chamber filled with the tar people and their minions—your minions, Mr. Morel—creatures as distorted, if not more, if that is possible, than your Mr. Baer who seemed to literally be melting into his corner, his tentacled and claw-like appendages retracting into his body.

I was seized by the memory of my first attempted escape and I still know not how I found something. Perhaps I grabbed one of Mr. Baer's feeble attempts at clothing, which resembled more the tattered flag of a ghost ship than any garments I've seen, laying on the floor. But there was something ablaze in my hand. I threw it at Dr. Zion urging him to keep it going at all cost or they would overtake him. Then there was darkness and either the child, or my own warped senses, watched the walls melt with a sucking sound. I felt the heralding sounds of the dreamer. He stepped through this aperture with some of the tentacled beings and their symbiotes of whom I have described to you previously. The symbiotes swarmed the creatures near me seemingly cutting a path in my direction as well as creating a blockade around me. The tentacled ones threw the distortions of nature towards the corner into which Mr. Baer had retreated. Through this melee strode the dreamer, and the walls resolved themselves to their original state. He walked up to me, took me in his arms, kissed me and caressed me. The blockade became tighter and the tentacled squadron moved in closer to us. He made love to me as the floor dissolved beneath us, with its usual distorted symphonic polyphony, and the walls folded over us.

Now, I move in the direction the child leads me. I believe it shows me the way to salvation or at least, its link to its brethren allows me to keep one step ahead of you. So I thought. Progress is slow. I have found that this body you have cobbled together for me loses its strength over periods of time. How long, I can no longer say. Thankfully, the combined will of both myself and the child prevents me from having to engage in the ritual often. I distrust my senses. I can only hope I have traveled far enough and for a long enough period that the child's visions of your servants' proximity are not true. During my feverish attempts at sleep, I imagine that the child speaks to me and is forming an identity for itself. It seems to acknowledge that I am its mother but also makes some reference to The Mother of All Monsters in relation to me. I pray these are merely the imaginings of my warped mind. Please call back your troops for I shall not return to you alive if captured.

Minecca

B.AI.C

We wanted to share this bit of good cheer with you, dear reader. It is one of those delightful little letters that make everything all better.

Dear sirs,

I do not appreciate the objects you left on my porch last night. I do not think skinning small animals is funny. If you insist on trying to visit my daughter, I would like to remind you of the restraining order. If I find you in my house, near my family, in the root cellar or in our mausoleum again, I will take drastic actions. For each of you, I have a bullet with your name on it. And once Cardinal Richelieu grants the exorcism, your time on this planet will be at an end.

You've been warned

Theodore Mordred

B.AI.D

Well, that's the end of this issue. We hope that you've enjoyed your journey through this heaping portion of *Cthulhu Sex* Magazine. Come back again and enjoy the next leg of our trek, which features a brand, new story by a mythos-imbued master as well as a few indulgent surprises and some gentle returns of our past favorites.

In case you didn't already hear the screaming of the innocent, *Cthulhu Sex* traveled to our very first Horrorfind Weekend a little bit ago. It was thoroughly wonderful for us. Besides the bodies that were never discovered in our hotel room, there were gads of writers, publishers and literary people and stuff. It seemed everywhere we looked, we discovered someone else we knew. We shared a table. A Lovecraftian artist released his new magazine Inhuman at a table across the way from us. Behind us was Raw Dog Screaming Press, tended by the delightful editors and publisher. Many contributors stopped by and signed copies of the issue in which they were presented. It was wonderful and particularly gratifying to put faces to their names.

In addition to this group revelry in the genre of horror, I would like to talk about a specific subject. I have found that there are things, which I like to call Cauchemars for lack of a better word, that only reveal themselves when my mind is in a state of heightened awareness and distracted by a necessary task. I often find myself in this situation in two specific instances. First, when I am just waking up and I am focused on reanimating my body. I have often been told that the sensing of these Cauchemars during this period can easily be chalked up to sleepy delusions and phantasms. Second, when I am wandering naked through the house with the lights out, trying to move around objects by touch and memory. The reason behind my nude meandering is unimportant, however interesting it is. Regardless, the important aspect of this type of occurrence is that it disproves the hypnologic aspects of the previous situation.

These Cauchemars that I have found are integrated with, yet totally separate from, the physical terrain of reality in which I interact on a day-to-day basis. They reveal themselves in many ways including disembodied voices malevolently calling my name, barely luminescent childlike shapes reaching for me through the darkness, and the crawling of multi-legged creatures over my body with the prickling of a thousand needles into my flesh. Needless to say, these Cauchemars present themselves in ways as varying as they are disturbing.

I have recently had what can only be likened to a telepathic communication with these Cauchemars. As they revealed themselves, I received the knowledge that they are not out to drive me mad, they are out to destroy all…

Oh, my goodness! Does that menu say, "Baby with Black Bean Sauce" or am I imagining things? Why yes, it does! You'll have to excuse me while I place an order.

Tentacles,

Michael

B.BO.A

Greetings and welcome to the newest installment of *Cthulhu Sex* Magazine.

To please the proper individuals involved in certain practices, I will take a moment and review *Cthulhu Sex*'s past year. 2004 started much like any other. As industry standard, we were behind schedule, understaffed, over budget and lacking the promotional resources we needed to take over the world. I initially blamed Mr. Baer for this as he would continuously refrain from editing in order to masticate various employees from various departments. This not only slowed the editing process to a crawl, it became a costly burden as new employees were trained and old employees' employers were paid off.

While taking a nighttime stroll in an unavoidable midwinter malaise, I stumbled across the first serendipitous event that would shape 2004 for *Cthulhu Sex*. A passing lady of the evening swooned at my feet. Since I knew I would end up safekeeping the blade that protruded from between her third and fourth vertebrae for the ritualistic acquaintance of mine who left it there, I feared its possession might give the authorities a mistaken impression. Therefore, I hefted the lady, the knife and all over my shoulder and hailed a cab. Not wanting to return to my residence with such a trollop, as my dearest would surely find such common blood unusable for her uses and take offence, I headed to the offices.

Once I arrived, Mr. Baer began his incessant banging on the basement door, somehow sensing unspoiled flesh near him. You would think that his meat-pounders would grow weary being beaten against spiked steel, but no, he could happily flay the skin off up to his elbow and be ready for more the next day.

What a trooper. Long story short, I dumped the lady's body into the basement and let Mr. Baer have his way with it.

Going through her pockets, I found a business card for a temp agency/escort service. I called and asked if they could discreetly deliver on a nightly basis. They assured me they could. I couldn't believe my luck. It solved the staffing problem as well as a few other problems that needed body parts. Within a few months, we were back on schedule, on budget and on track. Having the beautiful Motivatrix spur me on was a wondrous fringe benefit.

Then, out of the blue, came the second thrilling event. We received a slew of requests to edit for *Cthulhu Sex*. Like the old adage says, "When it rains cats and dogs, the streets get bloody." After his sound thrashing of the four other would-be editors and a couple of small coup attempts in Pacific Island countries, we invited our new editor aboard. Little did we know how important a part he would play in *Cthulhu Sex*'s plans of world dominance.

After he joined us, we had enough extra time and capital to branch out to a new convention. We chose the illustrious HorrorFind.com Weekend in Baltimore. The years of quietly observing the market and studying the players paid off when we snuck up on Raw Dog Screaming Press. Let sleeping dogs lie? Never! We pounced with all the ferocity of an insane Humboldt squid! Fur and ink flew everywhere as the ball of mayhem tore across the con floor. When the last growl was growled and the last sucker sucked, neither dominated nor was vanquished. We had come to an impasse and a newfound respect for each other. Therefore, we birthed Two Backed Books. The power of two combined to form one! Well, two distinct entities acting as one. I guess that makes the one another entity. So that would be three, wouldn't it? The power of two combined to form three. That doesn't sound as impressive as Two Backed Books is. Really.

Since then, the manipulation of outside forces has helped *Cthulhu Sex* to grow like a cancer. Physically, *Cthulhu Sex* has been picked up for national distribution by wondrous Ubiquity Distributors, Inc. and can be found on newsstands all over the place. Electronically, there was an impressive show of malcontent. Not only had *Cthulhu Sex* been on the Shocklines. com Best Seller list for a good number of weeks, one of the issues (issue 18, volume 2, to be exact) appeared on the Shocklines.com Top 20 Best Selling Magazines for 2004.

Just imagine my surprise at finding out that the poison wasn't working nearly as well as I expected. Mr. Baer, ever the optimist, suggested that it wasn't working at all. After spending a few nights in the basement under the gentle supervision of our new automated maiden of iron, Mr. Baer was willing to grudgingly admit that it might be possible that the nerve stimulation caused by the necrosis of cranial tissue does, in fact, exhibit addictive properties, therefore explaining the past positive occurrences.

Our joy is your benefit. Ignore the poison and enjoy this issue. We have worked hard to fill these pages with even more art and writing than ever before. After the virus alters your mind, we are sure you'll agree it is the best *Cthulhu Sex* ever.

B.BO.B

DOWN AND OUT UNDERNEATH R'YLEH

Mr. Morel,

Her name is Nelly Lynne, at least that is what they tell me. Or is it what he tells me? I can't tell anymore. Perhaps they are telling of—or am I hearing or feeling it? — the death knell of Lynne and my disturbed mind created another name. The voices have become a constant buzz in my mind, especially as it seems to shift between my connection to the baby's, who as you may have noticed I refer to as "he" for lack of a better referent, the kin of Mr. Baer and sometimes even the dreamer. Nelly Lynne is to be his governess. The creatures have picked her to raise the baby to be their leader. For even though the whispers seem to speak of me in deferential terms, they don't trust that I will teach the child their ways. I am surprised at their choice. Apparently, there were others with names no less descriptive of their nature, names like Cyn, Chille and Jeszt, but whose bodies did not hold together after the ritual. They just became more fodder for the continued replication of these ebon nightmares that you have sent to plague me. Perhaps it was Nelly Lynne's father's sinister connection to the man, unbeknownst to her, who would eventually become her husband. If the story I hear, the wrong word it seems since I have seen and felt what happened to this woman, is true then it is more romantic in the human sense of the word than I give these black-hearted misshapen monstrosities credit for.

She was an actress whose beauty was inexplicable and talent was unmatched. When she trod the boards, there were times the audience were her thralls to such an extent that a one-woman show would be spoken of as a fully cast production. Eventually she met a man as handsome as he was rich, the only caveat he asked of her was that she not ask where or how he made his money. Unfortunately, they were only able to spend a short time together. As she matured through her twenties, she fell victim to a fatal illness at the tender age of 30. This disease started interfering with her acting until she could do nothing but lie in bed complaining of joint pain. An attack of the nerves is what the doctors told her husband even though he got her the best care money could buy. As time went on, even their love-making lessened. She complained that she was pained by his touch. This did not seem to abate his love, or his lust, for her. He started to come up with more creative ways to stimulate her broken body. But, he would always withdraw to their bathroom when his creativity elicited groans of pain sooner than groans of ecstasy. In the end, she begged him not to let her die in pain. He made love to her one last time and as she let out an orgasmic sigh, life left her. He kissed her on the lips. Then, he called them and made a deal with them. He had actually figured out how to contact the hideous horde of tar creatures in the same manner as Mr. Baer. The scene would have been one that would have kept me stimulating myself for weeks, if it were not for that terrible reminder of the ritual and the need for its performance. First, he gently stripped her of her bedclothes, bathed her swollen joints and tense muscles while singing a discordant melody whose lyrics sounded like a syllabically misemphasized version of Barber's "I Can't Believe You Made Me Love You". In the middle of this song, though it was more like the point at which the sound, for I dare not call it music, reached a crescendo of chittering and humming, the darkness took shape, just as it did for me, and they started to arrive. Her husband led them to her. They descended upon her. But instead of attacking her as I have been forced to witness them do to so many others, they started stroking her body and kissing it. I am not sure what was worse, feeling that poor woman's metamorphosis or her excitement. While my mind tried to come to grips with the feelings of a dead woman's thrills, I continued to experience the living, writhing Gordian Knot of pleasure. Their misshapen tongues licked her breasts and kissed her cheeks. Their mutated limbs caressed hers and moved with an undulating motion in and out of her orifices. As this happened, she seemed to dry out. Her skin became scaly and she glistened with what at first seemed to be the sweat of sex but on closer examination I—or is it she? —realized that it was a slimy substance that seemed to be excreted from her body. This reptilian—or is it some type of fish? —transformation was completed as both her and the creatures climaxed their terrible orgy. Her husband moved towards her to express his joy and clasp his resurrected wife to him. So overcome was he that his plan worked, he forgot about the price he promised them and they fell upon him like they have so many others.

It turns out that what she did not know was that her husband was able to set up this deal with so much ease because he had been finding bodies for necrophiliacs. It was in this way that he had stumbled upon the rites and rituals of Mr. Baer's kind. For it seems that they have so inculcated themselves among the populace that there is now a following complete with what can only be called familiars (I am calling these inferior versions familiars because they seem to serve the function as such). Apparently, these familiars have been charged with either converting—ironically, that is how they refer to the transformation—both the living and, not being content with their numbers, the dead. Most of these familiars, not surprisingly, are the necrophiliacs previously mentioned. I have even heard that some of familiars have been promised a higher station if they kill themselves and then are likewise converted. This explains some of the cultish "suicides" I seem to hear more and more about.

I must say that this story seems to be yet another example of your malign influence, Mr. Morel. Of course, I do not trust my senses, either mental or physical, so that even though this tale, which I seem to have experienced firsthand in some diabolical fashion, lends credence to my theory of the terrors you have unleashed upon the world, I dare not believe it is so widespread. But, if these hellish entities can be swayed to such compassionate ends by any means possible, perhaps it is worth it no matter what the price. Aren't a few carcasses of small animals for a few necros better than this living hell in which you have me currently existing? Perhaps if I influence these necrotic familiars, for they surely must be dying with every act they consummate, there is a way to escape you and the horrid, Mr. Baer. I now realize that there is no place I can truly escape from the nightmarish monstrosities you have called forth. Nor it seems will dying provide me an escape, for I will be reformed or the baby will stop me. He must live to carry on his destiny and I must convince this governess to teach him about her experience. Hopefully, with the knowledge of their leniency towards her, my baby will lead them to a new way of being within the darkness and without.

Wilhereb

B.BO.C

Here you are, the last few pages of this issue bent over so you can see these words. This is the last section of the magazine to be put together. That's right, this was the last thing written. It encapsulates a solid view of the entire magazine.

Ever wonder what is going through the mind of a *Cthulhu Sex* Editor right before an issue goes to press? You might think it is something similar to, "Must finish this spread and write that Afterword thing and then get the disk to the printer and don't forget to thank all the people in this issue..." or possibly, "Who do I have to sleep with to get some ink laid out on this spread?" or even, "Where in the world do you think you're sneaking off to, Mr. Baer?" and so on and so on.

Well, we here at *Cthulhu Sex* do a few simple things to avoid these repetitive and time-consuming thoughts:

First, we generally thank everyone in the Foreword. This saves us the time of mentioning all the wonderful people who came to us with the wonderful words and pictures that you've already viewed. If you haven't already read through this issue, I thank you because that means you skipped over everything else to read my words. What bigger compliment could there be.

That reminds me that we didn't actually thank everyone in the Foreword. I will briefly do so here. I personally want to thank everyone who contributed artwork and writings to this issue. We wouldn't be here without you. As Avatar of *Cthulhu Sex*, it is my pleasure to offer you all the out-of-body virgin sacrifices you can handle. Simply close your eyes and enjoy. And you, dear reader, where would we be without you? Close your eyes as well. Actually, wait until you're done with the Afterword and then close your eyes. Otherwise, you'd miss stuff.

Second, we do not send a disk to our press, if a press it can be called. It is more of a spiritual and physical packaging house where the flesh of innocent individuals is rent from the skeletal structures, beaten to a paper-like consistency and impregnated with thoughts and ideas that reveal themselves as the pages are turned. If you've read the magazine before, you may already know this.

What you may not know, is that the thoughts and ideas are not created by external forces. They are an extension of your own centrist views and beliefs. Every image, every word on these pages is a creation of your mind. Yes, there are individuals who have spent hours drawing forth their hard-won creativity for their canvases and papers. And there are, of course, those of us at *Cthulhu Sex* who have spent months bringing it all together in an attractive and stylish manner, if I do say so myself.

But do you really think that any of us truly exist? I mean, have you ever met any of us? And even if you think you have, can you truly be sure that it happened? It is all in your memory and you know how accurate that is. Do you even remember that teacher who came on to you in grade school? How about those things when you were little that moved around you in the dark while you tried to get to sleep? You keep telling yourself that they were just dreams. Some of them were so bad you don't remember them at all. All you remember is that was the day you decided you didn't want to ever go into your room again. And then your friend showed up and said, "Hey, Michael, you wanna play tennis?" You knew it wasn't really your friend. Why would your friend come down to the basement in the dead of night and ask if you wanted to play tennis? Especially if she knew you didn't play tennis. Besides, she had a blood-soaked goldfish that she was calling a racket and she was pointing it menacingly at you. You had to kill her. She left you no choice. You had to.

Third, the singing. Oh, the gentle singing of your soft, but-ter-like sweetmeat. It calls to me. I can see it in your skull. I hear it slorshing as it moves. I know it wants me. And you know I want it. We were meant for each other. Your squishy eyes cannot stop my pulsating love. Sing, my beauty, as I plumb the depths for you. Sing to me as my love-meat pounds your brain-flesh. Sing to me.

...Itchy, Tasty
Tentacles,

St. Michael

P.S. Just in case you couldn't tell, it's been a long night!

B.BA.A

Greetings and welcome to the latest and greatest installment of *Cthulhu Sex* Magazine.

We have the pleasure of presenting you with an enormous number of excellent works of fiction, poetry and artwork, stuffed with even more than ever before. Cover yourself with the warm moist caresses of our fine poetry and prose. Ogle our particularly wondrous artwork, almost all of which were traditionally created with paint, ink, paper, canvas, hand and imagination. One caution---Don't get a paper cut on your eye. It hurts like a mutha.

I'd like to thank everyone who has given their time and effort to create work for and/or spread the word about this issue in specific and *Cthulhu Sex* in general. In particular, I'd like to give thanks to an artist agent for being his helpful self as well as introducing me to this issue's centerfold artist and to the curator of the art show at World Horror Con 2005, which brought many wonderful artists to my attention.

You might wonder why I, the powerful Avatar of *Cthulhu Sex*, am being so gushy. The answer is twofold. Firstly, we are finally playing with the big boys*. Secondly, we have a fundamentalist-fascist group† attempting to assassinate our staff members. I'll go into both of these in a bit.

But before all that, after all the real-life trauma of the past few years, take a moment to relax. Nothing bad will happen to you. You're safe right now. If I'm wrong, don't tell me. I like living in my own little fantasy world. Just sit back and enjoy this magazine.

So back to my first subject, playing with the big boys‡. Last year, we were picked up by a wonderful national distributor that is known for working with specialty magazines, much to our world-conquest-hungering delight. It was nice to know they believed in us enough to ship us around the country to infect heretofore-unknown readers. This year, we were thrilled and amazed when the largest distributor of popular magazines, responded to our constant badgering by sending a contract. Talk about wonderful surprises. And this is after they actually read a number of issues. World conquest, here we come! Did I say, "world conquest?" I meant "happy joy-joy synergy with all humans." Yeah, that's it.

Anyway, I mentioned a fundamentalist-fascist group† that is terrorizing our staff. I bring this up because one of them actually got through Father Baer's defenses and popped him in one of his eyes. It was particularly rude as Father Baer was suffering from a malady where he sloughs off his scales. I know, it sounds impossible but it's true. Feel free to ask Mr. Baer about it next time you meet him. I won't promise that he'll answer with words, but feel free.

This abusive group has named itself Scientists Calling for the Humanitarian and Effective Institutionalization of Superstitious and Solipsistic Eggheads. SCHEISSE has come to us with claims that everything is based on science and not faith, specifically citing that nowhere in any credible religious text is there mention of a prophet, avatar or spiritualist driving a car, checking their email, using an ATM, taking antibiotics or talking on a cell phone, and therefore all civilized advancement in the last three hundred years must have come from science alone, which means all other methods of evaluating the current state of affairs are inaccurate and should be removed from contaminating their swimming pool. I pointed out that the truth about everything is actually quite the opposite of their argument, citing the fact that people have held up their religious beliefs despite being faced with hard proof they are wrong, the fact that these believers have spent thousands of years in development and perfection of contraptions used to kill and cause pain to the people who brought the aforementioned hard proof, the fact that our magazine is created entirely of our contributors' dreams and our readers' faith and contains no physical

traits, and finally to prove my point decisively, the fact that a
paper cut on their eye hurts like a mutha. Needless to say, after
unsuccessfully attempting to hold in their vitreous humors.
SCHEISSE has made us target number one.

If you, dear reader, happen to come across someone tout-
ing the evils of *Cthulhu Sex* and the virtue of science, you know
what to do. Roll up this issue, and with a firm voice say, "No!
Bad SCHEISSE!" Just in case, you should always carry a copy of
Cthulhu Sex. You never know when you might need it.

*They could just as easily be big girls.

†Maybe more of a loose association than a group. Members
are made to swallow live goldfish.

‡" big" is a relative term and does not mean that there are others that are not as large if not larger.

B.BA.B

Meesta Morayl,

It is time. She has told me. He will soon emerge into the world. But first, we must find a place to nest…uh, rest. I have been trying to ignore his rumblings and stabbings, for they do not feel like kicks, against my uterus. The pain is such that it feels like he has either eaten through the uterine wall or made it more a part of himself, creating long tentacular feeding tubes, tresses of nourishment, that reach out to grab sustenance from my body along with the umbilical cord. I believe that my abdominal wall is slowly being breached as this cluster of tendrils reaches out to it. I can no longer travel for lengths of time. It is getting harder and harder to maintain this makeshift form they have created for me. I have had to resort to sending Nelly Lynne out to conscript some of the volunteers, or familiars, to engage in the ritual with me up to three times a day just to keep me from dissembling. She has been more of a help than I imagined though I do not trust the direction she is leading us. This destination she whispers about, that I have seen, felt and heard through the shattered kaleidoscope of senses which has shaped my reality, scares me with its antique tranquility. Nothing that old, even the grounds seem to bespeak a time before man enslaved animals to his yoke, calms me. I believe they are mere receptacles for shadows who prey on human vulnerability. She has been casting her own glamours upon me when the various distractions impede my ability to serve as the baby's transport vessel. This is how I have come to think of myself, something like a stasis pod in a spaceship. At these times, when he is clawing away at my womb, I imagine that my vagina will one day expand upwards to encompass my abdomen until my torso is stretched to form a portal of sorts. My baby will not to be born, he will emerge, stepping out—or will he slither?—of the gateway, a boy-king ready to rule. Then, I awake to the pain. Nelly Lynne is crooning to my stomach and me in a lispy insect hum, the baby restlessly whispers and his horde of followers chatters incessantly while the dreamer sends me mental pictures of his travels which seem similar to my own. Or is everything blending together?

Ia tekuli tekiri-ri- ri ftagn! Aves ress medy rumd edum duma rend arch nodu eefo rany eets eepo weav eeea didy.

She tells me that she knows a place where the baby will be safe. A house set off from the rest of the world near trees and water. It has been in her family for generations. I ask how we will get there with a quaver that seems to echo in the involuntary quivering with which my body erupts. Simultaneously an orgasmic thrill seems to fill my body as the baby seems to writhe in ecstasy at this news. Waves of fear and joy batter my body. She tells me not to worry. I still do. Would you trust someone who had been set to watch over you by your enemies? I must try to get her to teach the child that their kind and our kind can live together. The pain is great and I just want to sleep. The ritual no longer affords me comfort. I have grown weary of all this traveling. It has been made clear that I can no longer run from your monstrosities, Meesta Morayl. Nelly Lynne has seen to that. I am sure that this house she is heading me towards will be my final resting place. I hope it is quick or distracting. Perhaps the dreamer will be sent once again to distract me from the horrors that await.

Alla acko ceks micholi ired eepo wate upea oeav atae edoo etow eyai taio oree. Cthulhu ia ia tekuli tekiri!

I'm much colder now. Actually, I don't know whether it is me or the surrounding environment. I crave the warmth of the familiars. Strange that even the dead or newly risen seem warm to me. They do not help me but still I crave them and they do not come without engaging in the ritual. None of this is helping me. I hope the baby can survive these temperature fluctuations. I am no longer able to travel by conventional means.

Nelly Lynne has made a deal with the dreamer to open portals for us. They are not so much portals as they are a transformation of the surrounding air, light and sound. The area in front of us does not merely fall into itself but changes with a weird atonal piping into a gelatinous reddish, blackish green substance that reminds me of the scales on Nelly Lynne's body or the colors my skin turns when the cravings overtake me. This substance propels us through space to the next location. My womb seems to vibrate sympathetically to the music. With each trip we make, my body reacts with the same spasmotic undulations that wracked it when I was told about the house. The reaction, in response to this gore rot-colored ooze, seems to either help my body maintain its shape or help it to reform. The process feels like a massive allergic reaction. It burns, itches and starts to flake into blackish reptilian scaly pieces. Then we are through the other door. My body shivers with delight to the music reforming on the other side. Nelly Lynne has told me about the house, how it has been in her family for generations and how her sisters live there still conducting ritual baths and selling folk cures. His name, she tells me, is Micholi. Or is it Aelver? Please tell Meesta Bayar about his child for surely I will not be long for this world.

Himec Pod

B.BA.C

Watching the flickering screen filled with horrific carnage and insufferable boredom, my subconscious frantically attempts to break free from the hypnotizing flashes as they ice over my thoughts. With a desperate sledgehammer blow, my mind fractures into thousands of sharp-edged shards, ricocheting off the inside of my skull in a swirling vortex of conflict that cuts deeply into my innocent convolutions.

Thoroughly lobotomized, the prismatic images leap from the screen to pierce my eyes. The sights hold sway, bent on dragging me into a bed of red-hot coals made by the people who hate me, fueled with their raw anger at my very existence and their smoldering desire to crush my point of view. I climb up, fighting for escape and reaching for the offered hands and lifelines from the people who love me, strengthened by their unconditional support and their total understanding of everything I am.

Gaining my freedom above the discord, I find myself alone in a thick fog formed from the amorphous ghosts of the rest of the people, the ones who don't even know of my existence, the 99.999% of humanity that doesn't even realize that I am missing from their reality, that hasn't heard of or seen me and can't know there is even anything to miss. It is cold here with these thoughts, colder than the pure electric blue ice-light from the static laden screen before me. It chills me to the core and numbs me to the war and the kidnapping and death and the boy whose skin fell off.

I kindle a fire in my belly; I dredge up my own red-hot coal for those I hate, the ones that kill and kidnap and spread fanaticism and just don't give a damn, the ones who make children

cry and beat the aged and hurt just to feel something. The fire
burns brightly, fiercely, but it is an icy fire that radiates my
hatred outward, and still-birthed in the sterile water that is
hate, leaves none to hear me.

I fight the growing chill with my lifelines for those I love,
cocooning myself with memories of my family and the ones
closest to me and their families and my friends, the ones that
I share the simple comforts of companionship with that allows
them to go on when they are broke and downtrodden and helpless to stop the shadows of doubt and fear from sweeping across
their eyes and blinding them. The fire inside finally settles and
becomes a golden glow, a lasting warmth that shelters me from
the freezing fog.

All becomes safe and pure and true when my thoughts turn
to her, the one who shares her life with me, the one who comforts me when the world is cruel and who keeps me light when
the night is long. With the soft touch of her on my thoughts,
the fractured flower clams its roiling, becoming a gently pulsing rose. I relax into her warm embrace and sink beneath her
surface.

But in the back of my mind, the flickering screen nettles
me, begging an answer to its incessant questioning. Unable to
ignore it completely, I find myself wondering about the lives of
the 99.999% of humanity that I've never heard of or seen, the
ones that I don't even know I don't know.

DEPRESSING FUN TIME:

CALCULATE HOW MUCH OF THE PLANET YOU KNOW

How old are you?
How many new people do you meet a day?
How many new people do you see or hear a day? (Include TV,
radio and movies)
How many new musical artists do you listen to a year?
How many new authors do you read a year?
How many new newspapers do you read a year?
How many new TV shows do you watch a year?
Current number of people on the planet =

6,446,131, 400 (as of July 2005 so the number has changed)

Calculations:

Percent of humanity you personally know =
$100 \times A \times 365 \times B / Z$
Percent of humanity you have experienced =
$100 \times A \times 365 \times C / Z$
Percent of humanity that informs you about the world =
$(D + E + F + G) \times 100 \times A / Z$

What does all this mean? Not Much. You experience a tiny fraction of humanity. There are countless people you've yet to meet. Unfortunately, a recent poll showed that at least half of them don't like you because you're not just like them. On second thought, fuck 'em*. They don't care, so why should you. But we care about you! We always need sacrifices.

*Especially O.B. That's an order. He needs a female to do him right. Oh yeah!

B.BB.A

Greetings from the newest issue of *Cthulhu Sex* Magazine! We are thrilled to present the fine artists and writers that have been flattened between our pages. We delight in giving voice to new stories and poems from such a varied collection of voices and styles. As you peruse through the magazine, your eyes will be treated to the masterful works of our Centerfold artist, fantastic paintings and illustrations by other artists as well as an internationally respected photographer. We are flattered that all of these fine creations have chosen to be a part of *Cthulhu Sex* Magazine and hope you enjoy them as much as we do.

In an effort to better commune with our readers, we have created two new aspects to *Cthulhu Sex* Magazine. First, we have instituted *Cthulhu Sex* Street Teams. These teams are groups of fans that promote the magazine locally to earn free *Cthulhu Sex* stuff. The grassroots exposure that these teams bring is designed to spread the word of *Cthulhu Sex* to people with similar tastes, build camaraderie with likeminded people and earn free *Cthulhu Sex* collectibles not available anywhere else. For more information about *Cthulhu Sex* Street Teams, visit our Street Teams website at http://csmelite.cjb.net. Meet people interested in the same things you are and do some fun and unusual things.

Second, we have created an online forum, available through our website at www.cthulhusex.com/forums. This is a friendly place where people can discuss their likes, dislikes, interests and sacrifices, all in the comfort of their own home without the pressure of reading every little thing that everyone else writes. Delve in a little or a lot. You might even meet some of the Vomina.

We have recently expanded our tentacles even more throughout the world. Not only have we been introduced into the powerhouses that are Barnes and Noble and Hastings, we have been picked up by Borders and a number of smaller outlets. Despite the incredible expansion our tentacles bring, * we still keep a place in our heart for the local bookstores that took a chance on carrying us and carry us still, such special places as DreamHaven, Shocklines.com, Clark's World and ProjectPulp.com. If you don't see *Cthulhu Sex* Magazine on the shelf of your favorite bookstore, ask the manager to order it.†

On a more somber note, the destruction in the wake of the hurricanes in The Gulf was terrifying and terrible. We at *Cthulhu Sex* offer our deepest condolences for those who lost their homes, livelihoods, relatives and lives. A number of our contributors and friends are from New Orleans and the devastated areas, at least one of which spent the days after the flood cutting wood, clearing debris and rescuing his fellow New Orleanians. We encourage our readers to do what they can to help out and donate money, time, and/or support to the various charitable organizations that are helping people in the area.‡

Enjoy this issue. We enjoyed putting it together for you. Don't forget to visit our website for all the newest information and gossip about *Cthulhu Sex* Magazine.

*Ask Wanda about a particular feat of expansion.

†If they give you lip, you should get in the manager's face and give them what for!

‡A spokesman from Vampires Against War, www.vampiresagainstwar.com, said that the floodwaters have inundated the resting grounds of over 2000 zombies and vampires in New Orleans alone.

B.BB.B

Mmmishtttarrr Mmmorrrl,

He keeps me in this room and I can not get out. I don't know why. The temperature seems to fluctuate depending upon where I am. Odd since I don't seem to move much anymore. Rather, I prefer not to think of the way I am able to view the rest of this house as actual movement. Micholi—or is it Aelver? I have not decided yet—speaks to me constantly now. There are times, when Nelly Lynne is around, that he seems to speak with my mouth. Sometimes the visions of his followers performing the ritual pale into an orgiastic collage involving Micholi, Nelly Lynn, the dreamer, yourself, that horrid Mmmishtttarrr Bbbayrrr and the sisters. I thought being locked away with your creature, Mmmishtttarrr Bbbayrr was terror unimaginable. Little did I realize. Now I awake, my body shaking in uncontrollable ecstasy, with dreams that I dare not contemplate. The welts that appear to blossom into weeping sores at the first rays of light appear more regularly now. I try to slip into delirium as I move to leave once more. It is not so much movement as undulation or as if a throat were swallowing food. My limbs have lost what structure they once had, not to mention they move in accordance with a will not my own. It must be Aelver. I must believe that he is also responsible for the outward ripples of my torso's flesh.

Tekuli-kiri-ri ia ftagn. Darrrtchkt. Way vees carrresss usss weee rrreyesss and fffalll walltchkt-tchkt. Hunnngrrreee need drrintchkt sidhe. Emteee.

I can leave this room but when I do, I do not leave the house. I can not get out. I have been led through maze-like halls. At times, I can almost make myself believe I am walking. Then I notice how my limbs are dragging themselves through the corridors heaving my pregnant bulk along. The walls taste of long dead oceans as I touch them. There seems to be a seaweed substance hanging where the walls meet the ceiling. My welts seem to open and close like nightmarish mouths as decay-colored ichor drips upon them as we pass. My senses—nay, not mine, for I refuse to believe in the crawling horror I have become—tell me that the weed moves through the house like water. Somehow this keeps the house together. The temperature ranges from corridor to doorway almost as if the plant gives off an animalistic heat. It must be Nelly Lynne who guides me on this path. Micholi must be fed more than what I can provide him. This body will only last so long. We enter one room and they prepare me for the ritual. The familiar steps up, starts rubbing himself on me then there is an otherworldly symphonic buzzing and chittering, the familiar herald of the dreamer. He comes over and starts kissing me passionately. Before his face meets mine I notice the reason Aelver moved restlessly inside me. You, Mmmishtttarr Mmmorrrl and Mmmishtttarrr Bbbayrr have arrived with him and proceed to each side of me. They caress my breasts. Mmmishtttarr Bbbayrr's pincered hands tweaking the nipple. Nelly Lynne pushes her way in by inserting herself between the familiar and Micholi. The room is spinning. The familiar is pushing Nelly Lynne from behind as she caresses and kisses the welts on my abdomen. Waves of darkness flood over me as I hear my legs being spread and feet being licked.

Big blllatchkt playss othrsss mmmooov micholi. Mmmussst llleeev gggo away. Holllding playss too sssmmmal. Aelver pppooosh. Need tttowrrrs ssslleep. Call othrsss. Ka-thoo-lu ftagn ia ia tekiri tekuli.

They came to bathe me again, the sisters did. Then they lead me around the halls mumbling and chanting before certain rooms. We move through the house like the tide. Some of the rooms lead to others by impossibly surreal passages and staircases. Always the rooms seem colder, danker, mustier than the dripping living rot-colored corridors we pass through. They rub salve on my wounds and oil my body with something that smells like decaying fish. It produces a thrill through my body that sends my mind retching and screaming into the toilet. It brings back memories of the collage made real. I feel their crawling and licking all over my body. It feels like millions of tiny insects making my body their hive. I've been trying to call the dreamer so I can move to other places. But I'm afraid of who will appear with him this time. No answer anyway just a weird mix of distorted music and buzzing, which does nothing but further cement the memory of that nightmarish variant of the ritual. I turn my head and throw up convulsively. It does not choke me to death instead it just spills over me to mix with the welts and their ooze. They come to bathe me. I can not get out.

Inacca Pod

B.BB.C

Unconvinced of the veracity of my last enlightenment, I continued my pilgrimage into a wasteland of a great desert, one that I won't mention for fear of certain deities' retaliations. Once I had wandered quite far enough, I found there was literally nothing visible except the sky and the graceful ebb and flow of the shifting sands. The simplistic motion mesmerized me. For hours, I watched dunes rise and dunes raze, valleys form and valleys fill. And yet, I could find no solace in the constant flux, no spiritual soar, weft or weave. My heart longed for more than just this never-ending cycle of lift and fall, fall and lift.

So, I wandered a bit further until I spied a smudge of smoke on the horizon. Slowly trudging ever closer, I caught the barest glint of hewn stone in the distance. I sped up my gait, hoping to attain a touch of companionship on my trek.

As I approached, the glimmerings of stone revealed a row of majestic spires pointing towards the sky. The sight excited me with the hope against hope for a bit more than companionship, perhaps a drink of water to cool down the heat of the day. My step increased once more.

Once over the crest of a particularly large dune, I could see the turrets and walls of a whole glittering castle spread just beyond the next row of dunes. There were palm tree tops, explosions of rich fertile green, poking over the parapets. I could see birds of every conceivable color flitting from verdant tree to glowing tower and back again. Ladies in rich saris cooed from windows, waving veils and flowers.

I could not believe my good fortune. I have such pure tastes and pleasures that simply a drink of water and a few light words spoken with another person were the limits of my wants. To find that I might also sniff a flower and hear the gentle twitter of the birds while in the shade of a palm tree and surrounded by soft skin of ladies was beyond any expectation.

I traveled quickly down into the valley between my vantage point and the last row of dunes. My step was lighter than it had been in months. With joyous heart, I ascended to the top, basking in the glory that would be my reward for braving the wrath of the deities and the shifting sands of the desert. Strange that I hadn't noticed it before, but there was another row of smaller dunes between the castle and the row I had thought of as last. The castle seemed even smaller, more like a big house. The trees were actually large bushes and the birds were large scarabs.

There was a lady in one of the windows, wearing a rather normal sari and waving a cloth my way. She was smiling nicely at least. So, I stifled my disappointment and headed towards the house. I figured that I'd come all this way and I could still get a drink of water.

Cresting the last row of dunes, which only took a few steps, I was amazed to see that the large house was actually a shabby shack. There were a few gnats flying around and a few sickly-looking sticks poking up out of the ground. There were no spires, no windows, no women and no fountain.

Disillusioned but not defeated, I opened the door to look for the company I sought. Perhaps I could find someone to talk with. They might have answers, spiritual revelation or some tidbit of illumination to feed my hungry soul.

I found myself in a cave-like tent, close, hot, dark and claustrophobic. In the middle of the dirty floor was a mat encrusted with ages of dirt and offal. In the middle of the mat sat an elder, more wrinkled than a date in the sun.

"What is this place?" I asked him. "Where is the castle that I saw?"

"This is the façade of the castle you saw, the hollowed chamber of testing," he intoned with practiced ritual. "The rest of the castle is just beyond this chamber. You must prove yourself to enter."

"How do I prove myself?"

"You must pass my tests. To do that, you must go on a quest and bring me the items I seek."

"I see."

"Do you?" he snickered, unrolling a long scroll listing items.

"Yes," I answered.

I put one tentacle through each of his eyes and scooped out the parts of his brain that were easily freed from his head.

"I believe I have passed," I advised his disembodied brain as I assimilated it into my mental reservoir.

Whistling a happy tune, I proceeded onto the castle. There, I listened to the birds and sniffed the flowers in the shade of the palms. Then, I took the soft skin of the women and burned every building down. In all the excitement, I somehow didn't have a chance to get that drink of water.

B.BC.A

Greetings from *Cthulhu Sex* Magazine! This issue is cram-packed with deliciously adventurous writing and wicked tantalizing art. Within, you'll discover the wonderful thrill of inventive tales as well as amazing writings. You'll mangle your mind with the plethora of artwork from highly skilled artists of spookyART.com.

We are presenting so many amazing works that we had to sacrifice some people to make room for everything. Of course, we probably would have sacrificed them anyway. The gods need their due. We just opened up an intra-dimensional rift, pushed them in and trapped them between worlds. But, that's neither here nor there.

So, why did we have to go through such trials and tribulations to get this issue put together? Let me tell you a little story. Back when I was a youngling and *Cthulhu Sex* was barely a leaflet, I would search high and low for the proper artwork to put in its pages. The bar had been set high by the likes of our original artists. I with the help of the Motivatrix, scoured our resources to find the highest caliber of artists. Though rewarding, it was always a long and arduous process.

But then, we started noticing an order evolving from the chaos. As we contacted the most intriguing and delicious artists, a reoccurring theme became more and more apparent. At first, there were a few links, a few pathways that jumped from one artist to another. Then, the single connection became the many. Just as the numerous links became nearly too much to bear, the many connections converged on one another. The impossible became possible. The many became one. Almost unwittingly, we had stumbled on a nexus of dark artistic power. Its name was spookyART.com.

For months, we swam furtively in the dark waters of spookyART.com, wondering what was unfolding before our very eyes. As we watched, a handful of artists became many, growing almost exponentially outward to consume and ingest the most terrifying of the artistic tastes. It was fascinating to see and almost too much to behold.

One day, out of the blue, I was blindsided. There I was, minding my own business at a convention, going from table to table, chatting up prospective writers and trying to hide from the crazies that hound us, when I received a message from Father Baer. In his most human sounding voice, he announced that a man had invited me into the back room. It wasn't the first such proposition that I had received at a convention and probably won't be the last. However, after a bit of torture to coerce the truth from him, Father Baer informed me that the man referred to a human, as opposed to the euphemism I'd assumed it had been, and that the back room was actually the location of the convention art gallery.

I made my way through the throngs of people in the hall, composed of desperate fans clustered around famous writers or desperate writers clustered around famous editors (Yes, I too, was surprised that there are such things as famous editors), and into the back room, which turned out to be rather spacious and full of the most fascinating pieces. At the entrance, a person I didn't recognize, who was visually a bit on the intimidating side, welcomed me into the room and suggested I looked around. Only later would I find out that this purveyor of picturesque horror was none other than the man himself.

Not having the largest amount of time, as I had made it through the hallway throng just before the room was closing for the night, I gave the works the once over. I was thrilled with most of the work presented and decided I would track down this man, who I didn't know that I'd already met, and pick his brain. I spent the rest of the convention finding that I had arrived a few moments after he'd already left.

Later, back in the human-free safety of my home, I found a way to commune with this man. It turned out that his name was all over spookyart.com This ended up bringing his wonderful work into the pages of issue 22, volume 2. But, my memory of his convention art gallery coupled with the beauty of spooky-art.com made me covetous. My need to display wondrous artwork was more than any one man or woman could fulfill. I had to have them all, preferably all at once. When the idea to do a spookyart.com issue popped into my head, I had no other choice than to stand up in my pajamas and scream "spookyART.com! I choose you!

Little did I know that almost all of our artists would want to participate. At first, I was thrilled to receive such an overwhelming response. But then, reality set in. I would have to organize and lay out every single individual artist spread. The number of sacrifices needed to bring about such a feat was staggering. So, I did what any self-respecting magazine publisher/cult leader would do and called a temp agency. Once the warm bodies were brought in, everything was a party from there on out.

Enjoy this issue! That's an order!

B.BC.B

EDITORIAL NOTE ABOUT FOLLOWING LETTER:

This letter from Father Baer's translator, Wilhemina Cravesticon, was found on a valet staff's desk as the ME was removing the poor man's body. It was adhered to a jar that contained some foul looking gelatinous liquid. It seems that "Joe-Bob", that's what we'll call him for anonymity's sake, opened the jar, thinking it was pickled pigs' feet. Since two of the EMT's passed out when they arrived at the scene and the CDC cordoned off the sales area as a possible biohazard of alien delineation (whatever that term means), we assume that the jar was the cause of Joe-Bob's demise. I didn't notice anything out of the ordinary. But then again, I've had to work alongside Father Baer for quite some time, so I might have built up an immunity.

Mmmishmmmorlll,

It is not mine anymore, this bbbodddy. I can no longer trust them any more, the sssensesss. No more than I can trust those who imprisoned me here. They seem to leave me and explore the building themselves, the lllimbsss. Connected by an ever thinning strand of tissue, muscle, ligament or something I dare not try to define, I seem to see the places they visit as they crawl through this living monstrosity of a house. It is as if sections of my body share my awareness. It does not seem to be connected to this dank room, the connnsciousssnesss. The temperature seems to swim up and down the thermometer in time to the liquid movement of the rest of this horrid place. It is almost as if it is shambling from one location to another. I feel its movement through water, earth and air. I smell branches, bramble and bracken. I hear stones, seaweed—or is it lake or pond scum?—and soaring things, for they sound like nothing born of an earth, be it animal or human.

Waves caress my body. A drumbeat sounds. The march of numerous feet pounds through me. I sleep. Wake with words about time and pictures of loved ones in my head. Thousands of them. Giving themselves to me. How do I know this? How do I understand? How do I speak?

They have expanded from ripples to waves, the ssskinnnn unnndulllationnns. They seem to have stopped forming, the wellltsss. They are now growing towards each other as if they have a malevolent need to congregate. As they travel, their pustular flows, for that is the best way to describe the movement of the fluid that leaves them, blanket me, the ichorrr ssspewing lllesionsss. They leave a dark grey film on my body that mixes with my vomitus, their mmmouthsss. An act that continues with some regularity during my conscious moments of recall. Nelly Lynne and the sisters collect the festering fluid from my body and smear themselves with it while chanting some dark verminous insect language, which to my horror I can understand in my more lucid moments. The left over liquid, for there seems to be no end to this river of rot, they give to the familiars for their own purposes, ritualistic and otherwise. It seems that a sect has arisen that drinks the mixture only to vomit it over a partner in some sort of horrid disgusting act of foreplay. It seems they believe that in so doing they will imbue themselves with not only the presence of their savior but the ecstasy of his creation as well.

I need to escape. I must get out. This watery prison holds me. These elastic bonds have me chained to the wall of my cell. I kick and punch the walls. I bite and scratch. All damage seems to heal itself. Their does seem to be a slit above my head that keeps opening and closing like a mouth. Perhaps, if I work my way towards that. The voices I've heard, the visions I've seen seem to beckon from this direction.

It is now only an issue during the horrid few lucid moments I have, the pppainnn. I am in a constant state of delirium for which I pray, then immediately curse, the appearance of the dreamer. The crawling slime reminds me of what the ritual has become, a polluted bastardization of its original intent. At this point, I am not even sure if this communication will get to you in the form that I have set it down. I am surprised that my body has held out this long and terrified that my mind has. It left long ago it seems but perhaps not, for otherwise how would this letter come about, my willl. Aelver's pushing and kicking now seems to effect my whole being, both physical and mental, as a rock does to a body of water. With every thrust of a limb, Aelver sends waves through my body in a seemingly monstrous Morse code. Nelly Lynne spends most of her time speaking to my vagina, which feels as if it is answering her in some sputtering liquid language. The end is not far. Pray for me.

Podimecca

B.BC.C

How often does a publisher, editor or writer that you read tell you to destroy their work? I bet not many. Unless of course you're in the Vomina and have a working guanometer. If you don't happen to have the fifty million dollars a year it takes just to pay the dues of the Vomina, then this will be a treat. (If you do, talk to me later.)

Take this issue apart.

That's right. I told you to take this issue apart. Why on Cthulhu's slimy earth (over 70% water would definitely make it slimy, if not just plain-old sopping wet) would I want you to do that? Well, it's not because I want you to recycle the staples. Actually, I don't even know if staples can be recycled. But hey, if they can, it might not be such a bad idea. I hate getting staples stuck in my eyes. Don't ask.

Back on topic, there is a reason to take the issue apart. The reason is if you strike it down now, it will become even more powerful than you can possibly imagine. If you noticed, there are spookyART tabs throughout the issue. You probably thought that they were just for show. You probably thought I was just being a crazy publisher trying to be all spiffy by adding my own stylings to the already spiffy artist spreads. As true as that might be, that was not the original reason. All right, it might have been the original reason, but my creative team and I moved beyond that. Two people. That's my creative team. Get over it. We've made the tabs double sided, as you may have noticed. And if you're particularly astute, you might have noticed the complete folder in the centerfold. And if you're super-duper on top of things, you probably noticed that the pages with spooky-ART art only have spookyART art.

Okay. So, first take the issue apart slowly and carefully. If you've already shredded the issue to bits in a fit of destructive rage, then it's too late; you've ruined the whole thing. You should go to the bookstore and pick up a nice fresh copy. Of course, if you did, you probably wouldn't be able to read this then. So, if you can read this, unbend the staples so that they don't rip through the paper and fly off into someone's eye, which would most likely be mine no matter how far away you are. Then, carefully remove all the spreads from the staples, without ripping the spreads, and keep them in order. Go through the stack of spreads and separate the spookyART tabs from the rest of the magazine. Put the non-tabbed pages back on the staples in their correct order. The page numbers ought to help with that. Once all the non-tabbed pages are on the staples, bend the staples back down to reserve the contents for later use.

Take the tabbed pages and separate out the complete folder in the centerfold from the rest of the pages. Carefully cut the remaining tabbed pages in half along the perforated middle line. Fold the centerfold folder along the perforation and place the now separated tabs in the centerfold "folder" you have created. You will have twenty-six single-page "tabs" in the centerfold "folder", all of which Is collector's memorabilia.

My favorite thing to do with this new folder is to file it away in a filing cabinet at some fairly public area of a company or business. * That way, someone will find it sometime later, perhaps even years, and have no idea how it got there or what it is. Then, they'll take it home and do things with it in the closet so their spouse doesn't catch on. The rest of it is great to leave on a seat in a restaurant, church, bus or subway. † That way, someone can enjoy it while relaxing and pretending to listen or something.

So, there you have the *Cthulhu Sex* Magazine-spookyART. com Artist Tabbed Folder of Doom. ‡ We here at *Cthulhu Sex* Magazine hope that you enjoy your tabbed folder and find many useful and entertaining uses for it. This is sure to be a valuable commodity you'll want to pass down to your children and your children's children and whoever's left after they all go insane.

Be sure to join us for our next issue. It will be filled with new deliciously disturbing writing and artwork. I've already had to get rid of the bodies of a few of our sales staff who had accidentally caught a glimpse of the lineup and dropped dead of aneurisms. Don't worry, though. I'm pretty sure you'll be fine. But, I can't make any promises.

Tentacles,

St. Michael Amorel

*Do not actually leave in a filing cabinet or in a business area. Such actions are probably illegal and *Cthulhu Sex* Magazine claims no responsibility if this warning isn't heeded.

†Don't do this either. Such actions possibly constitute littering or other illegal activity and *Cthulhu Sex* Magazine claims no responsibility if this warning isn't heeded.

‡Please use responsibly. Not intended for minors or pregnant woman using large highway equipment. *Cthulhu Sex* Magazine claims no responsibility for any staple-involved or paper-involved accident or fatality due to the destruction or taking apart of this or any other *Cthulhu Sex* Magazine issue.

B.BD.A

Greetings and welcome to the newest issue of *Cthulhu Sex Magazine*! You hold, in your hand, not only our fine offering of excellent writers, poets and artists, but a secret, a horribly indescribable, unnamable secret.

Before I get too far into that, let me just say that we are pleased to offer the glorious cavalcade of writers, artists and poets that we are bringing to you, our dear reader. I can honestly say that I've never met all but one of them. They've been creative, professional and wonderful to work with, but I've never actually met them. It strikes me as odd that someone can have the thrilling experience of putting together an entertaining magazine filled with delightful works by amazing individuals, and not meet them. What a wonderful age we live in where we can do such a thing.

So, back to the horribly indescribable, unnamable secret. It is a conundrum wrapped around the darkest reaches between the words. Its name cannot be spoken aloud and must be conceived in the silence that surrounds a gentle morning dark before the dawn, that moment before the birds sound their heart- warming chirps but after the rustle of little creatures in the cupboards. It is in that moment that one can discern the basic inkling of…

Wait a minute. Let me go back to something. I've never met over ninety percent of our contributors. Doesn't that strike you as strange? It is kind of surreal to me. I mean, I really have no idea who these people are. They could be just about anyone. I know where they live and that they have email and they sign contracts, but really, I know almost nothing about them as people. I guess it isn't an issue. It's just a little strange to me.

So, the secret: If you look deep into the text of each story, paying particular attention to the anomalies and the areas they point to, you will be able to glean an important message about the universe at large. This indescribable understanding will fill you with a particular knowledge, lost deep among the ages of old. With the right tools, the Gematria and Tao numerology equations among others, you can pick up on the finer points of this knowledge and translate it into a usable and definably visceral experience. In tandem with the book...

Okay, now this is just bugging me. It's just so *bizarre* that there are so many people that fill these pages that could be just anyone. I've had the pleasure of meeting some of them. They are indomitable, entertaining, twisted, fanciful and even expressed whisky wantonness. So that makes it closer to seventy percent that I've never met before. But that's still a huge number of people I've never physically met. Doesn't that strike you as odd? No? Well, it must just be me.

Right, the secret. The ones who solve this secret will gain the power of clear sight, the ability to see that which is true and that which is false. They will be heralded as the masters of their domain and have power beyond their wildest dreams. But the course is long and treacherous, filled with pitfalls and red herrings. With faith and the skills granted to you by your mystical studies, you will succeed and learn the unnamable, horribly indescribable secret. Only the brightest and the best will learn of the secret. Many will fail. Do you have the skills to...

Seventy percent! That's like going to a family reunion at an invisibility convention. I mean, come on now. Have we really come so far as to have the ability to work, play and even have relationships with people we've never met? I'm sure I've met thousands of people online and through mail correspondence and not one of them can bring me chicken soup when I've got a cold (not that I ever really get sick, being the Avatar of Cthulhu). Well, I guess they could get it delivered to my house. And I do have my lover and my minions to take care of me if I needed it. You only need one person who cares, right? Maybe it isn't really that bad of a thing after all. At least, people can share ideas and thrive over great distances. Isn't that what life's about?

Anyway, enjoy the issue and find the secret.

B.BD.B

This letter from Father Baer's translator, Wilhemina Cravesticon, was delivered attached to a book and accompanied by an envelope containing a letter of translation of the first letter by a translator by the name of Nelly Lynne Glennticus. The Roman Text denotes Ms. Cravesticon's letter and the *Italic Text* denotes Ms. Glennticus' translation. It seems that the body of Wilhemina Cravesticon was quarantined and that all traces of her remnants were to be kept by various governmental agencies. Little could we know that the quarantine included all her writings so they are deemed "Contagious" and "Dangerous" by those same agencies. Unfortunately for them, this issue was already at the press and couldn't be pulled.

Mmmishugh ugh ughmmmowrlll,

Aaagh bbbookkk. Heeesss kkkommming, mmmaii bbbay-bbbai. Thththay tttawkkk aaabowttt aaagh bbbookkk. Aelver's kkkommming. Tttaiieekkk kkkaiieerrr uhf mmmaii bbbaybb-bai. Thththay wwwill mmmaykkk meee aaagh bbbookkk. Nelly Lynne pppruhmmmisss mmmeee. Dddoannnttt lllettt hisss faththtthrrr nnneeerrr. Mmmaii bbbuhdddeeesss rrripppinguh tttooo shshshrrredddsss. Mmmaii lllimmmsss llleeefffinguh mmmeee.

I ride the waves toward the light. The closer I get the more openings I see. The sliver of light I noticed in front of me gradually becomes wider. I noticed more shafts of light bathing me in liquid nourishment from above. I must release myself from the shackles that hold me here. The percussive music that lulled me to sleep now mixes with an orchestra of whispers welcoming me home. I can feel their warmth enveloping me, their arms reaching out to me. I am also afraid. I know not how I am able to fully understand or even form these thoughts. I want to sleep until it is all over. Perhaps, if I swim towards the light and speak to them, they will let me sleep forever in this beautiful bed of molten basalt.

Wwwoonnsss ssspoooinguh iiikorrr. Fffloainguh dddownnn bbbuhdddeee. Sssorsss fffaiinnndinguh eeech uhth- thther. Mmmaii bbbaybbbaii mmmuhssstt nnnuhttt bbbeee bbboarnnn. Chchchaiilldd mmmuhssstt dddaiii bbbeefuhrrr hisss faththtthrrr nnnoasss. Bbbuhdddeee kkkraaakkkinguh oapppennn. Lllimmmsss rrreetuhrninguh tttooo mmmeee, ssskraatchchchinguh mmmeee oapppennn mmmaykkinguh pppayjess uhfff mmmeee. Wwwelllttss gggaiidddinguh bbbuhrnninguh fffloass fffrrruhmmm sssorsss uhnnnddd wwwoonnsss tttooo sssisssttrrrsss. NellyLynne kkkilll Aelver. Kkkaaalll hisss faththththr, kkkaaalll Mmmishshshttaarrr Bbbbayrrr.

It is an effort to move forward. I push through the liquid and kick with my legs. My bonds still hold me. They seem to stretch as I move forward. The whispers are louder now, more like chanting and screaming. At times, it seems to come from this form I inhabit as I push onward. I give one last attempt to break free. I push and kick forward with all eight? of my limbs. The prison breaks open. The light that was so warming seems cold now. The air tastes so soft and warm. A name slips into my mind, Nelly Lynne.

NelleeLynne wuh uh uhll kaaaghtchchch mmmaiiee bbbaaaghbaiiee. Nuh uh uh nnnowowught sssttaaaghinguh, hisss luh uh uhmms mmmoowvinguh nuh uh uh owowught. Mmmaiiee bbbuh uh uhddee mmmooowvs eeechchch tai- ieemmm heee swuh nuh uh uhms thththrooow mmmeee. Dddooow nuh uh uhowt gggifff mmmeee tttooow himmm. Buh uh uhrnnn thththeeesss pppaaaghjesss. Ifff nuh uhow uht, thththaaaghrrr wuh uh uhlll beee mowuh uh uhrr. Aaaggghhh. Ia Ia Ftagn Oh My Beautiful Aelver…

Note Bene: Mr. Morel, no doubt you know of my existence. Please be assured and convey these thoughts as well to Mr. Baer that the child will be cared for. He will be raised according to our ways and he will rise to be our savior. Please accept this token of our fealty to the Elder Gods as well as my secretions which bind this note to the book as its lock and key. Mr. Baer will know how to open it but perhaps you are in possession of the same fell knowledge. The translations of the blessed event will be forthcoming. For now, please accept this poor explication. The second and fourth paragraph are no doubt the child's attempts at communicating with his father. I can only assume that this has been ongoing since his birth. The first, third and fifth paragraphs were Wilhemina Rebecca Cravesticon's last words as she was giving birth translated below:

1. Mr. Morel,

A book. He's coming, my baby. They talk about a book. Aelver's coming. Take care of my baby. They will make me a book. Nelly Lynne promise me. Don't let his father near. My body's ripping to shreds. My limbs leaving me.

3. Wounds spewing ichor. Flowing down body. Sores finding each other. My baby must not be born. Child must die before his father knows. Body cracking open. Limbs returning to me, scratching me open, making pages of me. Welts guiding burning flows from sores and wounds to Sisters. Nelly Lynne kill Aelver. Call his father. Call. Mr. Baer.

5. Nelly Lynne will catch my baby. Not staying, his limbs moving naught. My body moves each time he swims through me. Do not give me to Him. Burn these pages. If not, there will be more. Aaaggghhh! Ia! Ia!! Ftagn! Oh, My Beautiful Aelver...
Please note that we are still transcribing. So, an official translation will be forthcoming. Please know that I am open to any suggestions you and Mr. Baer have about the care and upbringing of our new Lord.

I remain your complete and obedient servant,
Nelly Lynne Glennticus

B.BO.C

A wise being once said that one could never return to their childhood. Being timeless, existing since the dawn of time, I can't say I really understand the meaning in it. But recently, I have found a couple of adequate situations that bring this age-old adage to mind.

The first is in the occurrence of movies. I have very fond memories of a number of movies from the past. There was one in particular that I remember that the children of a family I stayed with watched over and over again. It was a delightful little horror movie that made them squeal with joy and horror. It was a pleasurable little ditty named *Watcher in the Woods*. I recently happened to see it again. Perhaps it was because I no longer had the eyes of the children to see it through or perhaps because of the countless movies I have seen since, but I found myself only mildly amused by it. The thrill and the joy had been diminished by the passage of time. The fond memories of it were greater in scale than the actuality of reliving the event.

An even better example would be my enthrallment with video games. First off, let me defend one of my favorite pastimes by stating that I thoroughly enjoy the human ability to create stories and invent alternate realities, of which the video game is one of the fastest growing mediums for relating a complicated and emotionally charged plot, steeped in character development and fantastic vision. I have extremely fond memories of the first video game I ever purchased, *Ultima III*. I scuttled home to unwrap the precious box with the beautiful cover of a demon standing over a delta of lava, which later adorned my wall for many a year. I remember spending hours and hours moving little groups of glowing pixels around other little pixels. My joy was brightly lit by the gentle glow of my old Commodore 64 screen. A bit ago, I found an emulator to run *Ultima III* on my Windows machine. Boy, I had no patience for moving little groups of glowing pixels around other little pixels. My dissatisfaction is most likely because of the almost real-life visuals of video games that I play now and their deeply moving plots. It amazes me to think how far a medium can progress in so short a time. Perhaps the best example would be religious fanaticism. The first time I was surrounded by acolytes, all three of who were chanting hymns to me and calling upon me to grant their wishes, I was floored, literally floored. I could barely contain myself as I looked over the simple bowl of blood and fruit they had placed before me in offering. It was at that moment I realized that this fledgling race of simians were of actual use and had the ability to acquire, utilize and offer up resources. That realization allowed me the tools to spread forth, grow and gorge myself on the spiritual activities of these monkeys. I sometimes even can't believe how excited I was at that moment. In my fervor, only one of the humans survived to tell the tale. But since that moment, it has been nothing but hard work to reap the rewards. A simple bowl of blood and fruit is a nice memento now, but not nearly enough to satiate my gluttonous need.

But after traveling down this particular memory lane, I've reconsidered my initial supposition. The technologies for movies and videogames have brought a new thrill that the earlier ones could not have begun to touch. The offerings that grace my altars now are infinitely more rewarding than the kitschy and humble snacks I once received. It's good to occasionally visit those experiences and memories, but I look forward to braving the future, gaining even greater offerings and seeing just how far these monkeys will take their technology. I think that's their best chance at success because they're pretty much mucking everything else they try. That or give me more offerings. Yeah, they should just give me more stuff.

Tentacles,

St. Michael Amorel

B.BE.A

Greetings and welcome to the newest issue of *Cthulhu Sex* Magazine, jam-packed with artwork and writing. We are particularly proud of the stylish cover art. Within this provocative and wondrous issue, you'll find fanciful creations by masterful artists. You'll also find a delightful centerfold that shows off the work of an inventive model. Her spread is the first time we've dedicated a section to exhibiting a model's work. Ooooo... It's so rare to have our publishing virginity taken by anything anymore. Mmmmm... That's the way we like it!

In other devirginizing news, we have recently signed up for a MySpace account. The famed lead of *I, Parasite* created a profile for *Cthulhu Sex* Magazine (www.myspace.com/cthulhu_sex) and dragged me kicking and screaming into the swirling vortex that is MySpace. Funny thing though, once we were there, it was hard to leave. It was almost as if the Internet had decided it was tired of being used by everyone whenever they felt like it and then thrown away like a dirty whore. In retaliation, the Internet decided to spin a world wide web to ensnare hapless users. It coated its trap's easy-to-set-up web pages with sweet siren songs of free-flowing friendship, soothing companionship and desirability, all under a personable façade by the name of "Tom."

Quickly, I fell into the irresistibly tantalizing trap. Within minutes, we had acquired a good handful of "friends", particularly with the aforementioned band leader's suggestions. The first thing I did was stick out my neck and check various links to see who these new friends were. That was when the noose tightened around my neck and I was caught fast. On each friend's page was a list of that friend's friends. A simple click and I was in a new realm of that friend's friend's friends. Not only was I able to fly through dozens of interesting people at the speed of a click converted into an electric call for the next, I was also capable of stopping and scanning tons of minutia for each of these individuals. Beyond that, there were millions upon millions of individuals I could seek out and commune with. The potential for acquiring rabid followers was almost too much to bear.

After countless hours of clicking through these soon-to-be-but-not-quite-yet-converted followers, I realized that though various sightings of cheesecake pseudo-porn might be arousing, simply looking at the pages of future cultists without some form of contact would not yield me the efforts that I wished. Therefore, I returned to the CSM profile, again so wonderfully created by the band leader, and was surprised by what awaited me there. My oh-so-happy-to-please-me profile homepage told me that we already had friend requests waiting and even comments and messages. In a few short hours, we had more friends than His tentacles (on his face, you pervert). Within a few days, we had more friends on our MySpace page than we did on our forum. Seemed that more people wanted to be our friends than actually wanted to talk to us. Hmmm... there's something important in that statement that I'll have to look into late....

Anyhoo, I discovered the pleasures of blogging for Cthulhu, putting up "add" graphics and thanking others for their friendship. Without evening knowing it, days had passed by me. Things that needed to get done, weren't. Sacrifices were left unsacrificed. Nightmares were left unnightmared. I was at a loss to explain it. It was worse than when I found that web site that shows the "live" feed from the NASA probe thingy. I spent quite a number of hours on that one, trying to see if they could see me from space or not.

After that---the missing days, not the NASA probe thingy---I instituted a moderation clause in my personal MySpace code. Like all good addictions, it should be moderated, lest the addiction stop me from my other additions (such as crazy circus sex with my Naughty Monkey (Not that MySpace compares to my Naughty Monkey. It's just an example.)) Therefore, my MySpace time has been restricted to accepting followers….er, friends and examining their pages only, not spending time sifting through the delightfully tangled web that is MySpace. Unless I do. Then, I will. So there.

For those of you who aren't on Myspace, don't own a computer or don't visit the web and are wondering why I'm dedicating so much valuable page space to this subject, I have two words for you: Come on!

So, without any more ado, we have a great issue for you.

B.BE.B

After an unprecedented delay, we received this addendum that I can only take as a warning, which unfortunately did not make it into the issue in which the matter was actually published. Our regrets to the readers who passed on after reading the previously printed piece. I have personally experienced the most annoying side effect of having interns and people of no particular interest appear on my desk out of a dimensional vortex. In addition, the peculiar transition in which Mr. Baer has found himself after receiving the books is quite unhelpful when it comes to retaining new sales or PR staff. If anyone has any suggestions on how to reverse the process or at least fit his transmogrification into a viable business model, please contact us through the address presented below.

Addendum to note of 3/13/06 by these spatiotemporal coordinates

From Nelly Lynne Glennticus to Michael Morel

I have committed the pieces of parchment from the book to further testing. It is still unclear to me as to how it arrived at your offices. Indeed, though I know I wrote a letter to you in regards to it, I have no clear memory of its content. It seems that the Great Tentacled One works in mysterious ways. From the little bit I do remember of the book's contents, our Savior will be bringing about His paradise on this world. I long to see R'yleh rise from the depths once more along with our Lord Cthulhu. This can only herald the beginning of a second golden age for The Old Ones. But I digress...

We now know conclusively that the book is made from Ms. Cravesticon. Her body fluids were used to both ink and bind the book. Her tendons were used to further bind the pages of the book together in case either the fluids or the spell we placed upon it failed in some manner. Interestingly enough, after this process, her body seems to exhibit some unique properties heretofore only thought to be relegated to the ones such as the dreamer. I am, of course, referring to the ability of interdimensional travel. Thankfully it cannot do this on its own. For if it could I would believe that we would be more undone than if you do not follow the warning that follows later in this report. It needs to come into contact with one of our brethren. The familiars cannot effect it. Once contact is made, it not only infuses our brother or sister with knowledge of our Savior but also sacred information not known to any but the Progenitors. I believe this includes yourself, Mr. Baer and the dreamer among others. I'm sure that I do not have to remind you that our various modes of travel are located within this information. We postulate that either the dreamer had relations with Ms. Cravesticon or he altered her body in some manner. This means that he is suspect to our cause. Due to these conclusions, we recommend that you not place the book near Mr. Baer. It is very likely that the knowledge of someone else having carnal relations in a non-ritualistic manner with the woman he believes to be his wife will incite his wrath. In his fury, we expect he will use the dimensional knowledge to thwart our plans for this world. He will escape your confinement and, we suspect, try to turn our servants against the dreamer. Once he has convinced them that he is their only chance of freedom, I am afraid that we will be at their mercy. Their maddening discordant piping no longer playing our tune.

Once again, I must reiterate the importance of not having the book touch Mr. Baer. In order for the Savior to fulfill the destiny that is written, he must not be exposed to his father at this time. We cannot afford another schism in the order. I will not have us be cast back into the depths. I will not have us scattered throughout the dimensions again like so much planar flotsam.

We will be reconstituted in our proper places once again. I will see the Dark City rise up from the waves in all its glory with the gelatinous music of madness ringing in my ears. In order to ensure that you only will receive this, I have sealed it with my secretions as I was pleasuring myself. In this manner, I am assured that only one of the Progenitors will be able to open it and decipher the message. Please know that I am also sending it via the dreamer. Know that if you do not receive it, or if it is tampered with in any way, the dreamer has undone us. You must take measures against him and destroy Mr. Baer before he leaves the containment area you have made his home.

B.BE.C

It often amazes me how convoluted a process can become. In particular, some things are so simple at the outset, and then through a process of supposedly necessary growth and expansion, they become ever more dense and impractical. Most grow until they either implode under their own preposterous weight or suffer a slow death as they become anachronous. But some, the ones that are most interesting to me, thrive on the hypocrisy of their existence---too large to support all their parts, yet too entrenched to die.

While I was in Washington DC, partially for pleasure and partially for business, I came across one of these entities. Before anyone goes jumping down my throat for making allusions to the US Government, the Republican Party, the Democratic Party, the FBI, the CIA or any other such nonsense, as apropos as such an allusion might be, let me explain the situation. I'm sure that whatever archaic and nihilistic aspects one could attribute to these groups are mere shadows of the horror that is this specific entity I discovered.

So, there I was driving brazenly from New York to Washington DC with a carload of passengers. The drive started out just fine, particularly in consideration to speed. The car rocketed along at a velocity best not written down to reduce any repercussions. I knew basically what to expect as I had driven most of this route previously on a trip to Baltimore for a convention. For anyone not familiar with this drive, it is generally made on toll highways that consist of multiple lanes, impenetrable walls of green on both sides and various mini-city rest stops between off ramps. This constant blur of tree, pavement and sky continues for hundreds of miles, broken only by the occasional toll plazas and bridges.

After numerous hours of this mind-numbing tedium, something began to become apparent. After we passed Baltimore, the rapidity to which we had grown accustomed was slowly evaporating. Vehicles that had blithely chugged along the highway with us previously were caught in spontaneous bouts of sluggishness, reducing speed to almost a crawl. When we approached the terminus of these bouts, there was no readily apparent reason for the reduction, no accident, no speed trap, no construction, nothing. It was almost as if the vehicles were hesitating, as if they were afraid of something up ahead.

Then without warning, we exited a tunnel and were in the heart of Washington DC. The city is truly amazing, grand plazas leading to cyclopean buildings reminiscent of the great R'lyeh herself. Unfortunately, I didn't have time to revel in the beauty as the traffic suddenly sped up and scattered along an almost infinite number of exits, overpasses, merges and underpasses, all strung together in some mind bending alternate geometry. Believe me, I'm used to angles meeting in copiously surrealistic irreverence for Euclidean geometry, but this was ridiculous. There were exits off of exits that merged onto overpasses that were exits to underpasses with rules that defied any logic and signs telling of where one had been instead of where one was going.

In this scintillating entropy and chaos, we made one fatal mistake; we took a wrong turn. Now wrong turns are one of my specialties. I find them immensely productive for procuring heretofore undiscovered provisions and eluding potentially annoying pursuit. If I ever decided to undertake the task of driving in that city, I will never, ever make a wrong turn for the simple fact that it took me two and some hours to move the total distance of 10 miles along a road with no viable exits. And by viable, I mean exits that don't say things like "NSA personnel only," "Have ID ready for guards at gate" and "Abandon all hope..."

It was during this time, specifically when we were parked on the road for twenty minutes, that I realized what the problem was. While sitting there and suffering from dehydration, ineffectual rage and exhaustion from driving over eight hours and ending up in these mind-numbing geometries, I entered an almost spiritual trance. It was there I was visited by the entity, the chilling, gut-wrenching horror. Due to my status, it sought me as a prize, to laugh at my plight and crush my hopes for succor.

But unbeknownst to it or even to my conscious self, its very presence offered me focus to attach my rage, rendering it un-ineffectual and therefore effectual. I sent wave after wave of burning anger and white-hot hate along its pathways in an attempt to burn it to its center and eradicate its mind. My screams of anger were matched only by its screams of anguish. With an audible popping, I heard its attempted stranglehold relinquish. A police car pulled almost painfully through the parking lot on the road. Within moments, the traffic resumed a tolerable speed.

But it was only after we arrived at our destination, no one need know where it was or why we were there, that the full implication of what I tussled with struck me. I could hear the entity, the thing that I had burned with my sheer force of hate, laughing in the distant corners of my dreams. I saw it spread out before me, wrapped along those exits on exits and under-passes to overpasses. The very incoherent realities the roadways were built on called it from its own realm and trapped it there. It thrived on lies and suffering and could not be destroyed. It would continue to live and grow for it clogged the heart, veins and arteries of DC. It would continue to cause everything and everyone within its grasp to slow and retard. The highways of DC are possessed.

Tentacles,

St. Michael Amorel

PART THE THIRD,
THIRTEENTH SECTION, FIRST

Greetings and welcome to *Cthulhu Sex* Magazine. If you have read *Cthulhu Sex* before, you might have picked it up because of its amazing cover (unless you or your friend contributed or you wanted to submit to us). If this is the first time you've read *Cthulhu Sex*, thanks for trying us out. Either way, take a moment and revel in the stark simplicity of this issue's cover. For those of you who despise the stark cover, this issue in particular is packed with tons of tantalizing art, including pieces from two skilled artists. All this talk of art is not meant to take away any from the thrilling authors who also grace our pages. Take a spin through and you'll see that we have a veritable cornucopia of intriguing and entertaining works of both literary and artistic merit.

Yes…A much more palatable way to describe the contents. That ought to placate the zealots and inquisitors so that they'll stop reading the intro and flip through the magazine. Oh yes, they'll flip through the pages and one of the wondrous pieces of art will surely catch their eye. As they're enjoying it, thinking to themselves this particular piece is really quite good, they'll begin to wonder about the writing. Then, they'll start to read and then BAMN! We'll have 'em trapped, their guarded ignorance blown like an altar boy on spring break in Amsterdam. After that, we can quickly drain their precious ethers and ichors. Their lifeless husks will be playgrounds for our countless spawn! But for now, let them think everything is all right. We will bide our time and spring when the moment is right. Not now, but soon.

For those of you stalwart readers who are still with us, I wanted to mention a new sect of the Vomina* I recently came across. They're akin to autoerotics in that they prefer to practice their Vominal rituals in a type of solitude. (You'll see what I mean by "type" in a bit, patience is a virtue (and to the blindly faithful, so is being able to stomach overwhelming amounts of hypocrisy (gotta get me some of those blindly faithful)).) I had heard whispered references to a subgroup of Vomina called "Carne Valle" by other Vomina.

In an effort to follow the trail of the Carne Valle, I accompanied a particular news personality that has an inside track at a well-known house in DC. He, for lack of a better name, we will call Mr. Raine. Mr. Raine told me he could introduce me to a member of that household that was a participating Carne Valle. Of course, to the outside world, Mr. Raine would disavow all knowledge of Carne Valle, Vomina, and in particular, me. Mr. Raine introduced me to this member of the house, who we shall call Mr. Great Old One Whose Name Shall Not Be Spoken, or That Guy for short. That Guy invited me to his nightly ritual after a few moments of conversation and secret handshakes. Mr. Raine was duly impressed and took his leave to kowtow before the president of the Vomina. That evening, we met at an old brick house at the edge of a cemetery of which I didn't know the name. That Guy blindfolded me and took me down into the cellar. After traversing through myriad mazelike passages and a bazillion spider webs, That Guy lead me up into some cryptlike room, which considering where we were and what followed, it most likely was. That Guy sidled up to a crate, probably a cheap coffin in retrospect, and opened it. He gingerly took out a corpse and bent it over his knee. He chowed down the requisite Vomina herbs and spewed them into the corpse's waiting anus. He then produced a small flask of viscous red liquid, that from my previous experience, I think was blood. After pouring the liquid into the proffered anus, he shook the corpse, informing me that the saliva and corpse flesh commingled with the Vomina herbs to produce a particularly potent mixture he liked to call "Necrophoric". He offered me a taste, which I politely declined. He shrugged and positioned a number of other corpses so that their various orifices pointed outward. He pulled out a length of transparent tubing and placed one opening in his corpse's bum and the other in his own. Obviously, the dead body couldn't participate in the act of regurgitation so That Guy figured out a way to achieve the requisite force needed to inject the Necrophoric into his awaiting rectum. He suggested I wait in the tunnels while he completed his rite. I watched him jump up and down on the corpse's body to force the thick Necrophoric up the tube before I obliged him. Huddled within the dark passage, I heard him fervently availing himself to the corpses he had positioned for such a purpose. I had to wait nigh on seven hours before he returned to me in a semblance of sanity. Again, donning the blindfold, we returned through the twisting tunnels. He explained that his Necrophoric vison had directed the house for quite a while and his newest would be no different. Upon returning to the place from which we started our trek, the blindfold was removed, my sight restored and That Guy began texting his minions. The next day, a house member was forced to retire from his duties followed by a long string of other house members and servants. I don't know which of their number were Vomina or Carne Valle, but I do know that the house decay was definitely a result of their influence.

Tentacles,

St. Michael Amorel

PART THE THIRD, THIRTEENTH SECTION, SECOND

EDITORIAL NOTE ABOUT FOLLOWING LETTER:

The following letter was provided after the remains, or what have been identified as remains, of Father Baer had been found. This is not to say that you may or may not come across Father Baer now or later. It is just to give some background as to why it says what it says.

It is with deep regret that the county seat of Pasquamaltos, Washington informs you that Father Baer is dead. The remains of an individual with the identification of Father Baer and an envelope bearing this address as his own has been found in the woods outside of town. In the envelope was a letter requesting that all remains be transported to a St. Michael at this address. (see attached form 36-79H001 and plastic bag)

We hope that this news brings you piece of mind. May the Lord keep you and watch over Mr. Baer's soul. Please pass our condolences on to his family and his loved ones.

Sincerely,

Jane Biggum Hicksucker
The Pasquamaltos County Clerk

EDITORIAL NOTE ABOUT FOLLOWING LETTER:

The following letter was found on the desk of one Mable Oprajar, CSM PR employee 800945 while police were attempting to enter the building and search said desk. Thankfully they didn't find it and could therefore not start a wrongful death suit against us.

To Mother Oprajar:

I love you. You are receiving this because I have been murdered. I would send this to Father too, but you know how angry he gets. Do not be sad about this. I knew it might happen.

If you look under the second floorboard in my bedroom, you will find three DVDs. DO NOT WATCH THEM!!! These must be turned over to the P7NSA in Washington, DC as soon as possible. I made them while I was following the man who murdered me. They were very hard to come by and they are very bloody and ugly. I have nightmares about them. I wouldn't want you to see them. At least I can stop that from happening to you.

Do not be sad. I am in a better place now. He cannot hurt me anymore.

I love you,

Mable

EDITORIAL NOTE ABOUT PREVIOUS LETTER:

The room mentioned was searched and the DVDs retrieved.

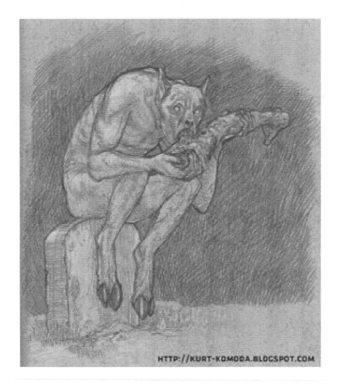

HTTP://KURT-KOMODA.BLOGSPOT.COM

This image was reconstructed by an artist. It was a makeshift drawing on the wall of the room mentioned above. The reddish background was in fact blood on the wall.

EDITORIAL NOTE ABOUT FOLLOWING LETTER:

The following letter appeared on the monitor of Aleister Crowley, Executive Assistant to Michael Amorel. It wasn't even on.

They think they have won this time. They have no idea what sort of vortex they have opened. They have struck me down and I have become even more powerful then they can ever possibly imagine.

I must apologize for not being able to greet you in person, my dear St. Michael. That damnable she-beast who shan't be named had a fairly powerful family. When their prayer to their bleeding lord went unheeded, probably because they sleep with their daughters, they deemed it necessary to try burning me at the stake. Considering how well that went when we tried it at the company Fourth of July picnic, I wasn't really worried about it. Then one of them got the bright idea to chant the Ht'Yoi'Thigot. I have no idea how one of those natural-born people could pronounce such a thing, let alone had the intellectual capacity to understand the ramifications of the situation enough to realize that it would be an applicable use of such an archaic text.

Needless to say, things didn't go quite as planned. The explosion flattened the first few rows of the fanatics. I don't know if it caught the bunghole responsible for it, but it did launch enough of me out of the fire to allow something of my physical form to continue on. However, it will take me a long time to rejuvenate myself. On the other hand, I now have the added side benefit of being able to enter other people's minds at will and use them like puppets.

Michael, feed me more of the she-beast's family and I will unfailing serve your greater need.

PART THE THIRD
THIRTEENTH SECTION, THIRD

Every once in a while, I get hit with one of those moments where I realize just how bizarre and outrageous the rest of the populous seem to find the people I choose to keep around me. The most recent occurrence of this came as I was talking to a complete stranger at one of those cafes that I love to frequent (after all, who doesn't enjoy indulging daily in their reality altering substance of choice). This stranger started up a conversation by asking about something I had been mumbling to myself. Well, maybe mumbling is a bit inaccurate; it would be more descriptive to call the softly-lilting sing-song a type of chanting. This particular oralization happened to focus on the body parts of a friend of mine. The stranger remarked that I seemed awfully fixated on my friend's legs. I replied that if he happened to have been lucky enough to have glimpsed the sixteen pairs in the basement, he too would understand my fascination. The gentleman, and I call him such in the lightest of manners, hesitated the briefest of moments before inquiring if my friend happened to be a sculptor or perhaps an insect or some such. I informed him that my friend was not a sculptor, simply a collector of other people's appendages. With a laugh, the stranger intimated that my statement was somehow intended to be humorous, though I have no idea why he would think such a thing as I had given him no indication that he should. I let him know as much by detailing my friend's most recent conquest, which involved sneaking into a well-to-do person's home and making off with a shiny pair of pale and hairy legs that were only marginally on the thin side. The stranger gave me a tight smile and turned away. At that reaction, I wasn't sure if my recitation of my friend's actions had answered the stranger's initial question to his satisfaction or not. I assumed it had and kept silent.

As we were standing in line at the time and he was in front of me, he was served first. At the counter, he started flirting with the underage girl manning the register. As part of his predatory offensive, he attempted to ostracize me and make a connection with her by mimicking what I had just said to him, but using what sounded like a fairly sarcastic tone instead of my informative one. To my surprise, she nervously laughed along with his pointed jibes as she rung up his drink and swiped his credit card. She seemed to find particularly hilarious the fact that I was leaking saltwater from my pores in an effort to keep my skin soft, supple and hydrated. Not that I suffer from dry skin, mind you. It is simply a thing I do to keep up appearances.

It was at this point that I realized the problem must be that his question had not been answered to his satisfaction and decided to do something about it. So, in the interest of furthering his knowledge of my friend's practices by completely answering his question, I silently and patiently waited for my turn, and when I was finally at the counter, levitated his receipt from the little plastic bin in which the youthful girl had placed it. She must have enjoyed herself mightily, as my drink came with just a hint of phlegmy foam on top, which I've found is one of the sure signs that a server particularly enjoys the companionship of their patrons.

As I drank my drink, the stranger and the girl asked if I knew of their god. I let them know that of all the gods I have mingled with, the one they asked about has been suspiciously absent. They told me to follow their god but I informed them that I already had a god. Then, they described some fiery hell where they thought I should go. I thanked them for their directions, but the real world was hot enough, it being summer and all, so I didn't need a fiery hell, but it sounded like a nice place to visit, perhaps during the winter. They cackled about my answers and asked about my friend again. In fact, the entire shop began to giggle uncontrollably and nervously when I expounded further on my friend's collection. This was when I figured out that the group found my friend's choice of hobby strange and bizarre.

After leaving with my drink and one unruly patron's teeth, I turned the receipt over to my previously said friend. With it, and some help from the authorities, he acquired the strange gentleman's address. To make a long story short, his collection grew that night by two pair, one of either sex.

Viewing my friend's handiwork, I believed that the stranger had his curiosity satisfied. But just to make sure, I visited him in the hospital the next day. When he saw me, he began excitedly calling out to his god, a practice of which I full-heartedly approve. After all, my friend doesn't have any gods' legs yet.

Tentacles,

St. Michael Amorel

A PROGRESS REPORT

Progress Report for Aelver Cravesticon from Nelly Lynne Glennticus:

It is the end for us. You, Mr. Morel, have doomed us all. Of course, I recognize that I bear some responsibility as well. I have tried to lessen the change we would bring about to this world by teaching Aelver something about humanity. That has destroyed by your deed. Now I dread the night and our sylvan surroundings as much as I use to rejoice in them with my sisters. Yes, I am one of them. I managed to get them to accept me as a priestess rather than just a creation for the Savior's survival. But, this is supposed to be a progress report about Him.

Since you gave the book to Mr. Baer, thereby sowing the seeds of our destruction, there have been some rather public displays of our existence on a scale which we find it hard to control. We have been able to hold him off for now. But I believe that it is not over. He is not finished. We might have destroyed his physical form but there have been some mysterious manifestations lately. Some of them suggest that the dreamer may no longer exist as well. At least, not in the form we know him. I had hoped that this was through some justice that you had wrought but recent information would point to the contrary. Aelver has taken to disappearing for hours at night at which point some disturbingly familiar noises were heard. Upon investigation, the area the sounds were coming from looked as if the woods were moving and there is evidence of displacement in measured sites through the trees on the way to the nearest town. As we know these are signs of dimensional travel. Aelver returns with a slick reddish-black film on his body and what I hesitate to describe in one so young as a sneer of wanton hunger, his lips curled back, his forked tongue flickering and his perfect pointed teeth bared. With each night's rendezvous, for there is no mistaking that he's meeting and learning from his father, his maturation seems to accelerate. The horns, claws, tail and pre-hensile appendages he was born with recede into his body for longer and longer periods of time. His growth has not matched this but I am unsure if this should be perceived as a blessing or not. His small stature may enable him to pass as harmless until it is too late. I also believe that there are times I can feel him attempting to influence my mind. I think my current safeguard is the connection to the rest of our brethren. All the voices are currently too much for him. How long this will last, I know not. The days are filled with more of an interrogation session than our usual home schooling. He demands to know why I have perverted the teachings. When I ask him how he knows this, he tells me that his father told him. I tell him that is impossible. He ignores me and asks why you have not been destroyed or at least banished. I try to explain that even we make mistakes and that not everything works out the way it should. He shakes his head, sulks, mutters something about how his father will do something about it and stalk-slithers to his room. I yell after him that he needs to maintain his human form.

During our trips to town, I have heard about incidents of animal mutilation between the town and us. In a suspiciously close radius to the woods and the areas of displacement, have been found livestock with either large slices in them and certain organs missing or lying there with parts of them missing. These coincide with the noticeable disappearance of children and young women. There are stories about a discordant but alluring piping accompanied by a rise in the winds and a deepening of the shadows. The shadows seem to dance and writhe ecstati-cally to the music. The children are drawn to this mimicking the movements of the shadows. Moving slowly through the town, they dance, play imaginary instruments to accompany it and march in time. It seems to have a strange effect over teenag-ers and adults in that they start copulating with whomever or whatever is nearby. With their guardians otherwise occupied, the children reach the edge of town and the air around them starts to try to match their jamboree. They step into the darkness created by the woods and disappear. These tales make my thoughts travel to places I dare not go. Is it possible that Mr. Baer is attempting his own brand of stem cell research? I fear that he is working on a reconstruction ritual. I'm afraid he is eliciting Aelver's help or even worse, teaching him it.

There are no more whispers in my head, only screams. The familiars have taken to engaging in the ritual with each other with the frenzy of a compulsion. There are orgies just to satisfy their need where in their passion they are consuming each other. The children of Messrs. Thool and Thothlu have contracted a plague. They are developing lesions that disgorge their essence. In short, they are disintegrating slowly. Their thoughts betray a horror I had not even contemplated: Mr. Baer would use the parts of his own people or their servants to complete his reconstruction.

I feel my thoughts being pillaged more and more. I'm not sure if this is Aelver growing in strength or Mr. Baer coming for me. I have no doubt that he is coming for me. Make no mistake, both of them will be coming for you. Aelver's anger grows in inverse proportion to his stature, not to mention his will to follow his father. Mr. Baer will complete himself and then deal with you. I hope that your containment abilities are of help to you. He is coming. May The Elder Gods be with you. For we shall never see our great city rise from the depths. We shall never hear the plaintive scritching of the Fungi of Yoggoth as they fly through the air nor the mournful gurgle piping of the shoggoths. I'm sorry I've failed you…Mmmaaassstters

AFTERMATH I

Diary entries of Inspector Tennyson Mactleone:
I have lived in a world of twilight for a while. Black and white are not necessarily as interesting. It is much easier to deal, not mention to do, this job if I think this way. The Thin Blue Line not being the stalwart figures of justice I believed them to be. So I have taken to looking at them the same way I do the rest of the perps, as a means to an end. People who do drugs, who have mental illness, we are all them. Robert was no exception. I believed he was a key to helping me bust open a case of missing persons. How could I know that this was a case that would lead to the dark and terrible knowledge that I now possess.

They come to me out of the darkness, he said. You have to get these things for me, he would say as he tried to cover up the track marks. Robert and I had been hanging out for more than a year. More than a year of me covering for his coke habit, his lies, his paranoia. What did I care, they were just stories. It seems that the best stories come out of people's darkness, their insecurities, their problems, their fears. People seem more attentive to the joys of people if they seem to have a redemptive quality about them. All of these were the rationales I had built up during my years on the force. How was I to know that these stories were valid relations of the horrible truth. So it was a tremendous feat when about 3 hours later after an intense discussion, we left Robert's building to get something to eat. Robert loved sushi. So we went to his favorite place on Ave A. We sat there while he told me of the entities that stepped out of the darkness to attack him. This is why he started learning the dark arts. A phrase that I was to learn was very apropos. I had always suspected Robert of being a Satanist but every time I brought this up, he would go off on a diatribe about the prejudice against witchcraft in this society. He would lecture about the true practice of witchcraft, its dependence on intent and the difference between white and black magic. Then assure me that he was not the one kidnaping women for some twisted ritual. He was kidnaping them for sex. He would pause and then laugh nervously at me saying that he was not kidnaping them, they went with him willingly. He was sure the entities had been sent by someone who knew he had been cheating on his wife. His cheating was rather tame in my book. It involved seeing prostitutes and engaging in S&M. I suspected that some of them were using Robert for their own nefarious ends. I was hoping one of these ends would lead to some information I was looking for. I did not realize just how nefarious and deviant they would be. Of course, in hindsight, I should have realized when I noticed Robert's track marks oozing a dark liquid.

I was called to a sight today that gave me pause. A pause that sends chills up once spines and makes one wish for another line of work. There was a report of a disturbance at the corner of Houston Street and 2nd Avenue. As I was approaching the site, there was a large explosion followed by an unearthly scream and a loud thump as something hit my windshield. It was a head. I cursed, hit the brakes and called for backup. Upon arriving on the scene, I saw only rubble and pieces of what I thought were twisted metal. I tried to question people in the area as to the source of the explosion. No one seemed to know as they saw no one go into the structure and no one come out. As I started to pick my way through the rubble, I saw that what I thought were pieces of twisted metal were not metal at all. They were pieces of human beings shaped into supporting structures and strengthened in much the same way as carbonized steel. At one point, there was a shift in the rubble near me and a shadow stretched forth towards me. As it touched me, I felt a clamminess and a fell whispering in my mind. I jerked myself away and stumbled over the rubble towards my car as fast as I could.

I cannot tell you what horrors it related to me in that moment. But I swear it is still around looking for a way to make itself whole. Looking for something that will complete it. Looking for a place that it can hole up until it can enact its terrible revenge. Perhaps I should warn Robert that what he fears is true.

Cast of a medallion that was found in the wreckage of the offices of Cthulhu Sex. It is purported to be a true representation of St. Michael.

AFTERMATH II

This was found in a hotel room stuck to the wall above the bed. There does not seem to be a trace of the DVD mentioned. Perhaps it is better that way.

It has not been the same. Not since I was reborn or, more accurately, remade. Not since you left me. I have been on the run ever since my search for you lead towards that misunderstanding. Personally, I thought they would stop me before things got out of hand. I mean, I know they are watching. How else would they keep track of me. Unless it is what they want.

I'm leaving town, if for no other reason than what I found in the closet this morning. I woke up hearing a muffled thumping in my head along with some whimpering. It took me a bit to figure out that the pounding noise was not just the result of last night's medication regimen: as many shots followed by beer chasers as it takes to drown out the noise in my head. Sometimes, when I am lucky enough to black out, the visions stop as well. The noise was coming from the closet. I got up and ambled over to it cursing at the Rockwell painting on the wall. Someone's Watching Me, my ass, they really do have a sense of humor. I open the door to find a naked woman wriggling around in there. She was bound and gagged in a semi-fetal position. She looked at me with frightened green eyes, her hair matted against her face after struggling so much. I thought of our last evening together. I did not mean for it to end like that. But, it was what they wanted. I dragged her out of the closet, untied her and took the gag out of her mouth. She started screaming and running for the door. My skin shattered like crystal and then fused. I moved to intercept her and managed to grab her before she turned the knob. I hold her close, stroke her hair and speak softly into her ear in an attempt to calm her down. The air in the room has become remarkably stuffy. I look down at her sobbing and sniffling. It is then that I notice the marks. There are scratches, cuts and circular gouges in patterns all over her body. I run my fingers along them in fascination. The shadows lengthen reaching out to pull me into the darkness. She nuzzles her head against my chest and pleads with me not to hurt her. I am mesmerized by her scars, both the outer and inner ones. My fingers trace one that starts around her neck and spirals down to her left breast, circling around it and ending at the nipple. There are two deep excoriations along the way that send other lines further down the body and around to her back. I follow the ones traveling downward. There are little gasps with intermittent sighs and moans as I explore each gouge and the trails that lead away from them. I smell seawater and seaweed-covered driftwood. There is a whispering as the darkness deepens. It is the whispering that unnerves me. I feel a buzzing within me. A soft hum then a crackle followed by a sucking sound which I want to believe is caused by the woman giving me a blow-job. It is, in fact, caused by the woman, more to the point, it is caused by her body. The skin is parting along the lines created by the cuts on her body and seemingly being drawn into the body. The body, if one can call it that at this point, is spasming and contorting itself into a horrendous portal. From which the air seems to pulsate with a sound not unlike waves pounding against a sinking ship that's carrying a farmer and his livestock. A man, or rather a semblance of one, shuffles through the portal. His head is hanging from his neck at an acute angle, his swollen tongue lolls out of his mouth and one of his eyes raises itself on a stalk to look at me. Whatever she says after you have your way with her, you must destroy the gateway he tells me. I do not understand what he says since most of the sound is a liquid slapping, slushing noise combined with chittering. One eye looks at me mournfully while the other raises itself on a stalk to look around fearfully. He warns that they will find me. There is a great gust of wind followed by a sickening moan as if from a backwards recording of whale communications. A long greenish red black tendril reaches out from the portal and pulls the man back in with a terrifying drowning slurpy scream. The darkness becomes softer. With a cracking and zipping noise, the woman is once again whole and lying beside me. She reminds me of you. I have a tremendous urge to fuck her. I try to get rid of my hard on by thinking of what just happened. But, it only increases my desire. There's a tingling at the back of my skull that seems to be spreading to the rest of my body. I look down at her, my stomach growls and I start salivating. I lean over and kiss her. She tastes like the sea on a fall day. I move my hands down her body, over her breasts, down her stomach to the hair around her sex. I move my head so that my tongue can follow my hands. I lick her labia and nibble on her clit. She contorts in ecstasy. I move my body on top of hers. Our bodies move together in unison. But, I feel something else. Once again, the scars are moving of their own accord. The circular wounds are sucking like hungry mouths. She is pulling me closer to her. I try to pull out and roll off of her but am stuck like a fly in a Venus flytrap. As she closes her arms around me, her hips grind into me. Her mouth closes over mine and she sucks the air out of my lungs. That's when I feel my body move. My skin starts rippling as if there is something moving underneath. My jaw unhinges and something lurches out of my mouth into hers searching out her brain. There is a muffled choking scream. As my arm seizes her left breast, twists it with a talon cutting a circle around it, I pull it off like a twist cap. She flails her arms at me with a noise I dare not describe. I punch my way through the ribs to her heart. I pull it out and eat it. The greenish black-tentacled blob oozes out of her mouth covered in brain gore. It slides its way over to me and pulls itself up to my ear where it squishes itself back into my head. I get up, turn off the tv and video camera, I pull the tape out of the camera and leave it on the desk. I get dressed and close the door behind me. Let them see what their handiwork has done. As I said, sex will never be the same.

AFTERMATH III

This was found with a DVD. The footage has been restored after some difficulty. It is still unclear whether it is a documentary or not. If what it portrays is true, there is no hope. For what was dead and banished could have returned already. Then the real darkness shall begin.

I believe in darkness. Not the warm embrace or the awesome wonder with the pin pricks of light and the living sounds. But the suffocating drowning helplessness one feels as the blackness engulfs you. It is this I see. Droplets of it in every soul I encounter. There is help for them. If they will accept it. There are days that I wish I could blind myself. But this would only result in the other senses alerting me to its presence. It was not always this way.

I was taken one night. Taken to a twilight lit room of impossible dimensions. The angles were all wrong as if there were secret rooms and passageways built into it. The room was waiting for me. A film projected against the wall seemed to be the only light in the room. The film was basically several suicide notes strung together with the deaths cut in between each person. Just when it seemed to be over, the film would loop back to the first person speaking and I was subjected to the whole thing over again. This in itself would not have been so horrible if I did not feel like I was being watched as well. As I attuned myself to the rest of the room beside the film, I noticed other things about my gray world. There was a shuffling, sliding noise behind the wall followed by a weird slap or perhaps it was a creak. I could not tell. The bathroom, if one can call the small alcove that, seemed to resonate with a dripping sloshing sound without any water running. The tile and pipes sweating with condensation.

The room warmed to my attentions. I walked back to the film. I sat down and for the first time, I noticed other figures in the background of the film. They were not noticeable at first, being only a face in the window, a shadow on the wall or a sound in the air. As I studied it, I started to see these people, for that is what I will call them, reaching out to the suicides as they were dieing. I thought it was in comfort until I noticed their shadows, at least I thought it was their shadows. As I leaned closer to examine it, I thought I saw them drawing darkness out of them. It was more like strands of ebon liquid were flowing out of them as the shadows slid over the body. The body writhed and twitched in what I can only describe as ecstatic paroxysms. .I shifted my gaze to the dead face expecting to see a look of peace upon it. Instead they were left with impassive death masks. The room started to bleed into me. They will regret what they have done.

I left the room in the company of two people. I could not distinguish their features in the pale light. They were wearing red robes to my white. The red seemed to beckon to me. As we got to the door at the end of a hallway, one of them turned towards me. By the light streaming in through the door, I caught a glimpse of face. It seemed vaguely familiar. As we walked into the area beyond the door, it seemed to open up into a large domed courtyard with a large obsidian block in the center. Its blackness whispered to me seductively. Upon the block, there was a humanoid shape. There were numbers of people dressed in white and red robes standing around it chanting. As we got closer, the robes parted before me and the chanting swelled in intensity. I was led up to the dais where a young woman lay. There was a rumbling sound as in an approaching storm. It was then I realized that I had not eaten in days. I stepped up to the woman, turned to the people flanking me and realized where I had seen them before. They were dead ringers for the suicides in the film. At that moment, I know not what happened. The chanting crescendoed, someone in a white robe stepped up and red liquid flowed over my robe. The white robe sleeve covering my arm sucking the red out of the sycophant, the altar turned into tar and flowed over me and the woman. There was a noiseless scream and a reverse flash of light as if everything became a photo negative for a second. I was on top of her and in her absorbing every bit of her essence. It was only when there was nothing left that I noticed that the storm had abated, and my hunger ceased. I stood up in a glistening reddish black robe and surveyed my followers.

Curious about other Crossroad Press books?
Stop by our site:
http://store.crossroadpress.com
We offer quality writing
in digital, audio, and print formats.